NATO and Terrorism

NATO AND TERRORISM

Organizational Expansion and Mission Transformation

James W. Peterson

continuum

The Continuum International Publishing Group
80 Maiden Lane, New York, NY 10038
The Tower Building, 11 York Road, London SE1 7NX

www.continuumbooks.com

Copyright © 2011, James W. Peterson

All rights reserved. No part of this book may be reproduced, stored in a retrieval system, or transmitted, in any form or by any means, electronic, mechanical, photocopying, recording, or otherwise, without the written permission of the publishers.

Library of Congress Cataloging-in-Publication Data
Peterson, James W. (James Walter), 1945–
NATO and terrorism: organizational expansion and mission transformation/
James W. Peterson.
　p. cm.
Includes bibliographical references and index.
ISBN-13: 978-1-4411-0907-1 (hardcover : alk. paper)
ISBN-10: 1-4411-0907-2 (hardcover : alk. paper)
ISBN-13: 978-1-4411-2976-5 (pbk. : alk. paper)
ISBN-10: 1-4411-2976-6 (pbk. : alk. paper) 1. North Atlantic Treaty Organization—Military policy. 2. Terrorism—Prevention—Government policy—Europe. 3. National security—Europe. I. Title.

UA646.3.P387 2011
363.325'1561094—dc22   2010027397

ISBN: HB: 978-1-4411-0907-1
　　　PB: 978-1-4411-2976-5

Typeset by Newgen Imaging Systems Pvt Ltd, Chennai, India
Printed and bound in the United States of America

To Bonnie,
The Love of my Life

Contents

Map 1. Europe   viii
Map 2. Central Balkan Region   ix
Acknowledgments   x
Introduction   xi
Abbreviations   xiv

Chapter 1	The Battle against Terrorism Reshapes the NATO Organization	1
Chapter 2	Partners for Peace after the Cold War	7
Chapter 3	From Partnership to Membership in 1999	20
Chapter 4	The Class of 2004 and the Post-9/11 World	32
Chapter 5	Further Class Memberships and the Traps of Southeast Europe	44
Chapter 6	Bosnia in the Lengthened Shadow of the Cold War	59
Chapter 7	Kosovo in the Shadow of Bosnia's Lessons	68
Chapter 8	NATO Applies its Capabilities in Afghanistan	81
Chapter 9	The War in Iraq Shakes NATO Capabilities	112
Chapter 10	European Security, East and West	126
Chapter 11	The Coasts of NATO, North and South	151
Chapter 12	NATO Missions Reshape the Battle against Terrorism	182

References   186
Index   207

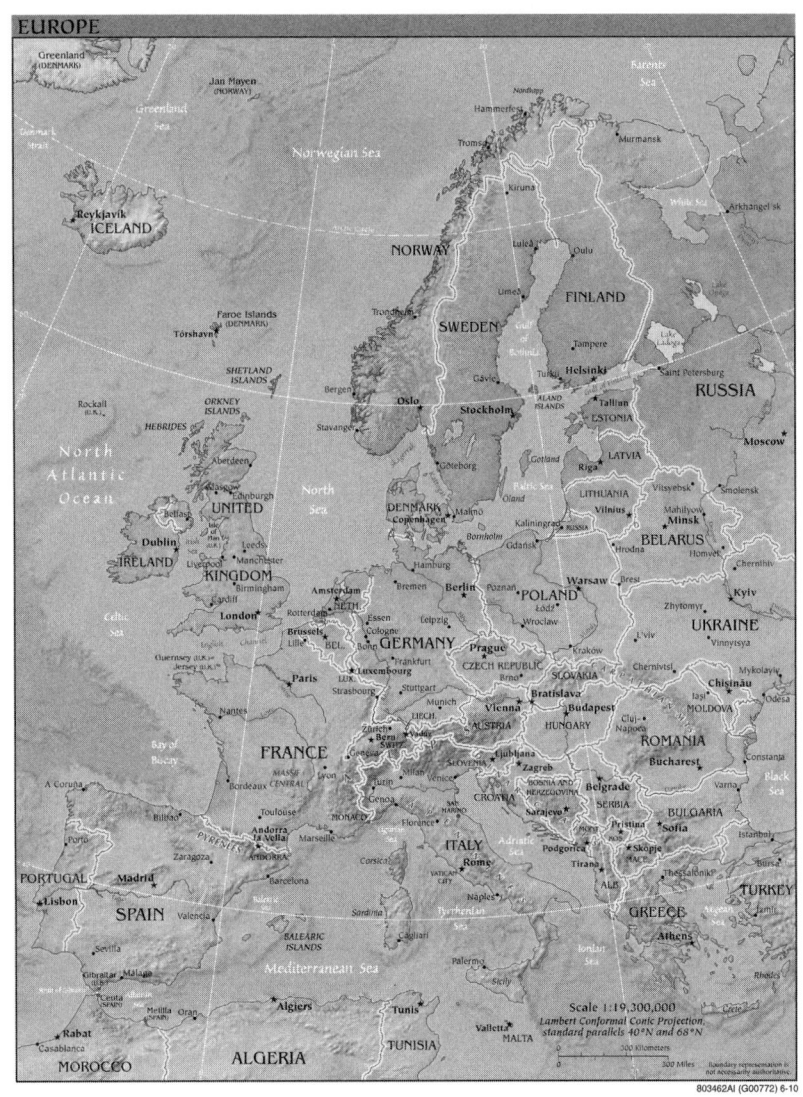

Map 1. Europe

Map 2. Central Balkan Region

Acknowledgments

I would like to thank Ms. Marie Claire Antoine at Continuum Books for supervising the entire project from beginning to end. She demonstrated great interest in the initial stages and worked steadily and patiently with me on all aspects of the book during the past two years. In addition, I am indebted to Murali at Newgen Imaging for his masterful and extremely prompt work on copyediting and page proofs. Further, I am appreciative of the continuing interest in the project demonstrated by my colleagues in the Department of Political Science at Valdosta State University. I would also like to express a special thanks to Dr. Ivan Nikolov, Director of International Programs at Valdosta State. He showed genuine interest in the book and sent me timely recommendations for sources, all of which I fitted into the book. My colleagues in the Department of Politics and European Studies at Palacký University in Olomouc, Czech Republic deserve special thanks. Discussions with them about key topics and use of their library have added a unique dimension to several chapters. Further, colleagues at the Department of Political Science and Sociology at Tavrida University, Simferopol, Crimea, Ukraine opened new windows of interest for me in the nations of the Black Sea Region. Finally, Bob Evanson of the University of Missouri/Kansas City offered his moral support and wisdom at several points during the completion of the book.

A version of Chapter Ten, 'European Security, East and West' appeared in The Carl Beck Papers in Russian & East European Studies, Center for Russian & East European Studies, University of Pittsburgh, USA.

Introduction

Capturing the changes in the North Atlantic Treaty Organization (NATO) in the two decades since the end of the Cold War is no easy matter. It is the thesis of this book that the capturing process entails three levels that have each been in continuous motion and that have together become inter-locked with one another. There is no chronological sequence to the actions of the three dynamic forces, and they impact one another without notice or warning. The level that ranks first and possesses the most force is clearly terrorism activity itself. Although the acuity of this factor is most evident in the post-9/11 world, its visage appeared in the previous decade in both sporadic outbursts and rogue state behavior. The second-ranked level is the transformation of the missions of the military alliance itself. Instead of the Cold War focus on the European theater, the missions expanded and multiplied to stretch from Bosnia to the shores of Somalia. The third level of analysis, most affected by the others but a powerful factor in its own right, is the organizational expansion of the alliance. Under the twin pressures of terrorist violence and changing missions, NATO expanded its membership by 75 percent in the two decades that followed the close of the Cold War in 1989. Interpenetration of these three levels set the agenda for NATO, but the constant uncertainties, disagreements, and explosions within this interactive system made it difficult to complete successfully and fully many of the ensuing challenges. However, a deeper understanding of this imperfectly functioning, three-layered dynamo can generate conclusions that will enable an expanded organization to be better prepared to confront, contain, and eventually defeat the most serious threat to the global community to emerge in the post-Cold War period.

The first and last chapters are bookends between which the topical chapters are arrayed and stacked. In Chapter One, the obvious impact of the increased pace and lethality of terrorism on the military alliance with its Cold War membership composition is at the center of the stage. In Chapter Twelve, NATO's assumption of very different kinds of missions receives analysis in light of their ability to reconfigure the machinery of engagement with an enemy whose terrorist tactics seem to have no civilized bounds.

The second and third chapters are also paired by theme, as they emphasize the process of expansion of the alliance from 16 to 19 members.

In Chapter Two, the efforts of the Clinton Administration to create a feeder system called the Partnership for Peace (PfP) Program receive analysis. His administration spotlighted those nations in the northern part of Central Europe that had acquired statehood in the formative period after the end of World War I. In Chapter Three, the three nations that navigated the process from PfP Status to full membership in NATO are the subjects of concern. Those new alliance partners included the Czech Republic, Hungary, and Poland.

Chapters Four and Five are joined in spirit through the spotlight that they cast on the more tricky membership questions that ensued after 1999, and especially after September 11, 2001. NATO took seven more countries formally into its structure in 2004, three years after the terrorist attacks on the Twin Towers and Pentagon. In fact, the key decision to bring them in was made symbolically in Prague, the capital city of a new member from the class of 1999. Further, the inclusion of Bulgaria and Romania as the twenty-fifth and twenty-sixth members of the alliance had much to do with confronting the increased terrorist threat from the Middle East and Persian Gulf region. On the map, the two countries look to be almost physical barriers against dangers emanating from the east. Inclusion of the other five members was also more problematic than the initial expansion of 1999. The three Baltic States of Estonia, Latvia, and Lithuania had been Republics in the old Soviet Union. Slovenia had been part of the Yugoslav Federation until 1991, while Slovakia had been left out of the 1999 class due to the rigidity and even intolerance of some of its domestic policies in the late 1990s. After a lull of several years, alliance expansion emerged as an important question at the Bucharest Summit in spring 2008. As a result, Albania and Croatia joined the military organization in 2009. Georgia and Ukraine did not receive invitations at that time, but the likelihood of their eventual membership continued to roil the waters throughout the period.

The image of a "shadow" is the unifying theme of Chapters Six and Seven. Bosnia, the subject of Chapter Six, had been the scene of a tragic civil war among Serbs, Muslims, and Croatians in the years 1992–1995. With a Russian blessing, the Yugoslav/Serb leader Slobodan Milosevic moved into Bosnia and pushed back the Muslims and Croats to the benefit of Bosnian Serbs. Thus, the shadow of the Cold War darkened the entire scene of operations and actions. NATO played a forceful role only in the last months of that war. Kosovo, the scene of much more intense NATO military action in 1999, was still part of Yugoslavia. The shadow of Milosevic was ever-present, as he sought victories for a local Serb minority that he had not been able to win in

Bosnia. In both settings, NATO troops worked with UN (United Nations) personnel after the wars to keep the peace.

Considerable NATO capabilities were involved in the American-led wars in both Afghanistan and Iraq early in the twenty-first century. Chapters Eight and Nine treat those wars from the vantage point of the effect on NATO as well as NATO's influence on their outcomes. The alliance formally took control of the Afghan operation against the Taliban/al Qaeda in late 2006, although many NATO partners had contributed earlier. The war in Iraq was quite a different story, as America clearly sparked that effort of a "coalition of the willing." However, the war drained United States and partner nation capabilities to the detriment of critical alliance objectives in Afghanistan and elsewhere. A number of NATO partners, most notably the Poles, took on major duties in Iraq right after March 2003, even though their alliance membership did not require such responsibilities. A formal alliance role emerged with regard to the great need for training police and military personnel through NATO Training Mission—Iraq (NTM-I).

Finally, Chapters Ten and Eleven are paired through parallel but contrasting regional thrusts. The regional dualism for Chapter Ten is East and West, and the theme is European security. To the east lies Russia with its unpredictable policies that eroded, in many ways, the sense of security in Europe. To the west lay the United States with its interest in both deterring Russian interests and protecting NATO partners in Europe. The 2008–09 Missile Shield Proposal lies at the heart of this regional dualism, and it will receive careful attention, as will successor plans outlined in 2009-10. In Chapter Eleven, the emphasis is on the North/South dualism with the image of coastal borders. NATO interests in the Baltic Sea region to the north and to the Black Sea region to the south will take the stage. Scandinavian nations see NATO as an important anchor in smoothly incorporating the Baltic nations, in light of Russian adventurous policies towards them. In the Black Sea region, Russian ambitions have been even more evident. This was especially evident in its war with Georgia in 2008, and then again in its cutback of natural gas supplies to Ukraine in early 2009. In these two chapters, NATO is engaged in a somewhat polarized struggle with Russia both on an east/west basis and on a north-south dimension. However, it would be a mistake to overestimate the Russian factor, for regional conflicts and perspectives added to the turbulent brew.

Abbreviations

BALTBAT	Baltic Battalion
BALTNET	Baltic Air Surveillance Network
BEAC	Barents Euro-Arctic Council
BSEC	Black Sea Economic Cooperation Pact
CBRN	Chemical, Biological, Radiological, and Nuclear
CFE	Conventional Forces Agreement/Europe
CFSP	Common Foreign and Security Policy
CIA	Central Intelligence Agency
CIS	Commonwealth of Independent States
CSCE	Conference on Security and Cooperation Europe
ČSSD	Czech Social Democratic Party (*acronym is for Czech words*)
CVVM	Center for Research on Public Opinion (*acronym is for Czech words*)
ESDF	Europe Security and Defense Force
ESDP	Europe Security and Defense Policy
EU	European Union
EUFOR	EU Force
FRTD	Facilitated Railway Transit Document
FTD	Facilitated Transit Document
GDP	Gross Domestic Product
GMD	Ground-Based Midcourse Defense
ICBM	Intercontinental Ballistic Missile
IED	Improvised Explosive Device
IFOR	Implementation Force
ISAF	International Security Assistance Force
JCS	Joint Chiefs of Staff
JIEDDO	Joint Improvised Explosive Device Defeat Organization
KFOR	Kosovo Force
KSČM	Czech and Moravian Communist Party (*acronym is for Czech words*)
KSF	Kosovo Security Force
MALT	Military Advice and Laiison Team
MAP	Membership Action Plan

MNBG	Multinational Battle Group
MNC NE	Multinational Corps North East
MNTF-C	Multinational Task Force Centre
NATO	North Atlantic Treaty Organization
NCO	Noncommissioned officer
NDS	National Defense Strategy
NeDAP	Northern e-Dimension Action Plan
NGO	Nongovernmental Organization
NRC	NATO-Russia Council
NRF	NATO Reaction Force
NTIM-I	NATO Training Implementation Mission—Iraq
NTM-I	NATO Training Mission—Iraq
OAF	Operation Allied Force
ODS	Civic Democratic Party (*acronym is for Czech words*)
OSCE	Organization for Security and Cooperation Europe
PfP	Partnership for Peace
PRT	Provincial Reconstruction Team
RAND	Research and Development
REFORGER	Return of Forces to Germany
SDP	Social Democratic Party
SFOR	Stabilization Force
SLBM	Submarine-Launched Ballistic Missile
SOFA	Status of Forces Agreement
START I	Strategic Arms Reduction Talks I
TMK	Kosovo Defense Force (*acronym is for Czech words*)
TTIU	Terrorist Threat Intelligence Unit
TTP	Tehrik-i-Taliban Pakistan
UN	United Nations
UNAMA	United Nations Assistance Mission in Afghanistan
UNPROFOR	United Nations Protection Force
WEU	Western European Union
WMD	Weapons of Mass Destruction
WTO	Warsaw Treaty Organization

CHAPTER ONE

The Battle against Terrorism Reshapes the NATO Organization

What was the shape of NATO prior to the replacement of the Cold War threat of communism with the post-Cold War challenge from both rogue state and cross-state terrorists? Shape can possess many meanings that include purpose, objectives, members, and missions. If it is possible to ascertain the shape of the organization for the four decades that span the years 1949–89, then it will be possible to examine the powerful and violent forces that both presented themselves to the organization and reshaped it in the two decades after 1989. It will be the contention that the first decade after the end of the Cold War was a time of terrorism that mainly emanated from a handful of rogue state leaders who designed atrocities against both their own population and that of nearby states. However, the years that followed the tragedy of September 11, 2001, were ones in which cross-state terrorists became much more active, prominent, and destructive. In 2002, President Bush used the term "axis of evil" as a reminder that rogue state terrorism was still a force with which it was necessary to contend and also a possible link to the cross-state perpetrators of violence (Chittick 2006, 204–5). However, the acts of violence that received the most attention in the first decade of the twenty-first century were ones committed by small cells that connected to one another in nebulous and hard to detect ways. The array of brutal activities after the end of the Cold War profoundly changed the shape of NATO in all four respects noted above. The goal of this chapter is to outline the impact of terrorist activities on the purpose and objectives of the military organization. Membership changes will receive attention in chapters two through five, while mission transformation is principally the topic of chapters six through eleven. The spotlight will then switch on to the final theme of how those changed missions, carried out by a renewed organization, then reshaped the battle against terrorism.

NATO's Shape during the Cold War

NATO's shape during the Cold War included a clear purpose, a derivative set of reachable objectives, an unchanging membership, and a fixed number of missions confined to the protection of West Europe.

The purpose of its creation in 1949 was clearly to prevent the spread of communist systems further west into the region that became known as West Europe during the Cold War. The abrupt transition from the common battle against fascism in Europe had given way most abruptly to renewed tensions between East and West. Importantly, the Soviet Union had only slowly pulled its military out of the belt of liberated states west of its own border. Some forces within those states welcomed communism as a fixed, predictable system with a vision of the future. In other cases, the force of the Soviet military underpinned the local communist parties that eventually came to power. Formation of NATO in 1949 was preceded by articulation of a containment doctrine that presented a rationale for preventing a further push eastwards of the Soviet-led Empire (McCormick 2010, 47–50). Thus, organizational origin combined with theory to create a sense of purpose in the exhausting aftermath of World War II.

NATO planners were able from the outset to extract a concrete set of objectives from this new purpose. Perhaps the Truman Doctrine of 1947 provided a recipe of practical steps needed to fulfill the purpose. In particular, communist forces had threatened to add Greece to the column of regional conquests immediately after World War II, and inclusion of Greece into the communist bloc would have made their controls cover the entire region from the Baltic Sea to the Mediterranean. Simultaneous threats to Turkey compounded the challenge (Jentleson 2007, 100–1). The Truman administration clearly took a stand to prevent the feared outcomes, and both nations remained not only noncommunist but excellent candidates for NATO itself. In the Greek case, it was Tito's Yugoslavia that gave sanctuary to those seeking the overthrow of the Greek government, but at that time no split had yet occurred between Stalin and Tito. The threat to Greece thus appeared to flow from the same source. Use of military force to defend European states against inclusion in the expanding communist orbit became a precedent for future objectives in particular settings. For instance, a series of Berlin crises a decade later evoked parallel NATO-led efforts to preserve the freedom of West Berlin and its lifeline to West Germany.

In terms of the alliance's members, there was a great deal of stability during the half century between 1949 and 1998. Steps to expand the alliance were not controversial and were based on practical needs of the moment. On the western side of the Atlantic Ocean, both the United States and Canada became part of the organization. Norway, Denmark, and Iceland chose to be the Scandinavian partners from the Baltic Sea region, while Belgium, the Netherlands, and Luxemburg rounded out the northern tier. In the Mediterranean Sea area, the alliance incorporated Spain, Portugal, Greece, and Turkey. The principal European powers also joined, and they include the United Kingdom, France, Federal Republic of Germany, and Italy (McCormick 2005, 49). The membership of Turkey was unusual, for that nation had firm links to the Middle East rather than to Europe. In the Western Hemisphere, exclusion of Mexico is understandable from the viewpoint of their lagging economic development. In addition, a number of familiar European nations opted out of the organization. Sweden had adopted a neutralist posture even during both World Wars, while Finland lay partly in the shadow of the Soviet Union. Switzerland, with its ethnic patchwork, had been, like Sweden, a traditionally neutralist power. Austria was on the cusp of the Cold War and still had a statue to the Red Army in Vienna. During the four decades, the overall membership patterns thus did not include all potential powers but did reflect both a representative sample and the strongest players in the theater.

NATO missions during the Cold war were congruent with purpose, objectives, and membership. In many ways, the missions included strong warnings in response to initiatives taken by the Soviet Union. Soviet and East German pressure on the city of Berlin in 1958-62, including the building of the Berlin Wall, elicited continuous statements and pressure by NATO. Both the Soviet crack-down on Hungary in 1956 and the Warsaw Pact invasion of Czechoslovakia in 1968 generated condemnation by the alliance. Strong international support for the Kennedy Administration during the 1962 Cuban Missile Crisis was part of this overall vigorous, verbal defense of western interests (Jentleson 2007, 107). In addition, there was a continuing preoccupation with alliance partners which themselves were afflicted by the presence of strong communist parties that often garnered as much as one-fifth of the vote in parliamentary elections. Particular targets of concern included both France and Italy. In addition, some of the missions were purely military and linked to the overall goal of preserving parity through deterrence of Soviet capabilities. For example, emplacement of cruise missiles and Pershing IIs in an assortment of West Europe states, principally West Germany, in the 1970s and 1980s constituted a response to introduction of short and medium range weapons by Soviet leadership earlier in East Germany and Czechoslovakia. Therefore,

Cold War missions entailed a mix of policy pronouncements about aggressive moves by the Soviet Union and Warsaw Pact, a studied focus on soft spots within the West, and deterrence through strategic emplacement of weapons systems.

An Alliance Reshaped by Post-Cold War Dynamics

The next question then becomes: How did the emergence of both rogue state and cross-state terrorism in the first two decades after the end of the Cold War change the shape of the alliance. Clearly, these powerful new threats affected the alliance's purpose, objectives, membership, and missions.

Many observers questioned whether there was a continuing purpose for NATO after the collapse of communism in 1989 and 1991. These doubts persisted throughout the entire twenty-year period after the end of the Cold War. After all, the principal target of NATO had imploded into fifteen nations, while most of East Europe had both thrown off communist rule and changed its self-perception to that of Central rather than East Europe. If the Warsaw Pact dissolved so quickly, what purpose could possibly keep NATO alive for more than a few years? By 2009, witnesses of the alliance's expanded membership base and missions worried that NATO was becoming internationalized to the point of meaningless. Chancellor Angela Merkel of Germany articulated this sentiment even in the middle of an election campaign and within one of NATO's leading partners. Writing in *Foreign Affairs*, Zbigniew Brzezinski wrestled with these doubts but ended up concluding that NATO "has the experience, the institutions, and the means to eventually become the hub of a globe-spanning web of various regional cooperative-security undertakings among states with the growing power to act" (Brzezinski 2009, 20). Such a precise statement offers a specific purpose that can generate expanded lists of objectives for the future. That image of a web can subsume the various, recent activities of NATO in contending with terrorist activities in particular hot spots at Europe's edge.

Whereas Cold War objectives had centered on containment of communist efforts to include more states in their sphere, post-Cold War objectives were firmly linked to blocking both rogue states and cross-state terrorist movements from including more states and peoples in the orbit of continuing fear, violence, and apprehension. Concrete objectives during the 1990s centered on containment of rogue leaders who challenged global order in a number of respects. In some cases, they attacked neighboring countries, often in order to protect a minority across the border. At other times, they attacked segments of their own population, many times in order to restrict and even persecute a minority within their own borders. Sometimes, they threatened or even commenced work on nuclear capabilities, in violation of continued warnings from the UN. Leaders who took all of these actions as a collective whole gave their countries and populations undeserved reputations as rogue states (McCormick 2010, 218). Leaders who most clearly merited the rogue state label included Yugoslavia's Slobodan Milosevic, Iraq's Saddam Hussein, and North Korea's Kim Jong-Il. While this decade was also a time of individual acts of cross-state terrorism such as the twin bombings by al Qaeda of American embassies in Kenya and Tanzania in 1998, this second type of terrorism took center stage during and after 9/11. From that point on, alliance objectives included close work with American leadership to search out the terrorists and prevent their actions in the future. While the hunt spanned the globe, the key issues that confronted NATO included the questions of how much and what to do about Afghanistan and Iraq.

NATO's shape also changed, under the pressure of the double whammy of rogue state and cross-state terrorism, in terms of its membership. All of the changes occurred during the second decade of the post-Cold War period. The first set of membership additions had much to do with the presence of Yugoslavia and Milosevic in the southeast corner of Europe. During the Bosnian War of 1992–95, western nations had done very little to contain the Serb pressure. European nations were reluctant to take things into their own hands, and the American public was not prepared for a wholesale involvement by the United States (Jentleson 2007, 441). Many often wondered why neighboring nations in Central Europe could not act as more of a police force in their own backyard. Thus, inclusion of the Czech Republic, Hungary, and Poland made sense in terms of erecting a regional deterrent. Symbolically, the inclusion of the three occurred at about the same time as the NATO bombing campaign in Kosovo. The second class of members entered in 2004, and five of those nations were also part of Central Europe. The inclusion Estonia, Latvia, Lithuania, Slovakia, and Slovenia completed the process that had started in 1999. However, admission of two Balkan nations was less connected to rogue state terrorism and much more closely linked to the emergence of cross-state terrorism after September 11. Bulgaria and Romania constituted a type of barrier against threats emanating from the Middle East as well as an anchor for NATO nations on their way to combat the trouble further east. Later, addition of Albania and Croatia in 2009, occurred at a time when the concentration of cross-state terrorist activity was at its high point, primarily in Afghanistan but also still in Iraq. They broadened that Balkan barrier whose construction had partially been completed in 2004.

Finally, organizational shape also means missions, and those changed profoundly under the pressure of terrorism. Alliance purpose, objectives, and membership all were streams that fed into that transformed set of missions. Cold War missions of NATO took place exclusively on the continent of Europe, although moral support given to the United States during the 1962 Cuban Missile Crisis was a partial exception. However, the list of missions in the post-Cold War included hot spots such as Bosnia, Kosovo, Afghanistan, and even Iraq. Increasingly, they shaded north occasionally into the Baltic Sea area and at times south into the Black Sea region. Both rogue and cross-state terrorism converged to drive these new missions. Activities of rogue leaders like Milosevic and Saddam prompted alliance concern and focus on the neighborhoods of their nations. The scattering of al Qaeda and the Taliban into many different nations gave a greater urgency to NATO preparations and dispatch of military forces. In a sense, both Afghanistan and Iraq became vortexes and magnets for a variety of terrorist and ethnic-based groups. It is also true that concern about Russian activities and threats in both the Baltic and Black Sea regions drove part of the NATO agenda. Perhaps, that portion of the agenda and set of concerns was more closely linked to the Cold War patterns. Such a perception seemed particularly appropriate in the months after the August 2008, Russo-Georgia War. However, Black Sea tensions were partly linked to the terrorist threat, for fundamentalism groups operating in several southern Republics of Russia were fully capable and willing to operate across state lines.

Over the course of two decades, therefore, the shape of NATO changed in major and significant ways. Its purposes moved from containing of communism to blocking principally two types of terrorist activity. Objectives of the organization shifted from the partly psychological deterrence of communist expansion to actual military containment of the perpetrators of terrorist activity. The organizational base of the alliance moved east and south, in a direction that positioned NATO to be both a stronger offensive force and a tighter defense against the new type of threat. Missions mostly moved out of the West European arena and into the Balkans and Middle East. This four-pronged new shape clearly bore the scars of 9/11 but also germinated in the soil of the widespread instability that crept in after the collapse of the Cold War rigidities of power.

CHAPTER TWO

Partners for Peace after the Cold War

Alliance Theory

Following the end of the Cold War, NATO's focus shifted from protection of the territorial integrity of West Europe to a political agenda of developing "new Euro-Atlantic security structures" (Balanzino 1995, 34). Instead of focusing continuously on the stalemate centered on the Iron Curtain, the alliance began to develop a theoretical basis for taking on challenges such as the management of crises and peacekeeping operations. Establishment of the Partnership for Peace (PfP) Plan in 1991 indicated a serious effort to embrace interested nations from the Conference on Security and Cooperation Europe (CSCE). NATO could gain important resources that would buttress capabilities in the new types of missions, while, at the same time, the partners would both develop more transparent planning processes and establish more "democratic control over their armed forces" (Balanzino, 35). Activities for the PfP members included dispatch of their liaison officers to a Partnership Coordination Cell in Mons, Belgium, representation at NATO headquarters in Brussels, and immediate participation in peacekeeping exercises. Additional important values for potential members included democratization of their governmental units, development of a market economy, increased protection of human rights, additional sensitivity to minority rights, and initial efforts to resolve border conflicts with countries in their region (Balanzino, 36).

Specific topics and issues also became central to the theoretical underpinnings of alliance development. One key issue for an expanding alliance has always been new costs to old and new members. Gates and Terasawa (2003, 369–83) suggest that collective defense expenditures can bear fruit for all concerned if there are common interests among the members. Obviously, this has been a challenge for an organization that expanded from 16 nations in 1998 to 28 by 2009. If certain new countries focus only on what they can obtain from the alliance, then private rather than collective benefits from the expenditures will result. Clearly, this has been an issue, for new NATO members have struggled and usually fallen short of the alliance goal that each commits at least 2 percent of Gross Domestic Product (GDP) to the organization. Another pressing theoretical issue has been expansion of alliance missions in light of changed international conditions. The 9/11 attacks certainly pushed defense against terrorism to the front of member concerns. The alliance's Prague Summit in late 2002, led to a changed policy agenda that incorporated a package of steps to prepare more fully for the battle against terrorism. Further, ethnic and religious conflicts continued unabated at the turn of the century. However, alliance processes and structures were not designed to deal with the kinds of challenges and threats that were emerging at that time. Thus, "organizational behavior and bureaucratic politics" skewed the ability of the alliance to respond effectively and crisply to each new challenge (Deni 2004).

In recent years, alliance theorists have called into question the capability of this alliance to remain credible in light of its defined goals. Divisions both within Europe and between Europe and the United States have created a certain amount of stagnation (Rupp 2006). Others (Moore 2007) have even questioned whether NATO will really be an alliance in the extended future. On the one hand, it may continue for a time as a genuine alliance with claims on and also benefits provided to all of its members. On the other hand, the organization might evolve into an "alliance with global partners" or an "alliance of democratic states." In this latter case, there are certainly common goals, but there will be great difficulty rallying nations for a common project or mission in difficult circumstances. The Iraq War generated another dilemma, as America worked outside of a reluctant alliance to connect, one-by-one, with states interested in becoming part of the "coalition of the willing." Many of the NATO partners were then left outside the planning process, while the effort to build common values screeched to a halt (De Nevers 2007). As the United States built ad hoc coalitions on a country-by-country basis, the leaders in the Bush Administration were transmitting the message that they could with impunity bypass the alliance and in effect declare it to be irrelevant (Hallams 2009, 38–60). Two writers (Noetzel and Schreer 2009, 211–26) contend that many observers then concluded that the alliance had changed from a unified organization into one with two tiers. For simplicity's sake, one could call the tiers the "new" and the "old" Europe. These authors prefer the label "multi-tier alliance" to a "two tier" one. They detect signs of three tiers to include reformist, status-quo, and reversal orientations.

Finally, there are alliance theorists who prefer the term "unipolarity" to the above more complex labels. From this vantage point, the United States has become the mover and shaker of the global system, at least on defense and security themes. Further, there is inertia within the international system that encourages the strongest player to consistently "seek further expansion"

(Jervis 2009, 188–213). There is a technical possibility that nations of medium military power may pursue alliances with one another to limit the influence of the unipole, but low-strength nations will find it difficult to resist the temptation to go along with the courtship of the lead nation (Walt 2009, 86–120). This depiction is on the surface much different from the more fluid alliance pattern portrayed by some of the writers mentioned in preceding paragraphs. However, it shares in the conclusion that new members will have an uphill battle to influence and obtain tangible benefits from the new organization that they have recently joined.

Historical Process of Enlargement

NATO has carried out six rounds of enlargement since its founding in 1949. At that time, there were twelve original signatories of the alliance pact. They included Belgium, Canada, Denmark, France Iceland, Italy, Luxembourg, Netherlands, Norway, Portugal, United Kingdom, and the United States. The first round of expansion took place in 1952, as the alliance strengthened its southern flank through inclusion of both Greece and Turkey. Following the armistice that concluded World War II, West Germany entered during a second expansion stage in 1955, and the larger Germany inherited that seat after unification in 1990. Internal changes in Spain led to a third enlargement round that included them in 1982. Fourth, the first bids to former communist nations occurred in 1999. The Czech Republic, Hungary, and Poland all formally joined the organization in part due to their economic strength and enacted political reforms. In 2004, a big group of similar countries entered NATO all at one time in a fifth round of expansion. That group consisted of Bulgaria, Estonia, Latvia, Lithuania, Romania, Slovakia, and Slovenia. The sixth and most recent process of membership selection culminated in 2009, as the alliance brought in Albania and Croatia (NATO 2009a). Each of these six rounds had its roots in security needs. Inclusion of Germany filled a huge alliance gap in the middle of Europe at a time when the Cold War was most intense. All the other stages of expansion brought in countries that were located on the edge of the European base of the alliance.

Following the conclusion of the Cold War in 1989–91, the direction in which former communist countries would travel was unclear. The Warsaw Treaty Organization (WTO) collapsed very quickly, as there was only a rationale for it when communist parties controlled the entire region. Initially, the Soviet Union put together the Commonwealth of Independent States (CIS) in an effort to keep some sense of community alive. However, the response to that proposal was not 100 percent participation. Certainly, the CIS never became a substitute for the WTO. Another option was expanded use of the Organization for Security and Cooperation Europe (OSCE) for nations located on both sides of the former Iron Curtain. President Havel of Czechoslovakia envisioned that organization as an ideal conduit between the two sections of Europe that the Iron Curtain had separated from one other. The OSCE had emerged from the Helsinki Accords of 1975, as the CSCE, but it underwent a name change as it became a more permanent fixture of the international landscape. Many former communist countries had been members during the Cold War, so they simply retained their membership after 1989.

At the same time, the Clinton Administration worked closely with the NATO partners to open the door of that organization to the former communist nations. The vehicle for this outreach was the PfP Program, and Vice President Al Gore had major responsibilities for the success of this project. The basic thrust of the program was inclusion of many of these states as alliance observers. A key point was that these new observers did not have a vote on actual decisions. However, they were able to become familiar with the policy processes, get acquainted with NATO's management teams, and send troops on peacekeeping missions. For example, a number of them sent troops to Bosnia in the mid-1990s and to Kosovo at the end of the decade. The focus will now turn to the question of what those PfP initiates brought into the organization in terms of their historical legacies.

Principal PfP Political Differences Inherited from the Cold War

The three Baltic republics had been part of the Soviet Union for about half a century. Prior to the Communist Revolution of 1917, they had been in a kind of gray zone among the Russian Empire, Poland, and Germany. Importantly, in the interwar period they had enjoyed independence as nation-states on their own. However, in the early part of World War II the Soviet Union absorbed them, and from then on they constituted three of the fifteen republics in the Soviet Union. Thus, their political experience differs from that of the other eleven non-Russian Republics. Those republics had been taken into the Soviet Union earlier in the twentieth century, and some had actually been absorbed into the Russian Empire much earlier.

The Baltic Republics thus had higher levels of historic resentment against the Soviet Union than did many of the other non-Russian Republics. For them, Moscow represented the force that had snuffed out their hard-won national independence. In the ensuing decades of the Cold War, the three northwestern republics were the targets of Russianization. Communist

Party leaders in Moscow established incentives that encouraged talented young Russians to move into the Baltic Republics for university education and later for jobs. Conversely, the Soviet leadership offered the same kinds of incentives to young persons from Estonia, Latvia, and Lithuania. The result was a permanent transfer of population of some significance. It may be that Soviet leaders had in mind a future in which later generations would be part Russian and part Baltic (Eglitis 2008, 236). In other words, there would occur a watering down or dilution of the Estonian, Latvian, or Lithuanian nationality. In fact, by the time of the collapse of the Soviet Union in 1991, the Russian proportion of the Latvian population approached 40 percent. That proportion was the highest in the Baltic region. Émigré groups in the West even talked of a purposeful Russian policy of "ethnocide."

Compounding the resentment of the three countries were the economic differences between them and the other republics in the Soviet state. Partly because of their long-standing links to Europe, and partly due to their natural resources, their developmental level economically was higher than the other Soviet Republics. In particular, it considerably exceeded that of the Russian Republic. Quality of their products and standard of living was comparable to that in the advanced states of East Europe. In fact, Russian military personnel often preferred to remain there rather than to be rotated back to their home area in the Soviet Union.

In light of these historical experiences, it is not surprising that the revolution that led to the breakup of the Soviet Union in a sense began in the Baltic Republics. Moscow's leaders in the Gorbachev period were most concerned about the ideas circulating and being publicized in Lithuania (Misiunas 1990, 225). Gorbachev even sent in the military to take over communication centers, and some loss of life occurred. Naturally, the three republics gladly shared the perspective of President Yeltsin in the Russian region that each republic should be able to keep control over the wealth generated by its own natural resources and productivity. This led to the decision to refuse to send tax revenues generated by their own profitability to the Soviet state.

Slovenia and Slovakia had shared the same experience of the Baltic states of being trapped into permanent minority status within a larger federation. However, they fit into a separate category because they had not been part of the Soviet Union. Neither had been subject to anything like Russianization. Each had been part of a negotiating process prior to entering their federations, and so they had not experienced conquest. In fact, each had been a voluntary part of the two federal states that emerged in East Europe after World War I. Based on their small size and permanent minority status, Slovakia and Slovenia were similar. However, in some ways their experiences had been quite different. Slovakia, for a variety of reasons, had been the less economically developed partner in the Czechoslovak federation, while Slovenia had been the most advanced economy in Yugoslavia.

Slovaks did play a central role in the negotiating process that led to the formation of Czechoslovakia after World War I. In fact, the founders of the state signed the official documents leading to its formation in Pittsburgh, Pennsylvania. That city was the site of a large Slovak population. In the Slovak view, President Masaryk and others promised them an equal share of political and economic power in the federation. However, by the time of World War II they felt a profound sense of betrayal. The Nazis exploited this resentment by setting up two separate protectorates for Czechs and Slovaks. When the communists took over, they promised a better day for the Slovaks. However, by the late 1960s, Slovak leaders felt a new sense of betrayal, as the system still seemed biased toward Czech interests and perspectives. The Slovaks pushed for and won passage of a new Federal Law in 1969, and that act accorded them more political equality in certain governmental organs. The top national leaders in 1968–87 were also Slovaks, and at least more of the military-related industry was located in the Slovak sector (Leff 1997, 64–66). However, the broad Czechoslovak federation survived the end of communism in 1989 by only four years. That unit quickly succumbed to the old resentments played out by a new generation of leaders.

Similarly, Slovenia participated in the negotiations that led to creation of Yugoslavia after the First World War. However, their situation differed from that of the Slovaks in that they were one of several junior partners. Also, whereas the Czechs had been a majority in the Czechoslovak state, Serbs in Yugoslavia made up only a plurality. In fact, there had been a significant debate at the founding of the Yugoslav entity. Serbs held that the federation should be a Greater Serbia in which they should naturally dominant. The Slovenes agreed with the other non-Serb groups that each nationality within the federation should have equal status (Banac 1984, 404). In one sense, the federation finally collapsed in 1991, due to the inability to resolve successfully that debate. During the communist period the Slovenes had mixed experiences. Prior to 1956 the Titoist leadership compelled them to share their wealth with the poorer republics in the south of the federation. This situation was due to Soviet insistence on central planning within each communist satellite. Once Tito veered from the Soviet-imposed economic alliance COMECON, the Slovenes did better. They had a greater ability to plan economically on their own and to retain the benefits of their economic productivity. However, in the period of the 1970s, Tito pushed some renewed centralization (Remington 1984, 245), and Slovenia was therefore ready for independence a decade after his death.

The third category of PfP states includes the three "early birds" who eventually gained entry to NATO in 1999. The Czech Republic, Hungary, and Poland all had achieved some status and respect even in communist times. As noted earlier, the Czechs themselves had enjoyed a privileged position within the Czechoslovak federation throughout most of its history. In the late 1960s the nation had responded to West German economic overtures with some, although limited, success. In fact, their achievements economically and politically in the interwar period had been some of the highest in the region. In particular, their industrial strength was significant throughout the entire twentieth century (Golan 1971, 13). When they threw off communist control in 1989 and separated from Slovakia in 1993, they were set to build on this strength. Hungary had also been one of the advanced states economically in the East European region during the Cold War. Particularly, after Kadar introduced the New Economic Mechanism in 1968, their economy took off. The mixture of economic incentives and some relaxation of political controls led to real prosperity in the countryside in the 1970s. They were able to build on these achievements rapidly in the 1990s (Heinrich 1986, 143, 160). Finally, Poland was resource rich, had a large population, and strategically was positioned to make a large, early contribution to NATO. Further, in communist times they had challenged the Soviet economic model of centralization several times, most notably with the Solidarity labor union in the early 1980s (Ost 1990, 138–41). All three nations won early entry to NATO principally because they had enjoyed a running start economically at the time of the anticommunist revolutions of 1989.

The fourth category of new NATO members includes Bulgaria and Romania. If the three countries discussed immediately above were "early birds' in terms of NATO entry, these two were "afterthoughts." Neither had achieved the economic success of their neighbors further north during communist times. Neither had the kind of tradition of limited political pluralism that the other three possessed (Ratesh 1991, 1–16). Neither had ever challenged the Soviet-imposed internal political model, whereas each of the "early birds" had. However, both became vital in the antiterrorist, American-led campaign that took place after 9/11. The prospects for their NATO admission zoomed after the beginning of the Iraq War in spring 2003. These geographically large states offered a kind of buffer zone as well as landing rights and resources for troops moving into the theater of operations. When Turkey pulled out of the planning process for the Iraq War, these two became even more geopolitically significant. Historically, they are quite different from one another. Bulgaria is a Slavic nation with ties to Russia that go back at least to 1877 (Brown 1970, 11–16). Romania has a Latin-based language that makes Mediterranean countries to its west look like natural friends. However, they are similar in having both a lower level of economic achievement and subject political cultures, and that makes them different from other nations that became part of the PfP program.

Impact of Historical Conflicts within and among the PfP Members

What kinds of inherited conflicts exist within the orbit of the new partners that could impact NATO planning after completion of the full admission process? Since many of the points to be discussed below pertain to ethnic and national conflicts from the past, it may be the case that actual NATO military exercises would be the arena in which some of those historical tensions might be evident. Creation of multinational units might put side-by-side soldiers who bring stereotypes and resentments from the past about one another. On the one hand, NATO planners may want to separate such troops into different operational settings. On the other hand, training and education can center on building mutual understanding. While some of these hostilities may circulate among different groups from within one nation-state, other sources of conflict and misunderstanding may emanate from past problems between the countries themselves.

First, there are a number of conflicts that have paralyzed these countries in the past. What is the nature and level of intra-national conflict on a nation-by-nation basis? The three former Baltic Republics from the Soviet Union inherited one basic split, and it flows from past pressures for Russianization. Each of the three has a substantial Russian minority within, and Latvia is the nation with the most sizeable such minority. In part, this ethnic diversity is an inheritance of the Cold War. During the Cold War, each of these three Russian minorities was in fact not a minority at all in terms of the overall demographic picture. Those groups represented the majority ethnic group within the USSR. Near the end of the Cold War the demographic balance was changing in the sense that projections indicated that Russians would soon dip below 50 percent of the overall population of the Soviet Union. However, Russians would still be a clear plurality of the population, in the face of many much smaller groups. However, the end of the Cold War reversed this Russian advantage, and Russian ethnic groups found themselves to be a minority in all of the new non-Russian Eurasian states. During the past 15 years, a number of those new countries have made efforts to restrict the rights of the Russian groups. Latvia, for example, has passed legislation that requires all students to be educated in Latvian after the middle school years. It is expected that all citizens will use that language in business connections and dealings (Goldman 2005, 54–55). As a result, Latvian units, as well as those from the other two Baltic nations, may bring internal resentments with them.

The two smallest nations that emerged from Czechoslovakia and Yugoslavia probably have less of a problem internally than the Baltics. Slovenia, for instance, does not have a distinct ethnic group that has serious claims of discrimination from the past. However, Slovakia has always had a notable Hungarian minority. If one penetrates back further in history, it is possible to see a parallel to the situation in the Baltics. Prior to World War I, Slovakia was part of the Hungarian half of the Austro-Hungarian Empire. As such, they were not a high priority of Budapest in terms of education and economic advance. In 1918 the tables were turned in Slovakia, as they would be in the Baltics in 1991. Slovaks became part of the Czechoslovak nation, and the Hungarians were now a minority in the Slovak sector. Even in postcommunist times that group has been the subject of discrimination (Goldman 2005, 137–8). For example, the Mečiar government in Slovakia made efforts to reduce or even eliminate Hungarian distinctiveness in their neighborhoods. These efforts focused on changes in place names and the schools. Slovak military units that included persons from the Hungarian minority could contain an atmosphere that would undermine unit morale.

The "early birds" have had some experience with past internal, ethnically based tension. For example, Czechs and Slovaks had stereotypes about one another that were challenges during the life of the Czechoslovak state. However, since 1993 the Slovaks have had their own country. The Sudeten German minority was expelled from Czechoslovakia much earlier, in the years following the Nazi defeat. Poland also had a large German minority, but they also were forced out in the mid-1940s. Hungary does have a significant Romanian minority, and its military units could have members of both ethnic groups. However, the main experience that these three advanced Central European nations have in common is the fact of a military crackdown at some point in their Cold War years (Volgyes 1986, 318–20). Hungary experienced this earliest. In 1956 a reform minded government experimented with ideas of independence from the newly created Warsaw Pact and with models of a multiparty political system. As a result, the Soviet Union invaded with its military forces, destroyed the backbone of the Nagy government, and imposed a recentralized, conformist political system. Czechoslovak reform communists pursued similar ideas during the Prague

Spring, and that generated a multinational Warsaw Pact invasion that the Soviet Union spearheaded. Finally, Poland seethed with conflict between its party leadership and the Solidarity leadership in 1980–81. There was no outside invasion, but Moscow ordered a crackdown by the Polish military under General/President Jaruzelski. All three nations thus have collective memories of military occupation, re-centralization, and forced conformism.

What might this common experience have to do with NATO operations and exercises? First, it may create skepticism among the respective populations about seeing their own troops head off to help control an internal situation somewhere else, for they themselves had been targets of occupation. For example, public opinion polls in the three would show much more skepticism about NATO after the beginning of the Iraq War than before. Second, their common experiences may instill more public queasiness about the location of other NATO forces on their own soil. If NATO bases ever were established in these three countries, their presence may remind populations of former occupation by Warsaw Pact forces. A memory of the departing Soviet Army after 1989 is not in such a distant past for any of those nations. Older citizens still recall the items taken by Soviet troops as they hurriedly left as well as the level of garbage and pollutants left behind. Third, connections with NATO may remind these medium-sized nations that they still do not have control over their national destinies. After experiencing Nazi and Soviet controls in the twentieth century, they now hear what NATO expects as well as what the European Union (EU) requires of them. In unpredictable ways, these kinds of experiences may influence future NATO activities.

Ironically, the "afterthoughts" may experience the fewest of these kinds of tensions. It is true that each has a significant minority group within. In northern Romania live several million Hungarians, while nearly 10 percent of Bulgaria's population is Turkish. The kinds of problems noted above for the other nations are potentially dangers for these two as well. In both cases relations with the minority group within have been extremely touchy at certain points in time. For example, Bulgaria expelled a large portion of the Turkish population just before the fall of communism (Goldman 2005, 119). Romania sent the military against its own Hungarian minority just before the fall of the Ceausescu regime in 1989, as they saw the resistance to the hard-line communist leader boiling up from that group (Stokes 1993, 162–3). However, both countries in communist times had no significant experiences of political pluralism. No consequential challenges emerged to the communist leadership for over 40 years, and there were no invasions by Soviet or Warsaw Pact forces. Both countries were willing to put in power after 1989 leaders who had roots in the communist past and were slow about democratization as well as about marketization. Thus, their military units may be less troubled by alliance requests and their eventual immersion in ethnically troubled or even failed states.

A second type of conflict entails those between and among some of the new members. Since an ethnic group is often scattered among two or three nations, some of these rivalries parallel those within the nations. The impact of these tensions on NATO is also possible, since units from several countries often work side by side in nations that have been torn apart by war and that are out of the normal NATO theater of operations.

There are a number of underlying national/cultural differences within the region that often play a background role to some of the ethnic tensions that are more evident. For example, most of the people in the new countries speak some variant of the Slavic language family. Thus, in military operations there may be some commonality and ability of the soldiers to communicate across national lines. Of course, at top officer levels the expectation is that English will be the common language, and so the problem does not exist there. Czechs and Slovaks will have no problem understanding one another. At the same time, several of the nations possess languages that are not Slavic based. Estonia and Hungary share a heritage in the Urguaic language family, and that is very different from the other Slavic based people. Romanian is rooted in the Latin language family, and so its younger soldiers may not be able to understand the Slavic-based groups with which they work. Another underlying cultural difference is based on religion. Church attendance is not the issue here, but rather it is cultural patterns connected with the East/West split that divides the region. Bulgaria and Romania are nations in which Eastern Orthodoxy has been the dominant pattern, while Roman Catholicism is the historical faith for the rest. It is not a good idea to try to link these particular religious faiths to distinctive political patterns. Both traditions have been linked in the past with political authoritarianism. However, the Czechs can point to the rebellious fifteenth century Jan Hus in their history, and they even have a holiday named after him. Poles can point to the role of their brother Pope John Paul II and recall his contributions to the collapse of communism in the late 1980s. However, these language and religious differences are clearly in the background and unlikely to have a direct effect on day-to-day military exercises and missions.

More central to potential misunderstanding within NATO operations are some of the nation-state rivalries and border disputes. For example, Hungary has been in conflict with both Slovakia and Romania over the treatment of its minority in their lands since 1989. Hungary passed a controversial Status Law in 2001 that was quite divisive. It guaranteed the right to work for those two sets of out-of-country Hungarian minorities for three months out of every year. The law also offered education and medical benefits for out-of-state Hungarians who were willing to travel to Hungary. Romania then passed its own Status Law soon thereafter in retaliation (Goldman 2005, 182). During the PfP period, careful balancing of these groups in alliance operations might have been necessary. Although the Czech-Slovak velvet divorce occurred in the early 1990s, the iciness between the two and frequent "putdowns" by individuals from each country can make specific missions more tension filled.

In sum, these two levels of conflict, intra-national and inter-national, can at times be mutually reinforcing. It would be a mistake to overrate their significance or underrate the ability of various units to overcome them. However, it was important for NATO planners to consider this complexity when planning activities that included the Partners at least in the 1990s.

Conflict between PfP States and the Traditional NATO Partners

Several long-standing alliance members have had historical differences with those countries that opted for the PfP Program. Do these conflicts have the potential to hamper future operations?

For example, Turkey is a long-standing member of the alliance, and clearly it has experienced tensions with Bulgaria. As noted above, this has much to do with the treatment of Turkish nationals within Bulgaria, but it also is related to historical differences that trace back to centuries of Ottoman domination of the territory that now makes up modern Bulgaria. At the southernmost point in NATO, Bulgaria has also been in conflict with Greece. These tensions in the Cold War centered on the Yugoslav Republic of Macedonia. Based on historic rights, both nations thought of Macedonia as part of their own country (Goldman 2005, 118–119). Due to Greek pressure, the post-Cold War name of the country must be The Former Yugoslav Republic of Macedonia. Further, the German conquest of East Europe during World War II occasionally brings to the surface antagonisms. There are nationalistic groups and leaders in Germany that continue to call for compensation to the families expelled from Czechoslovakia and Poland after World War II. Similar Hungarian groups occasionally make comparable claims about countries like Slovakia that sent their ethnic family members packing at the same time. Joint planning in NATO can be made more difficult by such historic differences between the traditional partners and the new recruits.

PfP Plan as a Lucky Transitional Step

Establishment of the PfP Plan was a lucky step in the early 1990s. It emerged very quickly in the wake of the Cold War's end, and the plan made sense in terms of the threats posed by rogue leaders who became more prominent in the ensuing fluid international situation. While the simple phrase PfP concealed a simmering pot of historical legacies of conflict among the partners, still all involved were looking for a fresh start. The need for some security anchor or center of gravity was evident in light of only the challenge to the region from Milosevic. However, the entire PfP project would have been much more problematic had 9/11 occurred one decade earlier. If the ensuing invasions of Afghanistan and Iraq had occurred at a similar earlier point in time, the process of NATO expansion would have been much trickier. Probably alliance expansion would have made sense. Perhaps it would have become even a higher priority. However, haste and quick planning would then have been the order of the day. It was indeed lucky that the partnership plan commenced in a decade that contained its own challenges and tragedies but not one that was filled with a whole new category of terrorism, cross-state threats, and suffering.

CHAPTER THREE

From Partnership to Membership in 1999

The partnership process resulted in actual membership invitations for the three nations described above as "early birds." Those nations included the Czech Republic, Hungary, and Poland, and the year was 1999. Weeks after joining the alliance, the Kosovo operation began and the new members realized the consequences of this new commitment. One Czech writer (Žižka 2009, 13) described that surprise as "The shock of Kosovo." However, NATO planners did not request much for Kosovo from the three new members in terms of equipment, troops, and operations. The military part of the Kosovo operation ended rather quickly, and at the time it seemed to be the last chapter of Milosevic's series of aggressive military acts. The alliance, perhaps, had compensated through this military operation for its inaction and passivity during the Bosnian War in 1992–95. However, from the vantage point of 10 years later, Kosovo was a harbinger of things to come and the onset of a new era of demands on NATO. The threat would be global terrorism rather than Serbian aggression against both its neighbors and one of its own republics, but the message for the alliance would be the same. The quiet first post-Cold War decade for NATO would yield abruptly to a noisy second post-Cold War decade.

The Czech Republic

For the Czech Republic, the anticommunist revolution that took place in 1989 was the critical event that made possible membership in western organizations like NATO and the EU. The western-leaning implications of that revolution echoed previous cycles of Czechoslovak history. For example, in the inter-war period of the twentieth century, the First Republic adopted into its political system many of the features of the western democracies that had emerged in the previous century and one half. After three decades of totalitarian rule between 1938 and 1968, the Prague Spring reformers again looked to the West and its democratic institutions for ideas and inspiration. Just as the seeds of the First Republic stayed alive beneath the permafrost of mid-century totalitarianism, so also the seeds that the Prague Spring reformers planted continued to germinate after 1968 beneath the veneer of normalization. In this sense, the 1989 revolution was the time when regional and global conditions made it possible for these two dormant seeds of western democratic ideas to sprout.

In many ways the revolution itself was a singular one that differed from the other rebellions that took place within the bloc during the same year. Massive, peaceful demonstrations daily in Prague forced the antiquarian communist structures to collapse. Step-by-step the percentage of communists in the cabinet was reduced to minority status (Ash 1990, 123–4). Alexander Dubček stepped out of the shadows that had encircled him since 1968 and became a visible symbol of the seed planted during the Prague Spring. More important was the strategy making role of dissident and Charter'77 leader Václav Havel, who coordinated the revolution from a back room in the Magic Lantern Theater. In effect, the power of the people combined with charismatic leadership to put the national value structure on a path to western institutions. With backbone and restored confidence, the transformed nation could take up an integral role both in its region and on the wider European stage.

Post-1989 foreign policy experiences also became pointers to future membership in NATO and the EU. First, the break with Slovakia was a foreign policy decision that located the Czech state a bit further to the west than it had been during the long Czechoslovak period. Further, the Czechs had freed themselves from the pressures represented by the Slovak nationalist and eastward leaning Vladimír Mečiar. Second, Prime Minister Klaus and his associates made the decision to convert the centrally planned economy to free market principles in a short time, essentially through shock therapy. Western economists such as Jeffrey Sachs were recommending this type of transition for the postcommunist systems, even though a number of key nations such as Russia eventually backed away from that advice. Third, western leaders deemed the Czech Republic as one of the newly postcommunist nations that was prepared to contribute to NATO very early. Therefore, the Clinton Administration welcomed the Czechs as participants in the PfP Program. Fourth, the two principal ideological threads in Czech foreign policy during the 1990s nudged the nation toward firm membership in communities of the west such as the EU. The thread of ideology symbolized by President Havel emphasized a "civic foreign policy." Based on his dissident experience, Havel focused on humanist aims, the common good, universal values, and good international citizenship for the new Czech nation. In contrast but in a complementary way, Prime Minister Klaus emphasized "free market values" as the foreign policy key that could unlock the doors to western institutions (Fawn 2003, 205–8). The forging of such values during the fast-moving events of the 1990s positioned the Czech Republic for invitations from the West into its inner circles.

The Czech Republic in the 1990s encountered a maze of external pressures and alliances that could become significant in its future historical experiences. President Havel initially had a real fondness for the OSCE, as that group of nations seemed to offer a useful middle course between the defunct WTO and NATO. Also, in 1991 Czechoslovakia, along with Poland and Hungary, signed the Visegrad Declaration. This neighborhood organization bore the potential to "maintain culture and national character" at a time when larger organizations loomed on the horizon (Ministry of Foreign Affairs of the Czech Republic 2005a). Another attractive organization in the early 1990s was the Western European Union (WEU). At that time, this long-established organization seemed to be the future EU military organization. All of these external pressures, however, had receded from view by the latter part of the 1990s.

Eventually, the PfP Plan of NATO became much more attractive as an external organization worth joining. Finally, on February 26, 1999, President Havel signed the agreement to join the military alliance (Ministry of Foreign Affairs of the Czech Republic 2005b). Very quickly activity commenced, for the Czechs needed to participate in planning the alliance's bombing campaign in Kosovo. Symbolic of the importance of the Czech Republic was NATO's decision to hold its 2002 conference in Prague. It was at that conference that the organization extended offers of membership to seven additional post-communist nations. By that point NATO overshadowed the OSCE, Visegrad, and the WEU as an external organizing focus for Czech defense plans.

Simultaneous with the opening offered by NATO were negotiations with the EU. On paper the discussions mainly centered on the economic goals that were at the heart of that organization's activities. However, the EU began to plan for its own military component, once the hopes lifted up by the WEU began to fade. Thus, they established a component entitled the Common Foreign and Security Policy (CFSP). After the Amsterdam Treaty of 1997, planning became more formalized. Brussels took additional control of policy formation, but the member nations received the right to veto CFSP missions if they conflicted with national interests. Within several years the Czech Republic included commitments to the CFSP in its National Program (National Program 2000). The eventual role of the CFSP in European military planning was then unclear, but it did offer promise as a military alliance that would be independent of American direction.

There were concerns from the beginning about the impact of joint membership in NATO and the EU on Czech independence and autonomy. Karlas perceives both organizations as emphasizing crisis management and conflict prevention. NATO, in addition, had a major role in providing collective defense. He concluded that both organizations were intergovernmental regimes in their essence and not designed really to dictate policy to the individual member states. At the same time, both did possess limited power to transmit authority with regard to the agenda. NATO planners were able to create an agenda for the member states, while the CFSP additionally bore the power to push for implementation of the agenda (Karlas 2006, 35–8). If that depiction squares with reality, then the Czech Republic would not be dealing with particularly intrusive external organizations. Czech reactions to Kosovo as their first NATO operation were mixed. Initially, they waited ten days to grant airspace rights to those countries actually carrying out the bombing campaign. However, the leadership eventually voluntarily supported the humanitarian goals of the operation, and this fitted in with President Havel's view that NATO in general expressed both Czech and European values (Fawn 2003, 219–21).

Attention to certain aspects of the developing political culture and of participant institutions reinforces the march of the Czech Republic toward the West and NATO. The Civic Democratic Party (ODS) headed by Václav Klaus endorsed all of the steps connected with the return to Europe in the 1993–97 period. The break-up of Czechoslovakia in 1993 hastened this process, as it pushed Ukraine and Russia further away geographically from the Czech Republic. Thus the Czechs had joined the PfP in 1994 and begun to stress connections with other Visegrad partners such as Poland (Szayna 1999, 112–48).

An analysis of political party positions during elections in the 1990s is very revealing in terms of the issues and debates that circulated throughout the Czech Republic. Political party leaders debated the merits of the move to the West but finally endorsed it. The 1998 elections are a useful example. The Czech Social Democratic Party (ČSSD) ended up technically in power, with Miloš Zeman as Prime Minister, but the party needed to establish a "Gentlemen's Agreement" with the ODS in order to function as a government. For the ČSSD there was less emphasis in the election campaign on hard-headed defense of national interests and more of a focus on living standards and the rights of citizens within the country. This priority on domestic issues led the ČSSD to upgrade the importance of North-South relations and the associated role of the UN. It concluded that Czechs should have a say whenever human rights were jeopardized in any part of the world. While it endorsed EU membership, it thought of it in terms of stimulating the Czech economy. While it favored NATO entry, it expressed grave concerns about the future location of nuclear weapons on Czech territory.

During the same election the ODS continued to give a "real-politik" cast to its statements on foreign policy. National interests rather than humanitarian concerns were its top priority. NATO membership could bring increased security for the country as well as trade and technological benefits. Heightened economic activity would promote development of the free market, a priority for Klaus since the early 1990s. National economic interests were of paramount importance, while crusades connected with globalization and human rights were to be carefully examined. Increased Czech exports through membership in international organizations were the desired outcome. Thus, the party said less than did the ČSSD about broader, western-based international organizations that could pull the Czech nation beyond the orbit of its national interest toward embrace of humanitarian concerns (Dürr 2000, 84–97).

One of the continuing political challenges for the Czech Republic during the 1990s was the issue of minority rights, a matter that affected the country's relationship with the outside world. The criteria for entering NATO, as well as the EU, required a record of fairness toward key groups within the population. One major conflict was the relationship between Czechs and Roma. A number of well-publicized incidents have raised questions about Czech attitudes and policies. For example, the erection of a wall by Czechs in Ústí nad Labem in 1999, became a foreign policy incident as well as an embarrassment in the year of admission to NATO. It was clear that the wall was intended to prevent Czechs from having to view the Roma population as well as their lifestyle. Attention to such issues was necessary in light of integration into western institutions. Development of a robust political culture on foreign policy questions remained another challenge to the new state. One significant new factor was the emergence of a visible public opinion on foreign policy questions. In general, the public was supportive of the new linkages with western institutions. However, there were some differences that were significant. Public opinion polls over time demonstrated a stable level of support for EU entry. However, before 1999 support for entry into NATO was less impressive (Leff 1997, 263). The Kosovo bombing campaign of 1999 made some difference in that. Their proximity to the Balkans made Czechs think somewhat more positively about NATO entry.

There were also unique efforts to build support within the political culture for certain foreign policy institutions that would be connected with NATO. One abiding problem was the negative set of Czech attitudes about the role of the military. Czech resentment of the military is understandable in light of the long years of the Soviet military presence after 1968. Also, after 1989, the Soviet military left a catastrophe in many Czech communities. The barracks and other facilities were in terrible condition, and individual Soviet units had taken anything of value from those locations. One effort to build more positive Czech attitudes about the military took place in South Bohemia. A citizen group called SAS was formed in 1997. The aim of the group was to demonstrate that the Czech military was a contributing instrument in a democratic state rather than merely an instrument of power. The SAS Institute established links to schools and universities with the objective of cultivating a more positive attitude about the Czech military. It set up conferences and also consulted specialists from other nations. In fact, one result of this activity was the creation of special ties between the city of Český Krumlov in the Czech Republic and Miami Beach in the State of Florida, USA. A public exchange of ideas about the role of the military could generate more informed Czech perspectives about the value of a strong defense capability to cope with new threats (Vondrouš 2002).

Finally, by the late 1990s, the spotlight shifted to the probability of NATO membership, and specific issues emerged. Earlier talk about reliance on the WEU for collective defense had disappeared. That organization had been born in 1948 and had become part of EU thinking in the early 1990s, in connection with European responsibility for its own defense (Pezl 1994, 25–6). As the date of NATO admission neared, Czechs began to focus on preparation of legislation that would move the Czech defense structure toward the level of NATO standards. New military personnel requirements mandated that the Czech defense sector prepare courses for all ranks about the changing role of the military. Training in the use of radar was also upgraded. Further, the Czech Republic would need to build a crisis command center that would facilitate the rapid sharing of information between NATO and the Czech Republic. It would also be necessary for the Czechs to build a system of command and control that paralleled the organizations in other alliance partners (Svěrák 1999, 13–31).

Involvement of the Czech military in the Kosovo bombing campaign brought home certain lessons that were pertinent to the defense sector. One was increased awareness of the asymmetry of capabilities within the alliance (Pick 2000, 25–32). America provided 80 percent of the bombs dropped on Kosovo in the spring of 1999, as well as 90 percent of the weapons. U.S. airplanes were the only ones that could operate in all weather. Lowered European defense budgets in the 1990s resulted in a situation in which all European NATO members contributed only two-thirds of the funding that the Unites States did to defense. The Czech Republic responded to this imbalance by developing a blueprint for change in 2001. That plan called for a rapid upgrade in maneuverability of units, logistical strength, placement of weaponry and personnel, ability to resist over a long period, and information command and control. Further, the Ministry of Defense drew up a list of four principles that would guide Czech participation in NATO. They included continued involvement of the two North American powers in the defense of Europe, reliance on NATO as the main guarantor of European security, subordination of the CFSP of the EU within the framework of NATO, and guaranteed access to NATO capabilities for all EU defense and security missions (Novotný, 2002). Recognition of the important Czech role in NATO was evident in the decision to hold the alliance's conference of November 2002 in Prague. That was the meeting at which an invitation was extended to seven additional nations to join NATO.

In fact, the involvement of the Czech Republic in mainly NATO missions was very broad in the two decades following the Velvet Revolution. They made their first substantial contribution during the First Gulf War in the 1990–91 period, as they sent 200 troops as part of the liberation unit. They followed up with a 320 person unit that was part of the UN Guards Contingent in Iraq from 1991 to 2003. These operations were part of UN rather than NATO activity, but they showed a sense of loyalty and responsibility to the kinds of missions that would characterize the post-Cold War world. Involvement in Bosnia after the Dayton Accords was even more extensive. Czechs committed 6300 troops to a combination of Implementation Force (IFOR) and Stabilization Force (SFOR) missions in Bosnia in the critical 1996–2001 period and the first few of those years predated their actual membership in NATO. Later, in the 2002–04, period, 42 of their soldiers took part in various command posts and civil cooperation units. After the EU took over the Bosnia mission from NATO in December, 2004, Czechs contributed several hundred troops through EU Force (EUFOR), to ALTHEA, in order to protect a camp and provide the services of experts. When Kosovo emerged as a major controversy in Balkan politics, the Czechs again were on the spot. They contributed 980 troops to the peacekeeping operation in the first three years after the NATO bombing campaign in 1999. Thereafter, from 2002 to 2005, their involvement included 2400 members of an entire Czech-Slovak battalion. During the following year, their Brigade/Task Force included 1438 military personnel.

Post-9/11 operations of the allies also engaged the commitments of Czech defense planners. Their well-known field hospital capabilities were requested and delivered in both major conflicts that followed the terrorist attacks on the United States. They sent the 6th and 11th Field Hospital units to Afghanistan early in 2002, a smaller Field Surgical Team in early 2003, and a Field Hospital and Chemical Detachment of 658 persons to the Kabul International Airport in 2007–08. Similarly, Czechs took part in the American-led invasion of Iraq through their 7th Field Hospital for most of 2003. Additional contributions to Afghanistan included a three-year stay (2004–07) by its 350-person unit for explosive ordinance disposal at Kabul International Airport, introduction of its 601st Special Forces Group for six months in 2004, a 600-person unit that became part of the German Provincial Reconstruction Team (PRT) in Feyzabad-Badakshan (2005–07), over 100 persons for protection of contingents in International Security Assistance Force (ISAF) URZUGAN (2008–09), and in the same two years 300 military personnel as part of the Enduring Freedom general operations. With regard to Iraq, they offered a small contingent of military police in Shaibah (2003–06) and a contingent of 423 to the NATO Training Mission (NTM-I) from 2003 until the end of 2008. Such extensive involvement demonstrated a consistent willingness to contribute fully at a time of several changes in domestic leadership and political party control (Ministry of Defense of the Czech Republic 2010a).

Poland

Like the Czech Republic, Poland was a likely contender for early membership based on its record in both communist and early postcommunist times. During communist times, the nation and its leaders developed a record of perhaps being the most consistent maverick within the communist bloc. In fact, Polish nationalism had been a powerful force historically over two centuries. The Great Powers had partitioned the nation in the late eighteenth century, and its disappearance from the map until the time of World War I intensified nationalist longings. During the communist era, Poles had resisted imposition of the Soviet Model as well as the emplacement of Soviet personnel in the highest levels of their political system. In 1956, Soviet party leader Khrushchev flew in his top leaders to negotiate with the Poles. Although the Poles won on some of their demands, the nationalist leader Gomulka turned out to be very antireform in his leadership style. Economic stringencies, mainly centering on drastic, overnight increases of the prices of basic commodities, led to the worker-intellectual revolts of 1970 and 1976. Of course, the Solidarity era reflected a powerful dose of Polish nationalism and very much caught the attention of the West. In 1980–81, Lech Walesa headed a workers movement that caught up into its net most employed persons both in the factories and in the countryside. Although Moscow orchestrated a crack-down by the Polish military in December 1981, eventual release of Solidarity personnel from prison and house arrest later in the decade set the stage for Poland to take the lead in the firecracker string of anticommunist revolutions in 1989.

Embedded within those nationalist outbursts and repressions over the stretch of two centuries was a conception that Poland was a European state that shared principally in the cultural traditions of the West rather than the East. In earlier centuries, Poland had been a vital trade route connecting East and West. Poles sold the products from their salt mines to many countries of West Europe to the extent that the natural resource became a principal source of their income after the fourteenth century. In later centuries, many Polish emigrants had moved to the United States, and so links between family members in American cities like Chicago and relatives back in Poland strengthened the tug of the West. In 1978, Karol Wojtyla from Krakow became the new Pope in Rome, and his international travels made him into a near international celebrity. Pride in his accomplishments cemented the leanings of many Poles toward the West and provided a ready forum for attacks on key aspects of Soviet control. Rome rather than Moscow became the central point on the Polish compass. Following the fall of communism, Polish political practices became quickly imitative of ones in the United States and Western Europe. The presidency of former Solidarity leader Walesa cemented the links to western personalities and practices. Although former communist forces had a mild resurgence in the elections of 1994, partly in reaction to the disruptions caused by adoption of capitalist principles, over the long haul this did not constitute a halt in the waves pushing Poland to the West.

All these efforts to reset Poland's location in the West encouraged NATO planners to conclude that this post-communist nation would have something of value to offer the alliance. At a time of great preoccupation with the civil war in Bosnia, Poland gained stature as country on the eastern side of Europe that had the potential to offer leverage in future situations that required deterrence of Milosevic-like aggression. A nation with such a large population would potentially have the capacity to provide significant military forces in the Balkans. As such, it could help provide an answer to those who were frustrated that Europe had done so little to contain the violence in the Balkans after the end of the Cold War. Eventually, Poland did take on a major responsibility when its leaders agreed to have it supervise a major sector of Iraq south of Baghdad after the fall of Saddam Hussein in 2003.

Hungary

Admission of Hungary in 1999 to the alliance was on one level more surprising than the admission of the Czech Republic and Poland. Like those two, Hungary had not been part of the Russian or Soviet orbit in its earlier history, but it also had been separate from the progressive Habsburg Lands until the creation of the Dual Monarchy in 1867. The territories under its purview and sway had not been targets of economic and educational upgrading to the extent that the areas under Vienna had been. This reality explains in part why the Slovaks, who had been under the control of Budapest, came into their federation with the Habsburg-ruled Czechs in 1918 in an inferior position. At the same time, Hungary had been a large and significant entity in its expanded state prior to the loss of territory that it experienced after the Peace of Trianon that concluded World War I in its areas. Of course, after Trianon it had the ambition to regain either its former Hungarian-populated territories or more influence over those populations. Such ambitions color Hungarian policy even at points in the twenty-first century.

Thus, Hungary's impact on the Central European region historically made it into a state of importance but one whose history differed from the somewhat shared experiences of Poles and Czechs. During the communist era, several leaders experimented with western models even more extensively than had the Poles. The 1956 revolt against Soviet control included demands by Imre Nagy to leave the just-formed Warsaw Pact and also to create a multiparty democracy. Freedom of speech developed in an embryonic way in circles that centered on coffee houses and pubs. Although the Soviet invasion brought a quick halt to these experiments, this brief dalliance with democracy made Hungary into something of a hero to the West. Following the reform episode and defeat, many Hungarians emigrated into the West and became a source of pressure that pulled the nation more into the western orbit. As mentioned in a Chapter Two, the introduction of the New Economic Mechanism by Janos Kadar after 1968 gave Hungarians some experience with capitalist incentives and the concept of a market. In 1989, it was not that surprising the Hungarians immediately followed the Polish example and opened their borders to Austria. Their economic system did reasonably well in the 1990s, and they joined the Czechs as the most likely future members of both NATO and the EU.

Hungary's geopolitical position in Europe offered an additional argument on behalf of admission to the western military alliance during the conflicts in the Balkans in the 1990s. Hungary was even closer to the rump Yugoslav state headed by Milosevic than either of the other two members of the class of 1999. In fact, all three received formal invitations to join the alliance two years after the end of the Bosnian War, in July 1997 (Ministry of Foreign Affairs of Hungary 2010a). If future military missions took place in the region, both over-flight and landing rights on Hungarian territory would benefit the alliance to a considerable extent. Its provision of troops might also be a bit less controversial than use of troops from the other two nations, for there was a remnant Hungarian population that was part of Yugoslavia. They had belonged to that nation since World War I, but they had retained their Hungarian identity and distinctiveness. In the end, the size, location, and economic/political strength of this nation made it a prime candidate for early admission to NATO.

Inclusion of Hungary paid off for the alliance in an important way several years after 9/11. Hungary decided to join the Strategic Airlift Capability in 2006. In the next several years, they gave NATO rights to a permanent base Papa in the western part of the country. C-17 cargo planes would utilize that base as their home and Hungary would itself be able to register the planes. In fact, the first planes arrived at that base in the fall of 2008 (Ministry of Foreign Affairs of Hungary 2010b). Such a contribution was important, for it provided the alliance with an enduring capability rather than simply a temporary commitment of certain types of specialized troops.

Model for Future Alliance Expansion

Above all, the admission of three new NATO members created a pattern that could be useful in future expansions. It was clear that the 1999 decision to include the Czech Republic but exclude Slovakia was probably only a temporary one. In addition, interest in Slovenia and the three Baltic states remained high, based on the same mix of factors that led to admission of the three in 1999. Those five countries also had progressive traditions during the previous century. The three Baltic nations had actually had experience as independent countries for several decades after the end of World War I. Slovenia had been the most economically advanced republic in the larger Yugoslavia during much of the twentieth century. Slovak economic prospects had considerably perked up after the emergence of the Husák regime in Czechoslovakia in 1969. While Husák masterminded the return of Czechoslovakia back into the Soviet orbit through post-Prague Spring normalization, he was a Slovak who located much of the armaments industry in that region and appointed many Slovaks to staff and ministerial positions within the central government. Thus, all five had something to offer the alliance. In part, it was their small size that kept them out of the picture in 1999, a year in which NATO planners made an effort to bring larger states with more weight and clout into the alliance. The three "early birds" that made up the class of 1999 could have the most impact right away, and the expectations were that the next emergency in the Balkans was not far off. They could also be a more powerful deterrent of Russian ambitions, in light of the wariness of that eastern giant about the whole series of events taking place on its western and southwestern border. Therefore, standards and procedures developed through the PfP process had culminated with admission of three new partners in 1999. Repetition of that model could become the formula needed for admission of additional states in the future, and NATO planners would thus not be always in the position of needing to "recreate the wheel."

CHAPTER FOUR

The Class of 2004 and the Post-9/11 World

Following the admission of the three nations to NATO in 1999, preparations began for the entry of several more. In the middle of those deliberations, the attack by al Qaeda on American targets took place on September 11, 2001. Since the source of the attacks was in the Persian Gulf region, further NATO expansion took on a greater urgency. In fact, Bulgaria and Romania were added to the list of potential new members in part because they offered a kind of buffer against the violence that threatened to flow in from the east. Although the Iraq War of 2003 would not be a NATO mission at the beginning or primarily, the organization and its Secretary George Robertson took responsibility for protecting alliance member Turkey from retaliation by Iraq (Hendrickson 2006, 117–41). The admission process was further complicated by the emergence of new nuclear powers at roughly the same time. Both India and Pakistan successfully tested nuclear weapons in successive weeks in 1998. Accelerated work on nuclear capabilities proceeded in Iran, North Korea, and possible Iraq (Terzuolo 2006, 45). The weak alliance reaction was partly based on its internal preoccupation with the complicated process of admitting new members. As a final result, NATO admitted Estonia, Latvia, Lithuania, Slovakia, Slovenia, Bulgaria, and Romania.

The current membership admission process itself is multi-pronged, tedious and lengthy. At the same time, its comprehensiveness ensures that successful candidates for membership will be prepared to contribute. Membership selection follows an extended process of discussion between both leaders and populations in the potential new member states and also in the existing alliance partners. Following an initial invitation to a potential member, the alliance conducts talks that cover "political, military resources, security and legal commitments." There must be at least two sets of talks between the leadership of the alliance and the target member. At that point, the focus switches to the current membership of NATO. The alliance prepares protocols that then become amendments to the NATO Treaty. All the allies must sign and then ratify the protocols. As the ball bounces back in the other direction, the potential member state must then present a letter of intent that includes a timetable for needed reforms. During recent rounds, states must promise to devote a certain percentage of GDP to their defense sector. Upon receipt of the letter of intent, the organization's Secretary-General then sends a formal reply. Completion of those stages in the admission process enables the potential new member to begin to play a role in NATO activities. However, each also receives at that time a "tailored" Membership Action Plan (MAP) that outlines their agenda for reform. Once all NATO partners have approved the accession protocols, then the Secretary-General is empowered to extend the official invitation to membership. The U.S. State Department serves as the official depository of the formal instruments of accession, and so their placement there ends the process (NATO 2009b). In sum, the process is a blend of advice from the alliance and participatory discussions by both new member and old member constituencies.

After NATO had expanded from 16 to 26 members by the middle of 2004, the alliance was positioned to confront in a more broad-based way the confluence of terrorism and instability connected with the Balkans, al Qaeda, the eventual war in Iraq, and nuclear proliferation. On the one hand, an enlarged alliance was able to manage the Kosovo conflict in the years following the NATO bombing campaign of 1999. Further, this enlarged organization planned the peace-making operations in Bosnia before turning over technical control in 2004 to the EU. Then in 2006, NATO took full charge of the military missions in increasingly troubled Afghanistan. Also, the ten new alliance members were more likely to feel some obligation to "help out" in the "coalition of the willing" in Iraq, in light of their recently acquired NATO obligations. On the other hand, the expanded alliance of necessity had more potential internal conflict to manage, and dissension might undercut counter-terrorist tactics if not strategy. For example, would Bulgarians and Turks work smoothly together when on the same assignment further east? Would the old ethnic conflicts between them or with other historically opposed groups compromise future military missions?

Alliance Summitry

Several NATO Summits underlined the importance of the new members for the continuing struggle against terrorism and instability. The 2002 summit in Prague was notable for several reasons. First, it was actually held on the territory of one of the new members admitted in 1999. Already, the Czech Republic had something of a track record of support for alliance activities. After extended discussion, they had given the green light to the bombing campaign in Kosovo the same year they joined. As the summit was held in November of 2002, it was clear that request would soon come to the Czechs for assistance in the form of specialized units in the upcoming Iraq War. Second, it was at the Prague Summit that the decision was made to expand the alliance during the next few years. Inclusion of the Baltic states of Latvia, Lithuania, and Estonia was meaningful, since they had formerly been part of the Soviet Union. Slovakia received an invitation that it had not obtained in 1999, the year in which the Czech Republic came in with Hungary and Poland. Elections had removed strongly nationalist forces from their leadership, and by 2002 their patterns of political and economic evolution matched those of the Czechs. Slovenia was the post-Yugoslav nation that was most prepared to contribute to NATO, and thus they entered the admission track. As noted above, the surprising choices were Bulgaria and Romania. Economically, they lagged behind the others being offered admission, and they also needed to make further progress in political democratization. However, they did offer a large buffer against the violence and instability so characteristic of the Gulf and Southwest Asian regions. Thus, their admission itself was linked to the new type of regional and even global war.

Another significant meeting was the one held at the end of September 2006, in Slovenia. Again, the site was the territory of one of the new members admitted only two years before. Much of the discussion centered on Afghanistan, and a key concern was obtaining commitments of more troops. In addition, pressure was put on all alliance partners to consider donations of equipment to the Afghan Army, even if it was not possible to increase troop levels from individual countries. Problems also existed in the restrictions or caveats that certain members had put on the operations of their own troops in the country. Some had prohibited their militaries from operating in the most dangerous parts of the country, and others had permitted their forces to operate only during the daylight hours. In particular, the American Defense Secretary Donald Rumsfeld pushed the new members to loosen these restrictions so that American troops should not have to bear such a heavy burden of risk (USATODAY 2007a).

In November 2006, Riga, Latvia was the site of another NATO Summit. Of course, Latvia was one of the new members admitted to NATO in 2004. In addition, some of the new alliance partners played a crucial role in the security arrangements for the meeting. Security was particularly challenging due to the existence there of a port. The renowned Czech chemical unit, for example, received the job of setting up a decontamination center in the heart of the city (iDNES 2006a). Crucially, the alliance made decisions about admitting additional new members. They invited Serbia, Montenegro, and

Bosnia-Herzegovina to become members of the PfP Program. However, they also warned both Serbia and Bosnia-Herzegovina that they needed to cooperate closely with the World Court at The Hague in turning over alleged war criminals from the Balkan Wars of the 1990s. Presumably, the PfP period would be a time of testing their resolve in those important matters. Alliance leaders commented on the progress being made by existing PfP partners Croatia, Macedonia, and Albania. However, they did not set any dates for the movement of those nations onto the NATO timetable (iDNES 2006b; SME 2006a).

Overall, it is clear that NATO used its summits both to cement the activities of the new members into the alliance agenda and to prepare the way for additional members in the future. Their newest PfP members were the strongest remaining non-NATO members in the Balkans, and their potential contributions to the battle against terrorism further east seemed to outweigh the decade-long resistance from several to overtures from the World Court to turn over suspected war criminals in a timely manner. Location of a number of summits on the territory of the new member states stood as a symbol of their military contributions and of their general support for U.S. operations in Afghanistan and even Iraq.

Potential Contributions of the Class of 2004 to the Alliance

The three Baltic nations strengthen NATO's flank in the important Baltic Sea region. As such, they offer support for the alliance in a delicate area that contains a range of touchy issues, many of which pertain to the presence of Russia next door. Each of the three contains a sizeable Russian minority, with that ethnic group being largest in Latvia. Language rights of that minority have embittered relations between all three Baltic countries and Russia. In addition, alleged mistreatment of Russian artifacts and historical statues important in World War II history has created tense situations and even stand-offs as well. The inclusion of the Baltic countries in NATO provides the three of them with a bit more leverage against Russia in these conflicts. In addition, Kaliningrad is a piece of Russian territory lodged amidst the Baltic nations and now separate from Russia proper. Since it is now surrounded by NATO members, there is another point of challenge to the authority of Moscow. However, from the vantage point of the Baltic nations, their new geopolitical position within the alliance strengthens their prospects for maintaining a strong foothold when conflicts of interest occur with Russia.

However, the Baltic contribution goes beyond provision of a bargaining chip for themselves and NATO in light of tension with Russia. Their potential for contributions to NATO's new type of missions is larger than their territorial size. Given their historical experiences during the past century, their military units and personnel would have unique understanding and sensitivity to the settings of those alliance missions.

First, each Baltic nation is small and has been through challenges in asserting its own values and autonomy within the immediate neighborhood. Similarly, Kosovo has been a nation only since February 2008, and the new fledgling nation has struggled to locate its bearings in the turbulent world of which it has been part. Second, each Baltic nation has struggled with its own internal ethnic complexity and diversity, primarily centering on relations with the Russian minorities. In a parallel way, Bosnia's central dilemma since its creation in 1991 has been to achieve a stable but delicate balance among Muslims, Serbs, and Croats. Third, Estonia, Latvia, and Lithuania have each wrestled with Russia in one way or another. They experienced 20 years of independence in the interwar period, were annexed by the Soviet Union, chafed under Russianization from 1940 until 1991, and then have engaged in occasional duels with Russia since independence. In some ways, the ethnic groups that struggle in Afghanistan share similar experiences and understandings. The Soviet Union occupied and fought in Afghanistan from 1979 until 1988, and in the last two decades tensions and conflicts have moved back and forth between Afghanistan and the Eurasian countries that now occupy former Soviet space. This was especially true during the tumultuous period right after 9/11. Fourth, the Baltic region has an anchor in the stable Scandinavian community of nations just to their west. Individually and through its regional organizations, the Scandinavian nations have inclusively reached out to the new Baltic nations and provided both a cover and specific assistance. As these three Baltic nations take part with other alliance partners in the technically non-NATO operation in Iraq, they can help to widen the horizons of groups within Iraq to the possibilities of engaging in positive ways with other nations in the region. Creation of new regional organizations in Southwest Asia could be a step that echoes the bonds that have been forged between the Scandinavian and Baltic nations.

How would such understandings be seen and shared though the prism of Baltic involvement in NATO-related missions such as Bosnia, Kosovo, Afghanistan, and even Iraq? Discussions between Baltic commanders and alliance personnel in the other four locations would be one means of contact, as would linkages with local civilian and military managers in the four. Most important might be the contacts that would result from interactions among members of the Baltic military units and citizens with whom they work on common projects. Among others, such projects may entail police training, reestablishment of effective educational institutions, and provision of high quality infrastructure that provides basic local government services. Empathy and cooperation between alliance military units and engaged personnel in the host countries would be enhanced by the mutual understandings that a common history provides. Thereby, the Baltic nations would be making a series of small, niche contributions to the ongoing battle against terrorism.

Slovenia and Slovakia are two additional members of the class of 2004, and each has the capacity to contribute to the larger missions and struggles in a unique way. Like the Baltic nations, the two are similar in their small size. Unlike the small northeastern European countries, they do not really share a common earlier history. Slovakia was under the control of Budapest within the Austro-Hungarian Empire, while Slovenia was a part of Vienna's orbit within the same larger entity. Thus, they had different developmental experiences, to the disadvantage of the Slovaks.

However, parallels reemerge when the spotlight shifts to the communist era, for both were the smaller pieces of larger federations. Slovaks perceived their situation to be a difficult one for at least the first two decades of that era. Between 1948 and 1968, Slovaks did not receive many top political positions or economic commitments. To them, this position of ethnic discrimination was a continuation of the Czech approach within the common state all the way back to 1918. The promises of the Pittsburgh Agreement of 1918 had never come to fruition, in the Slovak view. Conditions had improved in the 1968–89 timeframe, with two out of the last three communist leaders of the nation having been Slovaks. However, Czech-Slovak tensions broke out immediately after the anticommunist revolution, and the federation was dead within four years. Slovenia's situation in the Yugoslav federation was somewhat parallel to that of Slovakia's. Slovenia was one of several small non-Serb ethnic groups that joined Yugoslavia after World War I. Along with the Croats, Macedonians, Montenegrins, Bosnians, and others, Slovenia initially pushed for a true federation with some semblance of equal rights. The contrasting perspective of the largest ethnic group was that Yugoslavia should be a Greater Serbia, with Serbs in key positions of leadership within all major institutions such as government, the economy, and the military. In a sense, the federation leaders never satisfactorily solved that dilemma of what the internal power balance and configuration of the nation-state was to be. Therefore, Slovenia suffered under Serb domination for over seven decades after creation of the state and was very quick to opt out when the opportunity emerged in 1991.

Can these two nations in the middle of Central Europe offer much in the way of unique perspectives, as they participate in alliance missions that are caught up in the web of the struggle against terrorist strategies and attacks? First, the Slovak experience of receiving too little attention on key issues of economic development and political representation is one that is replicated in Bosnia. Muslims were subordinated to Serbian needs and pressures when Bosnia was a republic in the old Yugoslavia. Slovaks would share with them a mutual understanding of what kind of an impact such discrimination has on a small, economically less developed group nearly lost within a larger state. Second, Slovenia's historical situation, an advanced but subordinated republic in Yugoslavia when measured by the indicators of education and economic development could have a spill-over effect into target countries. Croats in Bosnia shared virtually the same experience as did their counterparts in the Croatian Republic and in Slovenia. They were successful on many indicators of progress but did not benefit in terms of either economic or political power. Third, Slovak and Slovenian experiences of being in subordinate positions during communist times was one that was replicated in some of the mission countries in recent decades. The Albanian population of Kosovo had been the subject of much pressure from both the Serb population in the northern sector of their republic and from Serbia proper, within the Yugoslav federation. In a parallel way, Shiites in Iraq had been subordinate to the Sunni's during the Saddam Regime of the last decades of the twentieth century. Fourth, the Slovenian experience of being one of several small groups in a larger federation approximates somewhat the overall situation of Afghanistan with its numerous tribes.

In all of these cases, the presence of Slovak and Slovenian military personnel would inject some element of common understanding. Slovak commanders and soldiers would understand the needs of Muslims in Bosnia, Kosovo, and Iraq. Of course, the basis would not be religious but situational. In addition, Slovenes would find the Afghan political landscape a familiar one, as its tribal divisions and infighting would look somewhat similar to the old Yugoslavia. The experience of having dealt with Serbian pressure from Belgrade would provide some common feeling with those in Afghanistan who had felt pressure from the Soviet Union, ambitious regional warlords, and even commandos representing al Qaeda and the Taliban.

Bulgaria and Romania were the last-minute choices for NATO membership in 2004, for there was a perception that their potential to contribute to the organization immediately was less than that of the other five potential entrants. In addition, the postcommunist revolution had come more slowly to their region than it had to the nations further north. In fact, the events of

1989 did not initially include much of a Bulgarian component. Clearly, their addition to the list was a direct reaction to the events of September 2001. Without them in the alliance, there would be a gap in protection and coverage in the southeast corner of Europe, and there would be an open gate across the Black Sea from violence-prone settings in Iraq, Pakistan, and Afghanistan. Iran, with its nuclear gamesmanship, was another threatening nation to whom the open gate would be a temptation. Thus, both nations received invitations sooner than expected.

Bulgaria had a unique experience as a member of the communist bloc, for they were the one East European nation that never challenged Soviet leadership of the bloc in a serious way. They remained loyal allies who assisted the Warsaw Pact with its invasion of Czechoslovakia in 1968, and yet there was no need for the Soviet Union to put troops on their territory in order to compel allegiance. However, their history between 1945 and 1989 was neither tension nor trouble free. Their population contained a 10 percent Turkish minority, and this reality became a challenging issue at times. In the 1980s, the Bulgarian government initiated a series of legal steps that put pressure on the local Turks. Some of those acts required conversion of place names in the Turkish areas into Bulgarian ones, and the result was considerable resentment by the minority. There was some movement of population back across the border into Turkey, and the tensions continued for a time after 1989. Further, although Bulgaria was not in the forefront of the 1989 anticommunist revolutions, a movement called eco-glasnost emerged in the early 1990s. The group was committed to a mix of issue positions that called more sensitivity on environmental issues and greater protection of civil liberties. These experiences positioned Bulgarians to make a unique set of contributions to NATO and its missions.

Romanian recent history was quite different than that of its neighbor to the south. Its leaders were one of the principal thorns in the side of the Soviet Union during the last two decades of the Cold War. Their challenge took the form of a different set of foreign policy priorities, while the regime itself maintained a pattern of control that satisfied Moscow. Basically, the Romanian Party resented economic pressures to specialize in the agricultural sector that had been their strength in the past. Their desire to create a more diversified economy clashed with Soviet desires to build an economic community based on distinctive contributions of each of its national members. Eventually, the Romanian leader Ceausescu endeavored to model his system on the Chinese Cultural Revolution. Romanian experiences during the anticommunist revolutions of the late 1980s were also a sharp contrast to events within Bulgaria. The Romanian Revolution was the last in the series of firecrackers but also the most violent. Revolutionary forces shot both Ceausescu and his wife on Christmas Day, after a quick convening of a kangaroo court. In fact, those bloody events were preceded by a crack-down on the Hungarian minority which had also taken a violent turn. In this sense, Romania's long-standing conflicts with the Hungarian minority in the north of the country were somewhat similar to Bulgarian tension with its Turkish minority in the south of the country.

Based on these historical patterns in the two "surprise" members of the class of 2004, what can they bring to the NATO table in various missions that combat the rage of early twentieth-century terrorism? First, their geopolitical position is ideal, for they complete a NATO dam that stretches from Estonia in the north to Turkey in the south. There are no chinks in that alliance suit of armor. In effect, the alliance has moved its entire protective shield considerably to the east. Just as it formed a continuing link whose Cold War centerpiece was the Berlin Wall, so now the long chain of protection was double-hinged on the eastern coast of the Baltic Sea and the western shores of the Black Sea. Second, both nations now could make available to NATO physical facilities that could be of value in virtually all of the key missions that included Bosnia, Kosovo, Afghanistan, and Iraq. Proximity to those theaters was enhanced for the whole alliance through the membership of these two Balkan nations.

Third, the consistency of the policies of these two in Cold War times provided a value to an alliance in which many members were dubious about certain missions or what they could contribute to them. Bulgaria had been unwavering in support for its Soviet partner during four decades, while Romania had dug in its heels in opposition to Soviet pressure for a quarter century. Even though the policy directions of both sets of communist leaders had pointed in opposite directions, the ability of leaders and peoples to stick to a designated course of action was clear. Fourth, the lessons learned from the conflicts of each of the two new NATO partners with its own specific minority group could be of value in certain missions on the ground. Such intra-national struggles may have made both members aware of the extra steps needed to bring about accords among the various groups in both Bosnia and Kosovo. Bulgaria's conflict with its Muslim minority may have sensitized at least its leaders to a comprehension of the special tools needed to deal with the precarious balance among various Islamic peoples in both Iraq and Afghanistan.

Overall, the potential contributions of the seven new members of the Class of 2004 to alliance missions in the fight with terrorists were substantial. Historical experiences, geopolitical position, and bargaining with minority groups gave them special understandings that would be particularly helpful in treating humanitarian situations in which NATO had taken on obligations.

Actual Contributions of the New Members Admitted in 2004

Bulgaria

Importantly, the Bulgarian leadership was willing to host the NATO Forum of Ministers of Foreign Affairs in April, 2006. This meeting entailed preparations for the important Riga Summit that took place in the fall of the same year. Bulgaria has also been particularly supportive of the alliance's open-door policy and encouraged NATO to improve relations with Ukraine (Ministry of Foreign Affairs of Bulgaria 2010a).

Estonia

The contributions of Estonia have been small-scale but wide-ranging. The nation has envisioned the open-door policy of NATO as an important lever for democratic reform in a variety of postcommunist countries. They have been particularly interested in taking part in Crisis Response Operations, and this led them to state their intention to take part in the NATO Response Force. Unique was their involvement in United Nations Protection Force Mission in Croatia (UNPROFOR) in 1995. They also have contributed to the full range of the four key alliance operations that have constituted the essence of alliance activity since 1995 (Ministry of Defense of Estonia 2010a).

Latvia

The early concerns of Latvia focused on making their military capabilities compatible with those of the alliance, and this process took a full decade prior to their admission in 2004. Alone among the Baltic nations, they decided to have a fully professional army with no mandatory military service. In addition, they needed to transform their military orientation from being part of large territorial units that characterized the Soviet pattern to a small-scale one that could contribute in a material way to crisis prevention and collective security. Their first actual engagement came in Bosnia-Herzegovina in 1996, but they also played a role in additional alliance-led missions in Kosovo, Afghanistan, and Iraq. In addition, their capital city Riga was host to a key NATO summit in November, 2006. Given their precarious location in the

Baltic region and close to Russia, involvement in air operations became a prime necessity. Thus, Latvia took its part in the rotational patrols that alliance forces participated in at an air base in Siaulia, Lithuania. The nation itself became the site of construction of an Air Operation Center at the Lielvārde airfield (Ministry of Defense of Latvia 2010a).

Lithuania

The country of Lithuania has participated in the NATO-led missions in Kosovo, Afghanistan, and Iraq. Approximately 200 Lithuanian soldiers and civilians have taken part in these operations, and the government made a specific decision to permit civilians to be part of the force (Ministry of Foreign Affairs of Lithuania 2010a).

Romania

The largest contribution of Romania was clearly to the Afghanistan theater, as they committed 38 troops to the initial Enduring Freedom operation. However, over time they later contributed nearly 1000 troops to the continuing ISAF mission. Kosovo was next in order in terms of level of commitment, as they sent 145 to that troubled Yugoslav Republic. Their involvement in Bosnia is interesting, as they sent only one person during the time of NATO management under the heading of SFOR. Following the EU takeover of the operation, their presence in operation EUFOR was a full 56 personnel. Their role in Iraq was quite small and confined to 4 personnel who became part of the NTM-I mission that the alliance had established to train local police officers (Ministry of Defense of Romania 2010a).

Slovakia

Slovaks participated fully in all four NATO-related operations that were in the center of the stage. At times, they engaged in joint operations with their former national partner the Czech Republic. Significantly, they were willing to work with the Poles in managing their sector of Iraq soon after the invasion of March, 2003 (Ministry of Foreign Affairs of Slovakia 2010a).

Slovenia

Involvement of Slovenes has particularly focused on the NRF (NATO Reaction Force). The nation has contributed military personnel to it since January 2005, and the personnel have included both military policy units and Chemical, Biological, Radiological, and Nuclear (CBRN) defense forces (Ministry of Foreign Affairs of Slovenia 2010a).

Pulling together the Strands

Taken as a whole, the nations that moved into full NATO membership several years after 9/11 are profoundly different along indicators such as size, historical experience, nature of their communist systems, and relation to Russia. At the same time, such historical-political differences have not prevented them from committing their military forces and ideas to NATO-associate activity to build more stability in the southeast corner of Europe and beyond. National differences among the new alliance partners have not faded away, but they have yielded to the common need to contain the explosive terrorist activity that emerged after the end of the Cold War with all of its predictable rigidity.

CHAPTER FIVE

Further Class Memberships and the Traps of Southeast Europe

NATO and its New Frontier

"For make no mistake: Evil does exist in the world. A nonviolent movement could not have halted Hitler's armies. Negotiations cannot convince al Qaeda's leaders to lay down their arms. To say that force may sometimes be necessary is not a call to cynicism—it is a recognition of history; the imperfections of man and the limits of reason" (Obama 2009). This remarkable passage from President Obama's Nobel Prize acceptance speech forges a powerful linkage between two major challenges to global order, spanning two centuries and separated by six decades. Both threats profoundly affected southeast Europe. In the 1940s, major struggles between local partisans and occupying fascist forces took place in Yugoslavia, Albania, Ukraine, and Greece. Further, Hitler's invasion of the Soviet Union included a "scorched earth" drive across Ukraine, a republic that was the key breadbasket of the USSR at the time. One of the significant allied victories during World War II took place at Sevastopol, in the Crimean region of the Ukrainian Republic. In a parallel way, twenty-first-century terroristic attacks by al Qaeda both emanated from and often occurred in the region next door to Southeast Europe. The presence of significant Muslim populations in three of the four countries mentioned above gave that threat an even more pressing dimension.

The definition of Southeast Europe used in this chapter is a broad and flexible one that is helpful in analyzing NATO's membership choices in the latter part of the first decade of the twenty-first century. At the alliance's Bucharest Summit in April 2008, the decision was made to admit Albania and Croatia to the organization in 2009. However, an offer of membership did not go out at that time to Ukraine, Georgia, the Former Yugoslav Republic of Macedonia, or Bosnia. The first two had been republics in the old Soviet Union, while the latter two held a similar status in the former Yugoslavia. While Georgia is technically beyond Southeast Europe and in the Caucasus, it will be included here for the purposes of this chapter. Both Ukraine and Georgia had been bidding for membership in the alliance prior to the Bucharest Summit, and their fates depended on a similar mix of circumstances that included domestic instability and Russian anxieties. The Former Yugoslav Republic of Macedonia will not be included in this chapter, for its exclusion was tied up with Greek concerns. Bosnia will receive only secondary attention, as its political management was shared among its own elected leaders and international organizations such as the UN, the NATO, and the EU. All the new and potential members given consideration here could strengthen NATO's flank in this corner of Europe and thereby create a more unified bulwark against al Qaeda-inspired disasters in the region immediately to the east. Thereby, membership selection was intertwined with realistic assessments of security threats from the east.

Keys from the Political and Historical Background

With respect to the admission process of additional states in the southeast corner of Europe, there were important distinctions between the position of the United States and NATO. In 2002, the alliance extended PfP status to Albania, Croatia, and Macedonia. However, they were unwilling to make the same kind of offer to either Georgia or Ukraine. In contrast, five years later in early 2007, both houses of the American Congress approved a NATO expansion process for the following year that included all five countries (iDNES 2007a). In 2008 at Bucharest, the eventual decision was more in tune with the alliance's moves in 2002 than it was with the American initiatives in 2007. Albania and Croatia received offers, while Georgia and Ukraine did not. The Former Yugoslav Republic of Macedonia question was tabled until Greek concerns were satisfied. At the end of 2009, positive statements emerged from NATO planners about the potential for not only Bosnia but also the relatively new state of Montenegro to join, once they had met the criteria (NATO 2009c).

In April 2009, one year after the conclusion of the Bucharest Summit, NATO Secretary-General Jaap de Hoop Scheffer gave a unique speech. He restated the conclusion reached the previous year that Georgia and Ukraine would be welcomed into the alliance once they met its criteria. In addition, he made pointed comments about the priority of the Black Sea region to NATO. In his view, admission of Romania to NATO in 2004 had significantly raised "the profile of the Black Sea area," and he further indicated that the alliance would soon be promoting regional initiatives that bore the potential to "contribute to greater cooperation among the Black Sea states" (IZVESTIYA 2009a). A week later the Secretary-General supported Black Sea partner Turkey after a terrorist attack resulted in the deaths of nine

Turkish soldiers in Diyarbakir Province (NATO 2009d). Both of these high-level statements constituted evidence of the elevated profile the Black Sea region held in the eyes of alliance leaders. In turn, such a priority spotlighted the importance of Southeast Europe in the alliance's evolving perspective and threat analysis.

Overall, the nations considered for alliance partnership after admission of the class of 2004 differed from the type of member included in the 1999–2004 period. All of those considered in the later period had suffered from serious internal turmoil. Georgia's turbulence led to the Revolution of Roses in 2003, while Ukraine's tensions produced the Orange Revolution in 2004. Bosnia, Croatia, and Macedonia had undergone civil wars, and the conflicts in both Bosnia and Macedonia centered on the presence of large Muslim populations within them. Although Albania seemed to have been less severely affected by that level of conflict, the war in Kosovo in 1999 had touched them and concentrated their attention on the situation in that Yugoslav region. Such a high level of internal tension and historical animosity weakens the potential of all of these nations to contribute to the alliance in significant ways at an early stage, for the residue from their civil wars still resonates in most of them. At the same time, these new members can offer the alliance important understandings about coping with domestic terrorism and conflict. As such, their insights can expand NATO's knowledge base as it undertakes future challenges.

The New Class of 2009: Albania and Croatia

Albania

Albania had a very unique position in the communist bloc during the Cold War. The nation had been liberated from fascist control during World War II through the assistance of Tito's resistance forces in nearby Yugoslavia. However, the reforms enacted by Tito in Yugoslavia in the late 1940s and early 1950s alienated the Albanian leader Enver Hoxha. He preferred an unreformed brand of communism and thus switched alliances to the Soviet Union. However, the Soviet Union itself began a series of de-Stalinization reforms after the Twentieth Party Congress in 1956, and the Albanian leadership again searched for a more orthodox model. They found one in Mao's China in the early 1960s. Both China and Albania offered scathing criticism of Soviet softness on the ideology throughout the 1960s and early 1970s. The Chinese Cultural Revolution, with its attacks on the pragmatists, inspired the Albanians to experiment with the same type of propaganda campaign. However, the death of Mao in 1976 led to the emergence of the pragmatists and the weakening of the ideologies in China. Albanian leaders still preferred the hard-line ideological approach and thus became quite isolationist, as there was no strong outside model remaining for them. Like its Balkan neighbors, the Velvet Revolution came very slowly into Albania's system after 1989, and the eventual process of change became quickly intertwined with scandals such as the pyramid scheme. In light of this political history and its low level of economic progress overall, its entry into NATO in 2009 is remarkable.

What does Albania bring to the alliance in light of its small size and rather eccentric historical experiences in the past 60 years? First, it is a country with a principally Muslim population. As such, it gives balance to an alliance that is engaged in a war with extreme Islamists in Afghanistan, that is concerned about the inability of Pakistan to control the mix of Taliban and al Qaeda operatives in Federally Administered Tribal Areas of North and South Waziristan, and that took some action on behalf of a Muslim population in the Bosnian War and related decisive action in Kosovo. In addition, many of the alliance partners are currently still engaged in the Iraqi conflict that bears the marks of an intra-Islamic battle. Second, the presence of Albania within NATO offers another degree of protection for Kosovo, in light of its declaration of independence from Serbia in February 2008. Many nations have not yet granted diplomatic recognition to that tiny enclave nation, and Russia's 2008 war in Georgia injects an element of unpredictability for similar microareas and states. Third, Albania's inclusion in at least one Black Sea organization is positive in light of NATO's current emphasis on that region. They are members of the Black Sea Economic Cooperation Pact (BSEC), an organization that is a decade old. Greece is similarly in the organization, even though it also is not on the Black Sea. Of course, Bulgaria and Romania are members, as they are littoral states themselves (Bremer and Bailes 1998, 131–47). With Albania in the alliance, NATO now has four members that participate in this important Black Sea economic organization.

Fourth, Albania has played a stabilizing role in the region since the end of the Kosovo War in 1999. They have made no effort to unite outside Albania minorities into a Greater Albania. During 2000–01, they were quiet during the civil war in neighboring Macedonia between the central government and the sizeable Albanian minority in the northern part of the country. In addition, the Albanian government did not make inflammatory statements on behalf of Kosovo's independence in the years leading up to its declaration of statehood. Further, they have taken some steps to cultivate U.S. support with an eye on the alliance connection. For instance, they contributed 70 noncombat troops to the Iraq War in March 2003. One result was that America included them in an Adriatic partnership that also involved Macedonia and Croatia (Goldman 2008, 110–11). All of these activities took place with the Socialist Nano government in power, a situation that could have resulted in some anti-American pronouncements.

In the end, Albania's inclusion is a further answer to those who thought that countries in the region should have made the key effort to contain the Bosnian conflict in 2002–05. Albania's Muslim roots, links to Kosovo, ties to the Black Sea community, and record of both stability and measured policies for the last decade make it into a valuable partner.

Croatia

Unlike Albania, Croatia had the reputation during the Cold War for being one of the more progressive republics in the Yugoslav federation. They had pushed for the decentralization reforms that Tito enacted for the first time in 1948. With Slovenia and Voivodina, Croatia had actually been part of the Austro-Hungarian Empire rather than the Ottoman Empire that had governed the Albanians, most of the Serbs, and others. As such, Croatia benefitted from the progressive policies of the Habsburgs and ended up with an economy and culture more like that of Europe than was true of the areas further to the south. Thus, its overall advanced status made Croatian leaders restless with the originally centralized Soviet-style system. Redistribution of Croatian profits to poorer republics like Macedonia created resentment and thus pressure for more regional autonomy within communist Yugoslavia (Remington 1984, 238–82). Their resistance to central controls also reflected a rejection of the concept of Greater Serbia that had been floating around since the creation of Yugoslavia in 1918 (Banac 1984, 141–225). The concept of a federation had more appeal to them, based on a reading of their self-interests.

Based on the historical record outlined above, it might be assumed that Croatia would be a very desirable alliance partner and might have earned inclusion in 2004, the year in which neighboring Slovenia entered NATO. However, their entry came five years later for several reasons. They had been damaged by the Serbian invasion and the ensuing war in the early 1990s. Shortly thereafter, their President Tudman took a turn in a very authoritarian direction, and their credentials for NATO or EU membership went downhill. In this respect, their plight was similar to that of Slovakia, a nation in which the Meciar leadership resulted in postponement of NATO membership from 1999 to 2004.

In Croatia, the death of Tudman in 2000 led to new possibilities for cooperation with the West. Immediately, their new leaders became more cooperative with the Hague Tribunal and its search for possible war criminals from the Croatian and Bosnian Wars of the early 1990s. After the November 2003 elections, Ivo Sanader became Prime Minister. While he represented the same Croatian Democratic Union Party that Tudman did, he was a different kind of leader. He had promised overtures to NATO and the EU during his election campaign. He had also averred that there would be positive steps taken to end discrimination against the Serb minority. In 2004, his outreach to the West also entailed a dispatch of a small contingent of troops to Afghanistan. At the time of the debate over replacing NATO management of Bosnia with that of the EU, he pushed for a continuing NATO role. When Secretary of Defense Donald Rumsfeld visited the country, Sanader made an open bid to join the alliance (Goldman 2008, 202–4).

Overall, the reasons for Croatia's entry into NATO in 2009 differed from those that supported Albania's selection. In fact, inclusion of Croatia meant that all of the former territories of the old Habsburg Empire had finally become part of the military alliance. Croatia had been the missing link in that set of states that were characterized by relatively high levels of economic development. Croatia's entry was really a case of delayed membership, in light of their political centralization and personalized leadership in the 1990s. At the same time, the nation's proximity to both Serbia and Kosovo meant that it was positioned to be a stabilizing factor as part of a broader alliance, in case trouble erupted in those two countries.

Waiting in the Wings

Georgia

Georgia's location across the Black Sea from Ukraine, Bulgaria, and Romania makes it at least a border state of Southeast Europe. Discussion of it here also makes sense due to the way in which its fate in terms of NATO membership has been linked to that of Ukraine. Both requested membership, were turned down in 2008 at the Bucharest Summit, and struggled with internal divisiveness over the value that the alliance would bring to their nations.

Georgia was an important Caucasus Republic in the Soviet Union. Stalin was a Georgian, and Politburo member. Foreign Minister Edward Shevardnadze was an appointed leader of the Georgian branch of the party in communist times and an elected leader of the nation after 1991. Its proximity to the oil-rich Caspian Sea and involvement in various pipeline projects and plans give it more importance as an economic link than might normally be the case for so small a country. Its ethnic divisions have been paralyzing during most of the period since independence. Abkhazia and South Ossetia have been Russian-linked enclaves that have kept a Russian military presence there longer than might have been expected. The combination of its outreach to NATO and the alliance's need for partners close to Iraq and Afghanistan make this unusual candidate significant.

Russia has had a long-standing concern about growing connections between Georgia's aspirations and NATO encroachment eastward. For example, after 9/11 the United States actually sent a small number of military personnel into Georgia in a hunt for al Qaeda operatives. The hunch was that they might have sought refuge in Georgia's remote Kodori and Pankisi Gorges. Also, in the fall of 2006, the Russian Minister of Defense Sergey Ivanov charged that NATO was providing illegal weapons to Georgia and thus strengthening the former Soviet Republic in its battle of wits with Russia. In fact, Ivanov pointed to the former communist countries that had joined the alliance recently as the key culprits (SME 2006b).

The Russo-Georgia war of August 2008 was a major crisis in many respects, not the least of which was its impact on Russian-NATO relations. The overall perception of the outside world was that Russia had either provoked the war or greatly overreacted to Georgian incursions into the enclaves of South Ossetia and Abkhazia. As casualties mounted, so did the mutual accusations. The alliance and Russia temporarily broke contacts through the NATO-Russia Council (NATO 2008a). Eventually, Russia declared the two enclaves to be independent and became the only nation to give them diplomatic recognition. NATO then warned Russia that their dual recognition violated the six principles agreement that President Saakashvili and President Medvedev had earlier signed (NATO 2008b).

More broadly, the Black Sea states and NATO worried about further Russian incursions into other surrounding states. The continuing presence of Russian naval personnel and ships in Ukraine's Sevastopol made this into a pointed concern. In a sense, the war made NATO membership into more of a must for Georgia. A NATO-Georgia Commission existed, and this would provide the framework for joint contacts. Even that Commission condemned the Russian recognition of South Ossetia and Abkhazia (NATO 2008c). In 2009, the Georgian Parliament further approved Grigol Mgaloblishvili as its representative to NATO (IZVESTIYA 2009b). It is possible that Kosovo's declaration of independence had something to do with the ferment in Georgia. That declaration preceded the war by only six months. However, the interpretation of that link is tricky. On the one hand, Kosovo's blow against Serbia might have inspired the Georgian move against Russian interests. On the other hand, Kosovo's break-away from Serbia might have inspired the two Georgian enclaves to seek Russian help in expanding their own sovereignty.

Georgian attitudes about joining NATO are more divided than they were in the earlier part of the decade. Some argue that the alliance can offer protection for them in an exposed and dangerous part of the world. Others worry about Russia's response and also wonder what NATO would expect. With the increasing pressure on alliance partners to increase their commitments to Afghanistan, what would that portend for Georgia?

In fact, Georgia had taken part in some NATO exercises. For example, in 2001, Georgia hosted a military exercise that included eight full NATO members and some who were PfP members. The latter consisted of four Black Sea nations of Ukraine, Bulgaria, Romania, and Georgia. Azerbaijan and Sweden also contributed to the operation. The exercise itself took place on the Black Sea and had the objective of developing "naval and amphibious interoperability" between NATO and PfP countries (Thompson 2004, 110). In the period after the 2008 war, Georgia was taking part both in the ISAF and in Operation Active Endeavor in the Mediterranean Sea. In December 2008 the military organization wrote an Annual National Program for Georgia and set up a NATO Liaison Office in the capital city of Tbilisi. Other important activities entailed the work of Georgian military troops in Kosovo in 1999–2008, and the participation of the nation in the Partnership Action Plan on Terrorism. In return, NATO partners and allies had assisted Georgia in demilitarizing ground-to-air defense and other missiles. As they had with many former communist countries, NATO also realized the need to build more positive views about the alliance within the Georgian public (NATO 2008d). More recently, in late April 2009, the military alliance decided to hold exercises on the territory of Georgia. They were held only 20 km from Tbilisi and included 1,300 soldiers from 19 nations. While the Russians saw these exercises as a consequence of the August 2008 War, the Western Alliance argued that they had planned them well before the events of August 2008 (SME 2009a).

In May of 2009, the NATO Military Committee made additional comments on the priority of the Black Sea region. That Committee met in Brussels with the Georgian Defense Minister. They encouraged the Ministry to continue with bold military reforms in spite of the economic setbacks of the previous year (NATO 2009e). This heightened involvement by the alliance in the region did generate a reaction on the east side of the Black Sea. Abkhazia's leader Sergei Bagapsh said he would turn over the province's railroads and main airport to Russia for 10 years. Russia's

President Medvedev began to talk about a new trans-Atlantic security treaty as a replacement for NATO (USATODAY 2009a). It was difficult to judge whether these were serious Russian policy indicators or whether they were simply additional reactions to the continuing military exercises in Georgia.

Later, much attention was focused on Georgia at the time of the first anniversary of the August 2008 War. Russian troops actually crossed the border from South Ossetia into Georgia proper, after reports emerged about grenades having been thrown into the separatist region (iDNES 2009a). Further, an opposition leader in Georgia, Nino Burdzhanadze, claimed that President Saakvashili had boasted a year earlier that the Georgian military could take Tsinvali in only one day (IZVESTIYA 2009c). Symbolically, Russia also put back into commission in early August the submarine *Alrosa* that could be submerged to a depth of 240 meters. This was its only real submarine in the Black Sea fleet. In early September, a promising naval exercise took place in the Crimean Peninsula, based on an agreement signed in 2002 in Kiev. Russian ships took part, along with Ukrainian, Bulgarian, Romanian, and Turkish vessels (IZVESTIYA 2009d). The exercise's inclusion of that particular mix of Black Sea nations was promising, although the one littoral state missing was Georgia. However, one week later, tensions re-emerged, this time centering on the enclave of Abkhazia. Russia issued a diplomatic warning that it would stop all Georgian ships that penetrated into Abkhaz waters, in retaliation for Georgia doing the same to a Turkish vessel the previous month (DN 2009a). By October, Russia had gone even further and made a decision to develop a military base in Abkhazia in order to assure its sovereignty (IZVESTIYA 2009e). Although possibly unrelated, a story emerged in the Russian press that the United States was planning to develop a base in Bulgaria for 2,500 U.S. soldiers and one in Romania for 1,600 U.S. troops (IZVESTIYA 2009f). The justification was the terrorist threat in the Middle East rather than Russia, but it would lead to more superpower military presence in the Black Sea region.

Therefore, it is clear that NATO was upgrading the profile of the Black Sea region in the 2008–09, period. This upgrade included broad policy statements about the importance of the Black Sea region as well as micro decisions about the transit of military supplies through Ukraine. This new alliance thrust also included a very special priority on Georgia, in the aftermath of the events of August 2008, and in the hopes of closer military cooperation and exercises with some of the states in the area. A number of these initiatives helped to knit portions of the Black Sea community together more tightly, but they also created more conflict with Russia.

It is also interesting to examine the reactions of surrounding nations such as the Central Asian states to the heightened tension between Russia and Georgia. For example, Kazakhstan made no accommodating statements to Russia after the 2008 war (Goldman 2009, 57–8). Leaders in Turkmenistan stated that they had nothing to fear from a potential Russian invasion of their territory (Goldman 2009, 83–4). Tajikistan was torn between the hope for U.S. support on their Afghan border and their resentment at American pressure for democratization. As a result, they provided some moral support for Russia in the war with Georgia (Goldman 2009, 113–14). Kyrgyzstan kept its ties to Russia through the crisis and even had some of its personnel visit the controversial enclaves. They may have done so to counterbalance the fact that the United States had a major presence at Manas Base in their own country (Goldman 2009, 183–4). In sum, the five Central Asian nations did not condemn the Russian actions in the August 2008 War, while at the same time they were careful to keep open their ties to America and NATO (Goldman 2009, 197–9).

Perhaps an optimistic concluding note for commentary on Georgia would be a reference to President Medvedev's statement at the end of 2009, to the effect that he was prepared to consider restoration of air traffic with Georgia and the opening of markets and goods for each other. However, he did not indicate an interest in talking with his counterpart President Saakashvili about these matters (IZVESTIYA 2009g). An improved atmosphere would provide both Georgia and NATO with time to think through their future linkages.

Ukraine

This former republic in the Soviet Union has had a powerful impact on its region since the 1940s. It's agricultural and coal resources made it into an inviting target for German forces during World War II, as they marched east into the Soviet Union. Even earlier, Stalin had tried to restrict its power through imposition of a mass starvation campaign that resulted in countless deaths. One reflection of its influence as a republic during the post-war period was its continued presence on the Politburo of the Communist Party of the Soviet Union. The republic had what amounted to an automatic seat on that very small inner sanctum of the party. In fact, both Nikita Khrushchev and Leonid Brezhnev, leaders who managed the Soviet system from 1953 until 1982, were both ethnic Russians who had spent much time in the eastern part of Ukraine.

Thus, it was not a surprise when Ukraine played the role of a spearhead during the collapse of the Soviet Union in 1991. The nationalist movement

Rukh called early and forcefully for transformation of the state into a real federation. This resource-rich republic was one of the first to back the demands of Russian Republic leader Boris Yeltsin for keeping economic profits back home within the various republics. The situation at the time was one in which Moscow skimmed off much of the profits from the more economically successful republics for the benefit of the central government's schemes and plans. The Ukrainian separatist movement contributed significantly to the fall of the Soviet system in December 1991.

This vast nation and former republic has always had a split mentality and ethnic makeup. Its eastern section includes a majority of Russians and leans in that direction, while the western part has a Ukrainian majority and looks to Europe and America. Those in the western regions would describe their country as the largest in Europe, but the easterners would be less likely to position themselves within that geographic unity. The Ukrainian-dominated central government in Kiev has passed legislation that makes signs in both Russian and Ukrainian mandatory in any publicly owned institutions such as libraries. Those in eastern regions such as Crimea often scoff at such legislation. Further, Russia often seeks to affect events in Ukraine by manipulating the Russian populations in eastern Ukraine and especially in the Crimean Republic (Balmaceda 2000, 231–5). Russian threats of a shut off or reduction of natural gas supplies obviously destabilize the economy (Baev 2008, 22–128). The most recent example of this exercise in economic blackmail took place in early 2009. Importantly, both the Russian naval presence at Sevastopol in Crimea and its use in the 2008 Georgia-Russia War keeps the pot boiling. Russian officers live scattered throughout the Sevastopol population and may be seen in uniform shopping along with the Ukrainian population. While this practice may be an effort by Russia to generate more understanding with Ukraine, the results are notably better in Crimea with its 60 percent Russian population than they are in Kiev much further to the north and west.

Ukraine's larger-than-life impact also was evident for the world to see during the 2004 Orange Revolution. This revolution was technically a reaction to corrupt elections that initially resulted in victory for the ethnic Russian Victor Yanukovych. However, the turmoil was also a reaction to a full decade of authoritarianism. One analyst (D'Arnieri 2007, 6) has described Ukraine in that period as an authoritarian country that has elections but is not really democratic. In his view, the key to understanding this phenomenon is that the 1991 events were an exercise in "national independence rather than political revolution" (D'Arnieri 2007, 14). In that sense, Ukraine shared the experience of many former Soviet republics as well as nations in other regions of the world. In such "hyperpresidential democracies," the role of elections is primarily to increase governmental power rather than to check it (D'Arnieri 2007, 16).

Therefore, the Orange Revolution constituted a rejection of all that legacy and residue from the communist era. People spent very cold nights huddled around barrels filled with burning firewood in order to make a difference. In the short run their efforts paid off, for the elections were rerun with the effect that reform leader Victor Yushchenko became President. His moral standing was very high at that point. Not only did he lead those who protested during Orange Revolution, but his face bore the deep scars that had resulted from poisoning, allegedly by the Russian Secret Service. At the time, many envisioned this revolution to be a second stage of the battle waged by Rukh in 1991. However, within a few years the anger about Yushchenko intensified and his approval ratings plummeted into the single digits. Hyperpresidentialism rather than true reform had reappeared, and his battles with Prime Minister Julia Tymoshenko and Russian leaders took on legendary proportions.

All of these events are important in understanding Ukraine's status as a candidate for membership in NATO. As early as 2001, Ukraine had taken part in the military exercise in Georgia that was shared between NATO and PfP members (Thompson 2004, 110). There was a debate soon after the Orange Revolution about the desirability of Ukraine moving in the direction of NATO membership. This debate followed publicity within the nation about the deaths of several Ukrainian soldiers in post-9/11 peacemaking missions in the Gulf area. For example, Ukraine had provided the second highest number of troops for the Polish-administered zone south of Baghdad in late 2003 (Czech Radio 7, Radio Prague, 2006). President Yushchenko dropped hints about a possible overture to the alliance, but the Russian Prime Minster Yanukovych was dubious. The latter was able to get the entire cabinet behind his recommendation that Ukraine was unprepared for alliance membership (IZVESTIYA 2006a). At that time, both leaders compromised on the idea of using a referendum within the country before a final decision about the desirability of a bid for membership (SME 2006c).

At the time of the Bucharest meeting of the alliance in April 2008, Ukraine as well as Georgia was expectant about a possible offer of membership. However, the alliance turned them down at that point, with a comment about possible inclusion at a later date. The invasion of Georgia by Russia a few months later had a double effect. It made NATO planners second guess their negative decision on Georgia and Ukraine at Bucharest, but it also made Ukraine worry more about Russian negative reactions to their potential inclusion in NATO.

By mid-2009, the controversy continued over the matter of what was best for Ukraine. There was a conference held in Berlin entitled "Russia, Ukraine, and 'Eastern Partnership' with the EU." The sponsor of the conference was the Institute for the Solution of International Problems, and its Director Aleksei Pushkov stated that the admission of Ukraine to NATO would not be advantageous to Kiev, Moscow, or the West (IZVESTIYA 2009h). At the same time, in March of the year, the Cabinet Ministers of Ukraine made an agreement that the alliance highly desired. They agreed that transit of goods to the ISAF Operation in Afghanistan could follow a path through Ukraine (NATO 2009f). It may have been coincidental, but a few days later the Ukrainians requested something, perhaps in return, from the United States. They asked for financial assistance in order to liquidate what was left of the Soviet nuclear arsenal. America had provided such assistance from 1993 to 2003, but the money had stopped at that point, probably due to the heavy investment in the Iraq War (SME 2009b).

When the NATO Military Committee met in Brussels in May of 2009, they spoke with the Ukrainian Defense Minister as they did with his counterpart in Georgia. They also encouraged Ukraine to continue with its military reforms. Significantly, Admiral Di Paola singled out Ukraine for special praise by applauding its role as the first PfP member to contribute to the NATO Response Force (NATO 2009g). Russian reactions included a threat to cut off natural gas exports to Ukraine, if that country did not pay for its May imports in a timely fashion (SME 2009c). All of these controversies and doubts create at least a temporary barrier to the alliance's efforts to create a dependable Black Sea linchpin in the struggle against terrorism.

In the last months of 2009, a number of small signs occurred that pointed in a direction linking Ukraine a bit more to the West. The swine flu epidemic hit western Ukraine very hard, and its Ministry of Defense asked NATO for assistance. They needed primarily medicine and vaccinations. NATO partners Poland, Slovakia, Hungary, and Romania responded in a positive way, as did India. In addition, the World Health Organization provided assistance (IZVESTIYA 2009i). Also, Russia decided to transfer its counter-intelligence unit from Sevastopol in Ukraine to Novorossiysk in Russia. They made clear that the Russian fleet would stay put in Ukraine, but they would need to operate without that important unit (IZVESTIYA 2009j). These were only small signs, but they became part of the larger dialogue about Ukraine's future with the Western Alliance. Election of Viktor Yanukovych as President in February 2010, added another element of unpredictability to the tense situation. He would certainly be more welcome in Russia, based on his Russian ethnicity, but he might sense a need to respond to Ukrainian nationalists on matters such as bargaining with Russia over natural gas deliveries, ownership, and price. In April 2010, he actually dissolved the commission that had been set up for preparing the nation for admission to NATO. He commented that Ukraine should be nonaligned and that public opinion was strongly opposed to membership in the Western Alliance (SME 2010a).

Conclusion

NATO placed the names of other countries on the table for potential alliance membership after the complicated admissions process of 2004. Again, the key summit that dealt with those future possibilities was the one held in Riga, Latvia, in November 2006. By that time, Croatia, the former Yugoslav Republic of Macedonia, and Albania had already become PfP members, but the alliance did not set any concrete timetable for their entry. However, they did extend PfP status to Serbia, Montenegro, and Bosnia-Herzegovina. This was significant in the sense that Montenegro had just become independent from Serbia earlier in the year. However, alliance planners also warned Serbia and Bosnia that they needed to cooperate closely with the World Court at The Hague in turning over war criminals from the Balkan Wars of the 1990s. Presumably, the PfP period would be a time of testing their resolve on that and other important matters (iDNES 2006c; SME 2006d). These newest PfP members were the only remaining Balkan countries that lacked any formal status with the alliance, and they collectively expanded the base upon which additional activities against the threat of terrorism further east could take place.

By late 2009, NATO had given signals about its connections with the three alliance partners admitted to observer of PfP status at Riga three years earlier. In December of 2009, the alliance offered Montenegro the chance to begin the membership admission process or MAP, and so they were free to begin those activities. However, Bosnia did not receive the same message. A "stalemate" had slowed down their progress both toward NATO and in the direction of the EU. Ethnic tensions were at the heart of its problems, and some observers pointed out that there might be a need for a constitutional reform to "improve the functionality of state institutions." NATO encouraged Bosnia that the nation would get a green light for membership after additional reforms (NATO 2009h). At the same time, they commented positively on Bosnia'. progress in military reforms and approved of the fact that its three armies were now under one Ministry of Defense (NATO 2009i). In fact,

Secretary-General Rasmussen had made similar comments in his visit to the Western Balkans one week earlier (NATO 2009j). There was no substantive discussion about prospects for the toughest case of Serbia. That nation had sent former Bosnian Serb leader Karadzic to The Hague in 2008, but there still remained much work for them. In addition, they had pulled back from the alliance after the creation of an independent Kosovo in February 2008. Thus, the likelihood of their entry was not high in the short run.

Overall, NATO's efforts to build a dike against al Qaeda in Southeast Europe in order to prevent damage of the type created by Hitler in the region in the 1940s were partly successful. For three nations of the region, the answers were clear. Albania and Croatia actually became full members of NATO in 2009, while Montenegro received a promise of membership in the same year. However, for other nations in the region, the picture was murky. Alliance hopes for both Bosnia and Serbia had receded, as both struggled with internal conflicts, while Serbia engaged in several psychological external battles as well. Negotiations with Greece over the status of former Yugoslav Republic of Macedonia had not proceeded far enough to end a decade of uncertainty about the prospects for that Balkan nation. Probably the biggest conundrum was the issue of what would happen with Ukraine and Georgia. Resolution of those twin problems rested on a mix of considerations that included domestic turmoil, Russian concerns echoing from the 2008 Georgia-Russia War, the policy stands of newly elected Ukrainian President Yanukovych, the fate of the Russian fleet at Sevastopol, the priorities of the Obama Administration, and the broader set of NATO attitudes reflected in the priorities of new Secretary-General Fogh Rasmussen. Another twist in the situation was the fact that Kosovo declared independence from Serbia in February 2008. Certainly, that tiny new nation could benefit from alliance protection, and its mainly Muslim population made it appealing to NATO as Albania had been at an earlier time. However, the hostility to such a move by PfP member Serbia and also from Russia, with its renewed participation in the Russia-NATO Council, made any overtures doubtful. In addition, Kosovo possessed only a diminutive capability to contribute to the struggle with terrorism that was taking place in the neighborhood to the immediate east.

CHAPTER SIX

Bosnia in the Lengthened Shadow of the Cold War

The Cold War Spreads its Shadows

During the Cold War Bosnia-Herzegovina was locked into Tito's Yugoslav state. As such, it shared with the other primarily non-Serb republics the fate of coping constantly with the pressures to make the country into a Greater Serbia. At the same time, Tito's reforms after 1948 injected considerable decentralization into the framework of governance. However, he backtracked on some of those changes in the early 1970s and centralized control in the hopes of avoiding a "Prague Spring" that had jeopardized the communist regime in nearby Czechoslovakia in 1968. The people and leaders in Bosnia were caught in the midst of those policy changes throughout the four decades of Cold War.

The ethnic configuration of the republic made it a potential site of contention that would entice outside forces to involve themselves. The ethnic breakdown was approximately 43 percent Muslim, 33 percent Serbian, and 10 percent Croatian, with assorted other nationalities constituting the remaining 14 percent. The Muslim population was far less than that of Kosovo's 90 percent, although the latter did not have full republic status within the Yugoslav federation. However, the proportion of Muslims did resemble the percentage in Macedonia, which was a full Republic. The difference in Macedonia was that the Muslims were in a minority, with the Slavs having the numerical majority. While it would not be fair to say that the Muslim populations in those three territories were a divisive factor, it is certainly true that the Islamic Revolution and victory in Iran by 1979 had an impact or at least an echo. The Brezhnev Regime in the Soviet Union worried about a replication of the Iranian events in nearby Afghanistan and decided to invade that nation at the end of 1979. Their occupation would last for nine years, until reform leader Mikhael Gorbachev withdrew them in order to preserve resources for the Soviet Union's needed economic recovery. Yugoslavia was quite distant from the critical areas of southwest Asia, but its ethnic configuration revealed the existence of pressure points and potential future vulnerabilities.

At the same time, the other main ethnic groups in Bosnia were potential soft spots in future controversies as well. For example, the Croatian Republic next door was more advanced than Bosnia on a number of economic indicators and had a protective attitude toward the small Croatian population that ended up trapped in the Bosnian Republic. Further, the horseshoe shape of Croatia was almost an invitation to squeeze in eventually its brothers and sisters in nearby Bosnia. From the point of view of the Croatian Republic's leaders and population, it was unfortunate many of its citizens ended up trapped in a much less developed republic across the Sava River, and in a place that had been part of the inattentive Ottoman Empire rather than the more committed and energetic Habsburg Empire.

It goes without saying that the large Serbian population in Bosnia was a troublesome point in light of both the proximity of the Serbian Republic next door and Serb ambitions to dominate the politics and administration in Yugoslavia as a whole. Tito was able to negotiate some of these controversies, in part due to the fact that his background was both Slovenian and Croatian. However, his negotiating powers could not overcome the fact that Serbs dominated the civilian bureaucracy as well as the officer corps of the military. In a crisis, the Serbs could exert more damaging leverage than could the Croats, given both their views about the nature of the Yugoslav federation and their large proportion of the Bosnian population.

In light of the interplay of these historical factors during the period of 40 years after the end of World War II, it is not surprising that post-1991 Bosnian political life would play out in the shadow of the Cold War. Patterns established within the Republic did not disappear but became intensified during the early 1990s. Western European powers and the Bush Administration across the Atlantic held a kind of nostalgia for the old Yugoslavia and its nonalignment during the last few decades of the Cold War. Thus, they were very slow to grant diplomatic recognition to Bosnia-Herzegovina, and their indecisiveness was a kind of invitation to outside interference. All three ethnic groups internal to Bosnia had real supporters in the outside world, and they included the new nation of Croatia, Serbs who were dominant in the shrunken nation still called Yugoslavia, and assorted groups and nations in the Muslim world who looked for patterns of discrimination against their counterparts who were residing in other nations. The fate of Bosnia really did hinge on a mix of outside forces such as the inattention of the West and the great interest of these three sets of concerned members of the extended ethnic families of the groups living in Bosnia. Of course, the end of Cold War and the fall of so many communist regimes lifted the lid of communist controls that may have bottled up some of the ethnic tensions that continued to exist during the Cold War. The three main groups in Bosnia could now express themselves without worrying about restrictions and pressure from Belgrade. Even though they had been living side by side in many scattered communities throughout Bosnia and interacting on a daily basis, their cultural differences seeped into the public arena after the fall of communism. Therefore, the recipe for a smorgasbord of trouble may have resulted from a very unusual mix of powerful external and potentially divisive internal forces.

Civil and Regional War

Between 1992 and 1995, Bosnia-Herzegovina experienced the most tragic of civil wars, as all of the above-mentioned conflictual factors converged at once. The Serbian leader Slobodan Milosevic in Yugoslavia next door decided to protect the allegedly threatened Serbian minorities in other pieces of the former Yugoslavia. This would eventually entail a short operation in Slovenia, a longer war in Croatia, and later incursions into Kosovo that NATO would quickly stop. However, the main battle was in Bosnia, and it lasted three full years. Serbian troops from Yugoslavia entered Bosnian territory from the east and worked with local Bosnian Serb troops to establish controls over the new country. In effect, the invading Serbs were trying to hold the old Yugoslavia together. Since that group held many of the civilian and military positions, they feared loss of those posts if a break up of the state occurred. Eventually, the goal changed to pursuing the old concept of a Greater Serbia. The wedge for that became the JNA (Yugoslav People's Army), and, by May 1992, JNA officials were in charge of the Bosnian Serbs. Further, Belgrade provided most of the supplies and weapons to their comrades across the border (Roskin 2002, 170). Eventually, the Serbs obtained control through force of 70 percent of Bosnia's territory, a percentage that was more than double their proportion of the population. Their rationale was that the departing Ottomans had much earlier left hill country to "poor Serbian peasants" in the Croatian and Muslim regions (Roskin 2002, 169). There was widespread international outrage over reports of Serb "ethnic cleansing," and the massacre at Srebrenica near the end of the war was one of the prime examples. Names such as Milošević, Mladić, Karadžić became rallying cries for international involvement. At the very last minute, the Clinton Administration and leaders of other members of NATO did engage in bombing selected Serbian targets in order to protect the Bosnian Muslims.

At the time of the break up of Yugoslavia in 1991, Croatian leader Tudman and Serbian leader Milošević made a tentative decision to partition

Bosnia-Herzegovina between their two nations. However, by the fall of that year, dynamics within Bosnia became to move to center stage. Bosnian leader Karadžić decided to leave the broad coalition that was endeavoring to determine the fate of a Bosnian nation (Baskin and Pickering 2008, 290). Early in 1992, objectives of the various actors within Bosnia began to diverge sharply into at least three paths. Leaders of the Serb Democratic Party aimed to carve out a separate Serb state that could unite with what remained of Yugoslavia. The Muslim Party of Democratic Action set the goal of creating an independent Bosnia-Herzegovina that would be unitary in political structure. At that time, the Croatian Democratic Union allied with them in pursuing the same objective. However, by 1993, their goal switched to formation of a Bosnian-Croat state, and during the next year the Croat and Muslim parties united to declare formation of a Croat-Muslim Federation (Csergo 2008, 97). Location of the 1994 signing ceremony in Washington, D.C. was a precursor of things to come in the following year in Dayton, Ohio (Roskin 2002, 175). In fact, an earlier Court decision from 1990 had made these ethnic divisions much more likely. The ruling had required that any election's results could not deviate more than 15 percent from the ethnic distribution in the census (Baskin and Pickering 2008, 298). The ruling had the net result of making the creation of ethnic-based parties inevitable.

The role of the UN was one of continuing interest but also one of only limited measures. During the Bosnian War, they passed 100 "normative acts" that resulted in imposition of an arms embargo. Since the Bosnian Serb Army was better equipped than the other two military units within the nation, they suffered the least from the sanctions. In addition, the UN was willing to create six safe havens for civilians but did not provide enough capabilities to actually defend them in the fullest way. When the related needs for humanitarian assistance and civilian protection emerged, the UN attempted to provide temporary solutions. In the end, the approximate 26,000 United Nations Protection Force (UNPROFOR) unit was too often at the mercy of the Bosnian Serb Army. One key problem was that the UN forces could only shoot if first attacked and could not even really fight in their own safe havens. Srebrenica was the symbol of the failure of this policy. In 1995, Bosnian Serb troops pushed aside the primarily Dutch UN contingent and marched thousands of innocents off to brutal deaths (Roskin 2002, 176). Of course, the resulting 200,000–300,000 deaths in the war provoked an international outcry at the weakness of the measures that the UN had taken over a three-year period of time (Baskin and Pickering 2008, 290).

NATO might have played a more forceful role but had pulled back from enforcement of the arms embargo in November, 1994 (Gnesotto 1997, 43).

In the first place, President Bush in the early 1990s had relegated any operations in the Balkans to the status of second tier operations (Snow 2004, 303). Thus, it was unlikely that he would have injected any substantial capabilities prior leaving office in January 1993. After President Clinton moved into the White House, the passivity continued. On one occasion, he sent Secretary of State Warren Christopher to Brussels for a NATO meeting on Bosnia. Participants expected substantial proposals from the United States, but Christopher said he had only come to consult (Hendrickson 2006, 48). During most of the war, NATO did what it could to maintain the air exclusion zone, upheld the naval blockade, and provided combat aircraft to support the UN forces in Bosnia (Zelikow 1997, 83). Finally, in August and September, 1995, NATO engaged in a twelve-day operation called Deliberate Force. That was probably the decisive event that drove the Bosnian Serbs to the negotiating table in Dayton (NATO 2010a).

The Peace Agreement

In the end, the Clinton Administration invited all parties to Dayton, Ohio in hopes that a very neutral site on the territory of a now-interested superpower would provide a quiet forum for rational discussion. At the time, there were widespread doubts that the conference would work or that any agreements would hold up, once the players and spotlight switched back to Bosnia itself. However, the Dayton Conference was successful in establishing the basis for a viable future for the Bosnian state. Serbian territorial gains were rolled back from 70 to 49 percent, and two territorial sub-units emerged. The Serbs had control in one, and Muslims and Croats in the other. In fact, the Bosniac-Croat Federation was able to retain ten individual, nationality-based cantons on its 51 percent of the territory, and Bosnian Croats could use them to retain close ties with Croatia itself (Csergo 2008, 98). Within the Federation, there were three Croation cantons, three Bosniac, and three mixed (Baskin and Pickering 2008, 291). However, there was still a nation called Bosnia, and so tough decisions were necessary on topics such as the right to return to homes that had been abandoned, division of population in cities that were ethnically mixed such as Mostar and Brcko, creation of a common driver's license, and design of a national flag. Pursuit of war criminals was part of the agenda as well, but it required several years before Milošević and Karadžić would make their way to the World Court. By the end of 1997, the High Representative of the UN received extraordinary powers to ensure that the Dayton Accords would hold. He was empowered to override Bosnian

Institutions, pass legislation, and dismiss officials from office (Baskin and Pickering 2008, 291).

In effect, Bosnia would be a nation under considerable international controls. The NATO alliance provided troops to police the settlement and work with communities to restore order and their lives. From December 1995 until December 1996, the NATO force was called IFOR. Under that heading, the alliance was to enforce the provisions of the Dayton Accords. One of its principal assignments was to maintain separation of the Federation of Bosnia-Herzegovina from the Republika Srpska. In that regard, NATO personnel worked closely with the High Representative, the UN, and OSCE. In December 1996, SFOR replaced IFOR, and that mission lasted until December 2004. The main goal of SFOR was prevention of the resumption of hostilities, and yet many other functions emerged as key necessities. They included patrolling, supervising demining operations, arresting war criminals, and assisting in the return of refugees and displaced persons. In 2003 alone, they disposed of more than 11,000 weapons and 45,000 grenades. SFOR also established a number of schools to train local personnel. One was a dog-sniffer school in Bihac, and others included demining schools in Banja Luka, Mostar, and Travnik. Another important goal was creation of a unified defense structure out of the three ethnic groups and two regional units. By March 2004, the two armies had been swept under a single command structure (NATO 2010b).

In 2004, the EU took over management of the military forces through the new mission EUFOR, and yet they continued to rely on NATO for equipment in carrying out operation ALTHEA. The decision to hand supervision over to the EU came at the alliance's Istanbul Summit of June 2004. NATO continued to contribute to reform of defense structures, erection of barriers against terrorist acts, and the capture of war-crime suspects. With respect to counter-terrorism, the willingness of NATO and the EU to share intelligence was a critical factor. The alliance also kept a military headquarters in Sarajevo (NATO 2010c). Really there was shared military administration, as so many of the involved nations were members of both NATO and the EU. In some regards, it was difficult to say how much influence local Bosnian managers had and how much the various instrumentalities of the international community had. In spite of that complexity, the peace surprisingly held.

In sum, for NATO, implementation of the Dayton Accords thus meant a huge involvement in that nation from 1995 to 2004, and considerable attention after 2004. The early period coincided with the years of the alliance's struggle with the tough question of admitting new members. At that time, the alliance instantly needed to embark on new projects and operations in a number of places like Bosnia. Mission transformation thus accompanied organizational expansion and at times even preceded it. Bosnia had become one such principal mission following conclusion of the Dayton Accord in 1995. Although the Accord called upon the UN to oversee the nation and be its custodian, the UN asked NATO to provide the security and guarantee of the Dayton provisions. At the time, there were real doubts that the Dayton Accords would hold, as infighting among Serbs, Croatians, and Muslims was expected to simmer and continue. Bosnia had also been a cauldron of ethnic tensions that pulled in outside powers. The neighboring Croatian nation acted in a protective way in relation to the small Bosnian-Croatian population. Russian-Serbian ties continued to be close, and that Russian embrace included both the Serbs of Yugoslavia and the Serbs of Bosnia. Much of Europe and the United States had perceived an obligation to offer protection to Bosnian Muslims, especially in light of atrocities that the Serbs committed against them in locations like Srebrenica. In this sense, after the Dayton Accord Bosnia lived in the shadow of the Cold War. The nation and its leaders felt the continuous tug of both both Russia and the United States.

IFOR/SFOR/EUFOR Operations

Immediately after the Dayton Accord, NATO utilized the IFOR unit to assist in maintaining the shaky peace in Bosnia. Several of the Central European nations received the call to take part in that mission while they were still only members of the PfP Program. For example, the Slovenian 15th Air Force Brigade flew missions into Belgrade in late 2002. This country was a logical choice, since Slovenian pilots knew the terrain well from their earlier experience as part of the Yugoslav military. The entire unit included 250 members, and they flew in helicopters and planes provided by the Slovenian Air Force. At the same time, Slovenian medics, doctors, and nurses were part of an important medical cell at Butmir (Ministry of Foreign Affairs of Slovakia 2004a). In the same year Slovenians and Romanians were included in a unit trained in riot control. Hungarians joined them later (Ministry of Foreign Affairs of Slovakia 2002a). As early as 1995, Hungary sent a contingent of engineers to assist in reconstruction of the Old Bridge in Mostar, and the group stayed until 2002. Soldiers from Hungary also worked with the NATO operation for its full extent from 1995 until 2004. They both sent a contingent and took part in the alliance's Sarajevo command (Ministry of Foreign Affairs of Hungary 2010c). From the Baltic region, Latvia contributed over time to IFOR, SFOR, and EUFOR (Ministry of Foreign Affairs of Latvia 2010a).

Slovaks made a number of key contributions in the period before their actual admission to NATO. They provided 600 volunteers for an engineering battalion connected with UNPROFOR. This unit was later actually transferred to terrain in the nation of Croatia. They also assisted in construction of refugee camps and road repair in 1998, and this was the first time that they were formally under NATO command. Within the framework of SFOR, they sent a helicopter unit to aid in providing security in Bosnia (Ministry of Foreign Affairs of Slovakia 2010b). Bulgarians also contributed to SFOR well before the nation's admission to the NATO alliance. They provided a transport platoon from 1998 to 2001. This included 26 servicemen and 10 cars in the area known as Hella/Beluga. Actual tasks included provision of fuel and work on bridges. An engineering platoon of 36 personnel also played an important role in construction and road repair from 1997 to 2001. Their mechanized platoon of 38 servicemen was part of the Dutch contingent that patrolled vital check points in the country. Finally, a Bulgarian Security Company of 149 personnel received an assignment to help guard SFOR headquarters. Their base for this operation was Butmir in Sarajevo. After the transition from SFOR to EUFOR in 2004, Bulgaria continued to provide personnel to the above-named units (Ministry of Defense of Bulgaria 2010a).

From the point at which all 10 new members were formally in the alliance structure in 2004, the alliance continued to ask for their contributions to Bosnia. For instance, in the summer of 2004, the alliance newcomers joined a specialized organization on crowd control. Hungary sent its 200-troop First Light Cavalry Regiment to an Italian unit that also had the capability to do hostage rescue as well as search and rescue missions (Ministry of Foreign Affairs of Slovakia 2004b). Another example of an important mission that included new members was Eagle Base. In July 2005, 50 Czechs replaced the Austrians in taking responsibility for security at one of the headquarters that the EU actually supervised. A NATO force had operated there previously, but that alliance turned over the security mission to the EU in December 2004. Thus, participation by Czech troops in the SFOR mission goes back to 1995 and they have been part of the EUFOR mission since December 2004. Czech airmen based at Přerov operate helicopters in investigative flights over Bosnia, and they also transport military material. There are also 80 Czech soldiers who work with the Austrians to protect the base at Tuzla (Ministry of Foreign Affairs of the Czech Republic 2005c). Additional goals include furthering European integration, rooting out corruption, and defeating organized crime (Ministry of Defense of the Czech Republic 2006a). By the end of 2005, all ten of the new alliance members had played a role in the

Bosnian activities. Only the three Baltic nations were not involved at that time, although they had been at an earlier point in time (Ministry of Foreign Affairs of Slovakia 2004c).

Discovering Meaning in the Shadows

Therefore, NATO operations to control instability and terrorism in Bosnia were meaningful for a number of reasons. Many observers had worried about the potential connections between the Muslim community in Bosnia and unrest in primarily Islamic societies further east. In a sense Bosnia is a microcosm of a larger struggle among some of the world's great religions and cultures. By playing a contributing role in 1995 and after, the alliance was able to assist in building a model of stability that differed from the examples that Iraq and Afghanistan provided. In addition, the Bosnian case study offers evidence of the different ways in which NATO involved its new members and thus meshed membership selection with involvement in a new type of mission. In fact, activities by new NATO members have actually occurred in Bosnia at four distinct points in time. First, all the new members contributed in that country while they had PfP status. Second, after 1999, the Czech Republic, Hungary, and Poland took on roles as full alliance members. Third, after mid-2004, all 10 members were part of NATO, and they worked under that label until December 2004. Fourth, after December 2004, the new partners provided assistance primarily in EUFOR and secondarily in NATO. In conclusion, an enormous tragedy that germinated directly in the shadows of the Cold War gave way to an imperfect but usable model of an ethnically balanced political system. At the same time, the territory of Bosnia became a display case for NATO's ability to integrate nations that had lived in the shadow of the Soviet Empire into an important alliance mission.

CHAPTER SEVEN

Kosovo in the Shadow of Bosnia's Lessons

Following his defeats in Slovenia, Croatia, and especially Bosnia, Serb leader Slobodan Milosevic set his sights on protection of the Serb minority in Yugoslavia's own Republic of Kosovo. He encouraged the ambitions of the Serbs in Kosovo, and their continuing atrocities against the Albanian majority provoked denunciations by the outside world through much of 1998. In September, the UN passed Security Council Resolution 1199, a declaration that condemned the Serb atrocities in Kosovo. However, Russian and Chinese opposition prevented the resolution from incorporating language that would call for use of force against the Serbs. In light of that resistance to the possibility of forceful UN action, the United States and the United Kingdom switched the discussion to NATO. NATO was willing to approve flyovers of the Serbian border in hopes that it might be a deterrent. The alliance also played a central role in organization of the Rambouillet Conference in early 1999, a conference that turned out to be the last diplomatic hope before the endorsement of military force (Hendrickson 2006, 94–105).

NATO and Operation Allied Force (OAF), March 1999

Use of NATO to forge a conclusion to the crisis raised the difficult issue of the use of force to protect an ethnic group against the use of terror and violence perpetrated by its own government. The fact that the conflict was totally contained within the borders of one country was a major reason for UN reluctance in these circumstances. In contrast, the UN supportive resolutions at the time of the first Persian Gulf War had been directed at pushing Iraq out of Kuwait. Defense of a nation against aggression was much more in keeping with the defined role and previous history of the United Nations. However, the Kosovo crisis did fit with President Clinton's criterion of a humanitarian crisis as a rationale for such intervention (Jentleson 2007, 288–9). Early in his administration, he had developed the theme of "Expansion and Enlargement." This foreign policy theme is understandable in light of the global situation at the conclusion of the Cold

War. It called for an active role by the West in expanding and enlarging the community of nations that nurtured free market principles and protected human rights. Obviously, major human rights abuses were occurring in Kosovo. In addition, the West had basically stayed on the sidelines during the great suffering in the region during most of the Bosnian War of 1992–95. In order to prevent similar scale atrocities, the decision of the Clinton Administration and NATO to take action when the UN would not is understandable.

Therefore, the conflict was a first in several respects. The alliance actually fought a war instead of defending against the prospects of one as it had mainly done during the Cold War, and the mission was directed against a situation of ethnic cleansing within a nation rather than against invasion of it by an outside force (Jentleson 2007, 442). In the end, 19 NATO members approved the decision to take action in light of the paralysis within the UN (Rees, 2004, 210). In a number of ways, NATO had taken upon itself the role of crisis manager through OAF (Mahncke, 2004, 54).

An additional unique feature of OAF was that NATO was on the verge of including three former communist countries in the alliance. Although they would not formally join until one month after the military operation, they felt special pressure to go along in the brief war of March 1999. Thus, Poland, the Czech Republic, and Hungary granted over-flight rights and made other contributions to the intervention (Terzuolo 2006, 49). Of course, the traditional alliance partners made more substantive contributions. For example, Germany and Denmark both took part in the campaign. In Denmark, the legislature had granted permission, and all the centrist political parties had been supportive.

Once the brief operation was concluded, a peacekeeping operation entitled Kosovo Force (KFOR) replaced the bombing campaign entitled OAF. Very quickly, the participant nations began to debate the political and military lessons of the intervention. European nations had learned that U.S. leadership had been required in the Kosovo operation in part because the EU lacked such capabilities. Therefore, the EU set up in the summer the infrastructure of its preexisting European Security and Defense Policy (ESDP). Germany considered upgrading its capabilities, and Denmark decided to modernize its Air Force. Interoperability among the various military forces had been an issue during the campaign, and a resolve developed to address that deficiency (Michta 2006, 52, 65, 105). American commanders had complained about the need for excessive coordination among the NATO partners. Some concluded that the European partners only contributed restrictions on the carrying out of policy (McGuigan 2007, 154). That concern was one reason that the Bush Administration decided to take the lead in the 2001 Afghanistan operation (Jentleson 2007, 334). In contrast, the United States did not turn over a large share of the Afghan peacekeeping force to NATO until 2006. On the other hand, a positive feature of the consultative feature of alliance planning during Kosovo was that it stoked the belief that NATO was becoming a political as well as a military alliance (Mahncke 2004, 73).

Another set of lessons pertained to the opposition that Russia had shown to the operation all the way from beginning to end. Russia traditionally had looked to Serbia as a smaller Slavic brother, and members of the Milošević family had at times taken sanctuary in that protective larger brother. In addition, Russia opposed the precedent that OAF might set for other regions of nations seeking border changes (Friedman 2008, 18; Jentleson 2007, 317). Russia had already fought one war in Chechnya (1994–96) and was beginning its second in 1999. In the shadows of its doubts lay also the seeds that the intervention was leaving for a later bid by Kosovo for independence. Russia feared outside pressure to grant the same eventual status to Chechnya. Another factor behind Russian rejection of a plan endorsed by either the UN or NATO was its own renewed push for Great Power Status. Their near financial collapse in 1998 convinced them of the need to take purposeful steps to restore their lost position, a move that resonated with popular concerns and interests. Vladimir Putin had become Secretary of Russia's Security Council in the same month that OAF took place (Baev 2008, 34–35, 82). He was thus thinking ahead to future chess moves when he espoused Russian opposition to the intervention. In addition, a consequence of the 1999 Serbian defeat was that it produced more evidence for Russia of "the political humiliation of its (own) impotence" (Gower and Timmins 2007, ixx).

Technically, both Russia and China also opposed OAF because of the conviction of their leaders that it constituted intervention in the internal problems of a sovereign state (Hendrickson 2006, 94). For them the operation constituted an illegal use of force. Chinese anger was fueled as well by the fact that NATO bombs hit its embassy in Belgrade (Pease 2008, 155). The budding refuge crisis made the image of Kosovo to Russia even more negative, especially since so many of them were Kosovo Serbs. The expressed concerns about sovereignty by Russia and China even resonated within NATO as it evaluated tactical decisions. The alliance had discussed the possibility of a ground invasion in addition to the air campaign. However, that would have entailed even greater interference into the sovereignty of an independent state as well as potentially higher casualties, and it therefore never took place.

Post-Intervention Management of Kosovo, 1999-2008

OAF was a success in achieving protection for Kosovo's Albanian majority in the face of Yugoslav interference in support of the Serb minority. However, it was not a panacea for an ethnic conflict that had raged since 1389. Kosovo quickly became an example of a situation in which peacekeeping forces can expect a long stay. Containing future ethnic conflict, rebuilding infrastructure, and reconstructing territorial integrity is no small matter (Rees and Mahncke 2004, 3). The primary responsibilities were on the shoulders of NATO. While the UN took responsibility for postoperation management of Kosovo, NATO organized the 17,000 soldier KFOR contingent. A third involved group was the EU, with its 1,800 person unit that engaged in important subsidiary functions such as training of the police (Štěpanovský 2008, 18–22). Altogether, 34 nations were assisting in Kosovo by mid-2008.

A unique feature of KFOR has been its inclusion of the troops of so many new NATO members. This inclusion helped to silence those critics who had expected European nations to do more during the Bosnian War. For example, the three Baltic nations all contributed in Kosovo after joining NATO in 2004. Estonia contributed a platoon to a police unit working in Priština (SME 2005a). Both Estonia and Latvia contributed to protection of the economically significant Mitrovica area in the northeast (Ministry of Foreign Affairs of Slovakia 2005a). Latvian forces had first come in 2000, and 15 of those troops served in Multinational Task Force Center (MNTF-C). Latvia had a total of 95 personnel in the region, and these yielded to Estonians in February, 2006 (Ministry of Foreign Affairs of Latvia 2010b). Estonia had been in Kosovo since 1999, but they did lower their flag at Camp Olaf Rye in Mitrovica in early 2010. They concluded that a decade-long mission had been successful and demonstrated the "efficiency of the activity of NATO." Their intention was to keep several staff officers in the nation after that point (Ministry of Defense of Estonia 2010b). Lithuanian troops operated in Urosevac and aided in the transfer of law and order functions from military to civilian units (Ministry of Foreign Affairs of Slovakia 2005b). They also had provided 30 soldiers to a Polish-Ukrainian Battalion (Ministry of Foreign Affairs of Lithuania 2010b).

Bulgaria and Romania performed different sorts of missions. In Prizren they assisted in protection of minority enclaves, patrimonial sites, and freedom of movement. Starting in 2000, a Bulgarian engineering squad of 34 soldiers and 5 staff officers also worked on deactivation both of mines and of unexploded ordnance in the same general area (Ministry of Foreign Affairs of Slovakia 2005c; Ministry of Foreign Affairs of Bulgaria 2010b). The engineers also rebuilt destroyed houses and bridges, repaired public buildings, constructed new housing, and helped build the bridge over Recan. In addition, a 51-person Bulgarian police contingent remained from the group that had originally entered Kosovo in 2000 (Ministry of Foreign Affairs of Bulgaria 2010c). Romania played an important role in Multinational Battle Group West (MNBG (W)) through the dispatch of their 498th Paratrooper Battalion from Bacau. Working closely with Italian, Hungarian, and Slovenian troops, they performed vehicle patrols, observation patrols, and observation posts (Ministry of Defense of Romania 2010b).

Czechs, Slovaks, and Hungarians also involved themselves during the decade after the alliance bombing campaign of 1999. Safety of returning Serb refugees in the border areas was also important, and Lithuanians, Czechs, and Slovaks all contributed in that project (Ministry of Foreign Affairs of Slovakia 2005d). For the Czech Republic, interestingly, their military contributions to Kosovo increased as a direct consequence of the 9/11 attacks. They perceived a correlation between the unpredictability of terrorism in these two disparate locations. In fact, they had also decided to increase their contingent in Kosovo three weeks before 9/11, because of the withdrawal of their forces from Bosnia (Ministry of Foreign Affairs of the Czech Republic 2002a). On March 1, 2002, they joined with their former countrymen to form a Joint Czech-Slovak Battalion for use in MNBG (C). At the time, the United Kingdom was in command of this overall unit that was based in the capital city of Priština. The Czech portion initially consisted of 400 troops and the Slovak of 100 (Ministry of Foreign Affairs of the Czech Republic, 2002b). This joint battalion was operational until July, 2005, but the Czech segment was continuously renewed for the next five years. From July 2005 until December 2006, Czech troops actually had command responsibilities of the MNBG (C). That unit included 1,600 troops with the responsibility of protecting the central hub of Priština (Ministry of Defense of the Czech Republic 2006b). The 500 Czech troops ended up being involved in a number of unexpected missions. For example, they presented school programs on the dangers of land mines, worked to protect the forests against illegal tree cutting, and endeavored to stop drug trafficking through the region (iDNES 2006d). By mid-2009, there were a full 550 Czech troops in this operation, and they included the 131st Combined Artillery Battalion from Pardubice and soldiers from the 14th Logistical Support Brigade also from Pardubice (Ministry of Defense of the Czech Republic 2010b). Finally, Hungary dispatched 470 soldiers as part of the overall Kosovo mission.

These new NATO members did not halt their contributions with the end of their specific missions or tours. With a certain amount of fanfare, they routinely welcomed home those who had served and those who became their replacements. In summer 2008, for instance, 60 additional Czech soldiers left to join the Czech 13th Contingent that already operated in Kosovo. Overall, that contingent included 402 military professionals. It had been operating under Irish command, but at the beginning of August it would be under the Finns. The center of its operations would be the base Šajkovac, in a region that included 130,000 citizens. Their mission included restoration of electric energy and drinkable water. The contingent was also tasked with fighting theft, domestic abuse, drug distribution, possession of illegal weapons, and illegal hauling of wood (iDNES 2008a). About the same time, Slovakia sent in another rotation of its soldiers. They would be contributing both to KFOR and to the EU's Operation ALTHEA-EUFOR. Slovak support for KFOR consisted of 134 soldiers who were mainly involved in assisting humanitarian organizations, particularly in protecting the Serb minority (SME 2008a). Clearly, international assistance would continue after Kosovo's declaration of independence.

The extensive involvement of new NATO members in KFOR made sense in several respects. Like the fragments of Yugoslavia, all of the new alliance members had been under the control of larger empires prior to 1918, on their own for two decades, in the grasp of the Nazis during World War II, within the communist bloc for the next four decades, and then in the process of renewal since 1991. The postcommunist states that had joined NATO were closer to the troubled Balkans than were either the West European nations or especially the United States. Many of these new alliance partners could also offer positive models of postcommunist development both to Serbia and to Kosovo.

Independence and a New Constitution for Kosovo

Independence

The Parliament in Kosovo declared independence on February 17, 2008. Just as in 1999, this new stage in Kosovo's history was not one that traveled through the UN. Again aware that Russia and China would veto any Security Council Resolution, the leaders of Kosovo reached out to individual nations with a request for recognition. By early October, forty-seven nations had done so. They also displayed a new flag that was bright blue, contained a golden map of Kosovo, and included six stars for each of Kosovo's principal ethnic groups. In an echo of the 1911 International Exhibit in Rome, the leaders signed their names on a large iron sculpture that spelled out

"NEWBORN" (MSNBC 2008). Whereas the Rome exhibit had given Serbs a chance to celebrate their heritage and dreams, the 2008 piece provided the same opportunity for the Kosovars.

This new state was unique in a number of ways. Outside powers had given Kosovo more than a nudge toward independence, especially during OAF in 1999. A number of nations granted it recognition in a short space of time, and 65 had done so by early 2010. Its boundaries were "something other than the internal borders of a highest-level administrative component of a pre-existing federation" (King 2008, 2). A number of factors were pointers toward this event at the time that it occurred. Shortly before the independence declaration, Boris Tadič had won the election for President in Serbia. His platform had been a pro-West one that contrasted with the nationalistic platform of his rival Tomislav Nikolič. Tadič would emphasize continued talks with the EU about a future relationship, and he was unlikely to agitate Kosovo Serbs in opposition to the independence of Kosovo (Štěpanovský 2008, 18–22). Such intrusion into the new state would have reminded EU negotiators of Serbia's effort to protect Serbs in Bosnia in the 1990s and the enormous bloodshed that ensued as a result. That kind of interference would surely have set back any productive discussions with the EU. Other precedents for independence existed in prior historical periods. The focus on self-determination of nations after World War I heartened the Kosovars to apply that principle to their own territory many decades later. A series of UN resolutions in the 1960s that supported national liberation declarations in Africa seemed to offer a parallel to the Kosovo situation as well.

At the same time, other winds prevailed against the logic of a declaration of independence. Both the Helsinki Declaration of 1975 and a resolution by the OSCE in 1990 supported the inviolability of existing borders such as those of Yugoslavia. Then in 1999, the United Nations Security Council passed Resolution 1244, a declaration that gave Yugoslavia the right to determine questions of autonomy within its own borders (Štěpanovský 2008, 18–22). For smaller postcommunist nations that had just joined NATO, recognition of Kosovo also seemed to be too much of a knee-jerk response to American interests. They had not intended to replace reflexive support for the Soviet Union with too frequent acquiescence with American preferences (Rychlík and Zrno 2008, 20).

In spite of the doubts, Kosovo did continue on as an independent state, and so related questions about the role of the international participants emerged. First, would the outside troop presence continue into the indefinite future? American Secretary of Defense Robert Gates said that the 1,600 American troops in the international contingent would remain at least in the near future (Washingtonpost 2008a). Second, would international judges and prosecutors in the troubled north of Kosovo be able to continue on with their work? In fact, violence had forced their evacuation shortly after the independence declaration. By early October, UN justice workers returned to the courthouse in Mitrovica, the key city in the Serbian north. Those who returned first would deal exclusively with the worst criminal cases. Eventually, the EU would send 2,000 judges and prosecutors to replace the UN officials, and at some point in that transition justice workers would take up civil cases as well. Third, would Serbia succeed in getting the UN to investigate their questions and doubts about the new international entity? They had submitted a resolution asking the General Assembly to request an advisory opinion from the International Court of Justice (USATODAY 2008a). Any positive reaction by the UN to their requests would roil the waters even further.

The New Constitution of the Republic of Kosovo

In light of the above analysis, the features of the Constitution that pertain to matters of ethnic balance and relations deserve attention. Chapter I is entitled "Basic Provisions." On the matter of official languages at the national level, both Albanian and Serbian have coequal status as official languages (Article 5). At the municipal level, Turkish, Bosnian, and Roma also have that status. With regard to religious differences, the document simply states that Kosovo "is a secular state and is neutral in matters of religious belief" (Article 8). Chapter II on "Fundamental Rights and Freedoms" spells out more fully the possibilities for the various religions within the new state. Each religious denomination has the right to set up its own schools and charities (Article 39), but the government may also restrict religious freedom if there is a threat to public safety, health, or individual rights (Article 33).

Chapter III on the "Rights of Communities and their Members" is particularly meaningful to the conflictual situation in Kosovo. Article 59 enumerates 12 separate rights that each community possesses. A community has the right to education in one of the official languages of the Republic. Each has the right to use its own language and alphabet in public as well as in private. They may do the same when dealing with municipal authorities and local offices, as long as they represent a sufficient share of the population as deemed by law. If an interpreter or translator is needed, the public authorities will bear the cost. Personal names also receive attention. Citizens may register their names in the original form and script of their languages. Meaningfully, they can revert to their original names, if they had earlier been changed by force. Place names should also duly reflect the multinational character of the particular area. Each also has the right to broadcast programming in their own language, and Serbs could license their own Kosovo-wide television channel. Finally, each community would have the right to "free and peaceful contacts" with persons of the same ethnicity in any state. All of these provisions certainly reflected the best intentions of local leaders as well as the norms of the UN, EU, and NATO. Again, on national issues the above provisions pertain to two official communities, and on local questions they are relevant to five.

The Constitution also says much about ethic balance in governmental institutions. At the local level, if 10 percent of the population belongs to communities that are not in the majority in that municipality, those communities have one special Vice Presidential position for themselves (Chapter III, Article 62). Article IV on the "Assembly of the Republic of Kosovo" goes into great detail on the parliament at the national level. That parliament contains 120 seats, and 20 are reserved for communities that are not in the majority. For example, the Serbs will have no fewer than 10, the Bosnians 3, and the Turks 2. In addition, Roma, Ashkali, Egyptians, and Gorani are reserved at least 1 each (Article 64). The Assembly also selects a President and five Deputy Presidents. Basically, the dominant Albanian group controls selection of the President and three of the Deputy Presidents, while Serbs have one Deputy and the other communities collectively also have one (Article 67).

Features of the Executive Branch are outlined in Chapter VI "Government of the Republic of Kosovo." The President will propose a Prime Minister to the Assembly (Article 95), and following that the Prime Minster selects a Cabinet. If the Cabinet contains twelve or fewer positions, Serbs are guaranteed one position and the other nonmajority communities a second. If the Cabinet consists of more than twelve, then all the nonmajority communities select a third. A similar principle applies at the Deputy level. Cabinets numbering twelve or fewer positions will contain two Serbs and two persons from the other nonmajority communities. Cabinets with more than twelve positions grant a fifth deputy position to the nonmajority communities (Article 96).

Chapter VII is interesting both for what it contains about the "Justice System" and what it does not. At several levels, the nonmajority communities are served by a 15 percent guiding rule. For the Supreme Court or for any appeals court, they will collectively be guaranteed 15 percent of the positions (Article 103). However, there is no mention of a guaranteed seat for a Serb, a principle that appears in the chapters on the legislature and executive. The final Chapter VIII presents a complicated formula for choosing members of the Constitutional Court. Essentially, the nonmajority communities do not have a guaranteed seat of any sort. There are nine judges on the court, and the Assembly picks seven by a two-thirds vote. The Assembly then picks the other two judges by a majority vote, and the Albanian community would obviously win these as well. However, for these last two judicial positions, there is also a stipulation that a majority of legislators from the nonmajority communities must also vote for the winners (Article 114). This final provision seems to make it impossible for an Albanian who is totally unacceptable to the nonmajority communities to win a position as Constitutional Court judge. Presumably, the nonmajority communities would boycott or vote for one of their own candidates, if the Albanian candidate was totally unacceptable. This provides a sort of indirect safety valve for the nonmajority communities (assembly-Kosovo 2008).

Overall, the document looks fair to the disparate communities within the new Republic of Kosovo. Of course, the question for future study will be the extent to which it operates as equitably as it appears on paper. Will local officials really take the time to hire translators if nonmajority persons come in on public business? How much impact will the nonmajority Vice Presidents actually have on policy? What will be the role of nonmajority legislators in the committee and party structures of the Assembly? Will Serbs be content if they are not successful in obtaining important judicial positions, given the lack of any guaranteed positions on them? The answer to such questions will emerge in the political discussions and battles of the future. While the outside monitors are still there, they can act in an advisory capacity and perhaps give the new Constitution time to penetrate at least some roots into the soil of Kosovo.

Impact of Kosovo Independence on Other States

Fears mounted in many quarters about the effect of Kosovo's independence on other nations and regions. The variety of those fears paralleled the variegated nature of the sources of them. The EU had a concern about the impact on Cyprus with Turkish and Greek claims, on Spain with its Basque challenge, and Romania and Slovakia with their Hungarian minorities. Russia prophetically feared the impact on the fragile situations in Georgia and Moldova (Štěpanovský 2008, 18–22). Even though it would be Russian minorities that might rebel in those two states, Putin claimed to not want another issue that would pit Russia against both the EU and the US. Others were concerned about the impact on the Balkan neighborhood itself. Might the Kosovo model be emulated in Macedonia by the Albanian minority there?

Further, might it also encourage Bosnian Serbs to try for independence, and will Serbia itself move closer to Russia (Rychlík and Zrno 2008, 20)? The list of concerned observers also included Metropolitan Amfilohije Radivič of the Serbian Orthodox Church. Ironically, his base was now Cetinje in the new state of Montenegro. He predicted that a new phase of conflict, battle, and war was likely in the region (SME 2008b). Others compared the Kosovo situation to the 1991 breakaway by Lithuania from the Soviet Union. That separation had the ripple effect of breaking that giant state into 15 new countries. In a similar way, might not the Kosovo precedent have similar impact on countries like China, India, Mexico, Brazil, South Africa, and Ukraine (Zachar 2008, 37–9)?

The Kosovo Model and Regional Instability

Many of the above-stated fears have not materialized into substantive problems. However, it is true that a key determinant in Kosovo's fate was the continued involvement of outside powers. King (2008, 2) centers his conclusions on the fact that Kosovo came into being at least indirectly because of the actions of external nations and alliances. He identifies four entities similar to Kosovo in postcommunist space as the ones to watch, and he invents the term TAKO to describe them. They include Transdniestria, Abkhazia, Nagorno-Karabakh, and South Ossetia. It is the outside intervention of Armenia into Azerbaijan that is the factor for Nagorno-Karabakh, while Russia is the key external player both for the Transdniestrian sector of Moldova and for the Abkhaz and South Ossetian regions of Georgia. In a sense, King was prophetic about the two components of Georgia, for war developed in both units in August 2008, only six months after Kosovo's independence declaration. Obviously, the situation was complicated, for the Georgia troops first hit those two pro-Russian enclaves. However, the result of the massive Russian response was that both enclaves ended up with more autonomy than they had before. The conundrum in this situation is whether the true Kosovo parallel is to the existence of Georgia with its two northern pro-Russian communities that lie on the border with Russia, or whether the genuine parallel is between Kosovo's push for independence and the separatist tendencies in South Ossetia and Abkhazia.

The above-mentioned primacy of outside factors in a multiplicity of case studies requires consideration of the question of whether the 1999 protective NATO bombing campaign was the event that was most responsible for the 2008 declaration of independence by Kosovo. The preponderance of historical and political evidence does point in this direction. Outside pressures on

Kosovo had made a difference since 1389. However, until 1999, they always resulted in subordination of Kosovar interests to larger forces. In the fourteenth century the Ottoman Empire became dominant. In following centuries, the only additional outside forces were provocative movements and parties based in Albania and Serbia, and their intent was to keep the pot boiling. After the collapse of the Ottoman Empire, the new Yugoslav federation subordinated Muslim interests to Slavic ones. Once Yugoslavia itself experienced the communist takeover and revolution, the Kosovars did not even enjoy the full republic status that tiny Slovenia did. During most of the 1990s, Kosovo watched as Serbia moved forcefully through its wars into Slovenia, Croatia, and worst of all Bosnia. The Serb shadow in Kosovo at that time was large indeed and became a physical presence in mid-1998. Historically, none of the above-noted outside pressures promoted the interests or autonomy of Kosovo. However, OAF was an external factor that, for the first time, repelled the invader on behalf of Kosovar rights. The ensuing management of Kosovo by the UN, EU, and KFOR both continued that protection and directly breathed life into the dreams of those who called an independent republic into existence in early 2008.

Post-Independence Security Issues

Nearly one year after the independence declaration of 2008, the government itself established a new Kosovo Security Force (KSF) that consisted of 2,500 professional soldiers and 800 specialists. They replaced a Kosovo Defense Force (KDF) that had included former Albanian rebels. The newly formed group would only carry light weapons and would primarily deal with natural catastrophes and disasters. British instructors would provide the training, while the United States would give the forces uniforms and Germany vehicles. The contingent would have a multiethnic character, although the response of Serbian and Kosovo Serb leadership was to recommend that no Kosovo Serbs join it. KFOR, under NATO leadership, would still have overall control, and that force still consisted of 15,000 troops in early 2009 (SME 2009d).

In February 2009, Kosovo celebrated the first anniversary of its independence. Gatherings surrounded the monuments built to the casualties of the 1998–99 war. In the intervening year, the UN had handed over supervision of the nation to a 2,000-member EU mission of police officers, judges and advisors. That group would work closely with the much larger NATO force. Serbs continued to reject the existence of the new nation (USATODAY 2009b), while issues and questions from the 1999 war continued to percolate. For instance, in April 2009, Amnesty International called upon NATO to take responsibility for civilian deaths that resulted from the bombing of Serbia's state television station during the war. NATO defended its actions by pointing out that the Hague prosecutor had declared the bombing to be "legally acceptable," and by observing that the station had been part of a communications network that directed Serb attacks on Kosovars (USATODAY 2009c). Then, at the beginning of 2010, Serbs withdrew their diplomatic representatives from Montenegro in retaliation for the latter's recognition of Kosovo (IZVESTIYA 2010a). Overall, there were still 127 nations in the UN that had not recognized Kosovo as a nation. Serbia continued with its legal challenge to the existence of the new country at the World Court in The Haag. The new country wrestled with a 40 percent unemployment rate and an exodus of many young persons from Kosovo into other nations (iDNES 2010a). Attention to these simmering questions required attention from the UN, NATO, and the EU.

During the summer of 2009, NATO found it possible to scale back its force from 15,000 to 10,000. The rationale was that Kosovo now had its own force of 2,500, and that the EU had upgraded its initial contingent to 2,500 as well. Thus, the number of military personnel would remain the same, but a portion of the NATO group could be available for use in Afghanistan (USATODAY 2009d). The increased terrorism in Afghanistan was having an echo effect on force maintenance of Kosovo, although the security situation in the latter was by no means calm or without danger. Ironically, the new nation of Kosovo had in a sense been born in the shadow of the Bosnian War but was also affected by the shadow of the Afghan War.

CHAPTER EIGHT

NATO Applies its Capabilities in Afghanistan

In October 2006, NATO took formal control of the ISAF in Afghanistan. This was a remarkable step for an alliance that had been formed nearly six decades earlier to counter early Cold War threats by the Soviet Union toward West Europe. In 1949, no one of its founders would have dreamed that the alliance would eventually be operating in a country in the Middle East. To them, it would have been incomprehensible that a force of 40,000 in that year would be attempting to stabilize a country that had succumbed to an extreme, militant, Islamic movement like the Taliban. No doubt, equally surprising would have been the fact that the militant movement had both harbored and refused to surrender a terrorist whose commands had resulted in attacks on key buildings in New York City and Washington, D.C., with the ensuing deaths of about 3,000 persons. Probably, NATO founders would also have been amazed, when they realized that contributing members of the alliance in Afghanistan included ten nations that had formerly been part of the communist bloc that the architects of 1949 were establishing NATO to contain.

Primarily, this chapter will focus on the nature of the mission since October 2006, the point at which NATO took over the operation in a formal way. At the same time, it is important to examine certain aspects of the operation as it evolved after September 2001. Attention will focus in the first section on evaluation of the foundation document transferring control of ISAF to NATO. Second, the concerns will center both on the makeup of the military force itself and on the changing strategies in which it has been involved. Third, there will be some analysis of the degree and amount of economic assistance provided by the various national members of the allied forces. Some nations that have supplied troops have also provided economic aid and assistance in rebuilding facilities that would nurture further economic growth. Others, however, have preferred to assist with economic resources as a substitute for troops. In a number of cases, public opinion within those nations would not have supported dispatch of military forces. Fourth, political development in terms of institutions and the machinery of democracy have also been part of the effort in Afghanistan. What role have NATO nations played in that challenge? A fifth section will examine briefly the related areas of policy decisions, current issues, and visions for the future. Sixth, there will be an extended section in the paper that treats the individual contributions made by the member states. All new alliance partners have contributed in some way on the ground in Afghanistan. What have been their specific contributions, and what has been the overall division of labor? A conclusion will then present several challenges that need continuing attention by NATO planners in Afghanistan.

Declaration by the NATO and the Islamic Republic of Afghanistan: September 6, 2006

The initial document bears the signatures of Mr. Jaap de Hoop Scheffer, Secretary-General of NATO, and Mr. Hamid Karzai, President of the Islamic Republic of Afghanistan. A first section presents a framework for cooperation between the two entities. NATO-enunciated goals center on creation of more "security and stability" in both Afghanistan and the wider region. Successful completion of the 2005 National Assembly elections had established a basis that such a hope could be realized. The Afghan Government looked at the official alliance support as a step on the path to the eventual taking of "full responsibility for its own security." NATO's cooperative role would not just concentrate on military capabilities, but it would also include progressive measures to assure good government and the rule of law. The triple battle would be against "terrorism, extremism, and drug trafficking." Interoperability between Afghan and NATO military capabilities was also part of the process.

Second, certain agreed upon principles would underpin this framework. Realism was essential, especially in light of the imperative of maintaining the current NATO budgetary ceiling. Control and ownership by Afghan authorities was also significant, for they needed to play a central role in determining priorities. Both units needed to preserve firm connections with the security and defense institutes in Kabul. Links with other key programs such as those of the London Conference were also on the agenda.

Third, the document outlined a number of concrete activities that would flow from the cooperative framework and principles. NATO would welcome Afghan participation in activities that took place elsewhere, such as Central Asia. There was an expectation that Afghan expert teams would visit alliance headquarters in order to learn more about defense reform and institution building. In addition, NATO would set up special short courses for Afghan participants at the NATO Defense College, NATO School Oberammergau, and elsewhere.

Fourth, the agreement looked also at the related matters of assessment and implementation. The key players in that vital process of assessment would be the NATO Senior Civil Representative and the Afghan Mission in Brussels. Allies involved in the Afghanistan mission would also be invited to provide bilateral aid, and in some cases PfP funding would be added in a supplementary way. Fifth, planning and assessment would target, in particular, improvements in the Afghan National Army. Goals would include increased professionalism and hence credibility of the military force.

Sixth and finally, the landmark arrangement enumerated a number of key areas of cooperation. Selected themes included more openness in the democratic foundation of the Afghan military, a more transparent personnel management and training system, joint participation in NATO/PfP military exercises, assistance that ranged from aircrew training to military equipment, greater emphasis on border security, cooperation on civil emergency planning, language training of security personnel, civil/military coordination of air traffic management, increased public understanding of security issues, and use of the Virtual Silk Highway to enhance access to information (*Declaration by the North Atlantic Treaty Organisation and the Islamic Republic of Afghanistan* 2007).

The document summarized above was a path-breaking one that involved NATO officially in a very new type of military project. Instead of countering threats that emanated from the heart of Europe or even from the Balkans, the alliance would now manage military and related projects far from its previously defined orbit. As the U.S. Permanent Representative to NATO put it in a speech given in late 2006, the original Cold War goal of protecting national territory had yielded to the objective of transferring power to the place where threats originated (Nuland 2006). In that sense, it was very important to lay out the new objectives through a joint statement that was as specific as possible. Similarly, in early 2007 President Bush argued that the NATO takeover of ISAF had made a real difference. A result had been creation of a "robust security force" that operated throughout all of Afghanistan rather than in only several regions and that also managed twenty-five PRTs. The injection of NATO's management role into the quicksand of Afghanistan had enabled the Afghan central government to at least reach out to all corners of this complicated nation (Bush 2007, 5–10). Thus, official governmental leaders of NATO made positive assessments in the early months of the new NATO operation. The "Declaration" was a meaningful one that had led to improved conditions in the Afghan battle against global terrorism. However, such optimism would not last very long.

Composition of the ISAF Force

Creation of ISAF had taken place in December 2001, at the time of the struggle against the Taliban regime in Afghanistan. From 2001 until October 2006, ISAF reported to the North Atlantic Council in Brussels (Saikal 2006, 525–34). The NATO takeover of the ISAF operation then occurred on October 5, 2006. Under NATO control, the force increased to 36,000, and a full 37 countries took part in the mission. All 26 NATO members were part of that contributing team. The workload was divided up into 25 PRTs. This is a significant NATO commitment in light of the fact that it is the first alliance operation outside of Europe (NATO 2007a). New programs have also been added. For example, in the summer of 2007, the alliance set up an Operational Mentor and Liaison Team, and its responsibilities were provision of specific advice to the Afghan military (NATO 2007b). In the end, there were five regional commands under NATO. They included North, South, East, West, and Kabul (NATO 2007c).

A number of key developed nations assist in the ISAF operation. Saikal (2006, 525–34) suggests that both France and Germany took part in ISAF operations in order to compensate for their unwillingness to participate in the 2003 invasion of Iraq. In effect, several nations took up specific functional areas of work in the overall Afghanistan activities. For example, Italy was a key nation that took responsibility for meeting the challenge of reforming the judiciary. Germany provided assistance in training the police, and the United Kingdom had primary responsibility for counter-narcotics. Japan's functional areas included disarmament, demobilization, and reintegration. Uniquely, each of those activities was suited to the particular strengths and historical experiences of the countries themselves. Of course, the United States took on overall supervision of training and building the Afghan National Army. These integrated efforts combined with expansion of the military activities to cover the entire country. Presumably, the net benefit would be penetration of control from the Kabul area into every corner of the country (Saikal 2006, 525–34).

Several participants called for even higher levels of involvement. For instance, in the summer of 2007 the consensus emerged that NATO was short two battalions. This shortage resulted from the restrictions that member nations were putting on their troops in terms of mission and military activity. The restrictions were intended to save the lives of their own personnel and thus avoid the inevitable public criticism back home (MIL 2007a). Karel Schwartzenberg (2007, 43–5), the Czech Foreign Minister, envisioned a situation in which the European nations would take over the PRTs in the near future. He saw this unique, expanded operation in Afghanistan as a "self-defining mission for NATO."

Finally, calls emerged for growth of the Afghan National Army itself. In a nation with 31 million people, some wondered why the army consisted of only 30,000 troops. Plans developed to increase that number to 70,000 in the near future. Inclusion of Afghanistan in the PfP process was also a key ingredient in the discussion. Thus, NATO's takeover of the ISAF operation involved more than added military muscle to the battle against terrorism. Both coordination with other allied nations and increased contributions by the host nation itself were essential needs.

Economic Assistance

The nations allied in the effort to both stamp out terrorism and rebuild Afghanistan contributed enormous sums after 9/11. By June 2007, the total package of economic assistance provided since 2001 amounted to $26.8 billion. Nations that had attended the 2006 London Conference pledged nearly 40 percent of that total assistance package, so much of the aid was earmarked well after the liberation of the nation from the Taliban. Specific areas designated for receipt of the assistance included health, the economy itself, the private sector, infrastructure, security, refugees, women, schools, and media (NATO 2007d).

A particularly interesting discussion of future needs took place within the German government in September 2007. The Foreign Minister Franz-Walter Steinmeier called for a 25 percent increase in the amount of Euros from Germany earmarked for Afghanistan. Specific areas that would benefit from this increased assistance entailed the building sector, income creation, and cross-border projects that touched on Pakistan. None of this would come to pass, however, unless a security foundation was first established. Only within the framework of security would economic aid have any impact (Ministry of Foreign Affairs of Germany 2007a). Germany's record on both counts between 2002 and 2007 was commendable. They had provided 38 million Euros to assist in clearing of land mines, and that project extended back into the 1990s. Understanding that return of refugees was vital in restoring a sense of economic momentum, the Germans had also channeled 20 million Euros to that endeavor (Ministry of Foreign Affairs of Germany 2007b). Overall linkage of aid to projects that intertwined security and economic considerations made great sense in such a threatening and fragile environment.

A related issue that emerged was the role of nongovernmental organizations (NGOs) in assisting NATO governments and militaries in the campaign. In many ways, the work of the NGOs adds the potential ingredient of winning "hearts and minds." These workers are not part of any perceived occupying military force and thus can add a human face to the NATO presence. However, there are several pitfalls that accompany injection of this dimension to the turbulent Afghan setting. Military forces often complain that the NGOs are in the way of their missions. NGO leaders sometimes feel exploited when the military channels assistance in directions that serve only strategic goals rather than human need. NGOs also fear for the lives of their workers as the enemy may mistakenly target the aid workers as in fact part of the military force. For example, a total of 68 aid workers died in conflicts in Afghanistan between 2003 and 2005. Finally, the Taliban may be well aware of the distinction between military personnel and aid workers. However, they may target the aid workers since they are doing the work of the hated American government (Lischer 2007, 99–118). In sum, use of NGOs in the economic assistance effort is a double edged sword. They offer the possibility of humanizing the face of NATO's military intervention, but they also can inextricably become involved in the various battles and conflicts in ways that undermine their purpose.

Political Development and Infrastructure

The takeover by NATO of ISAF brought one significant new political player into the picture. The office that then became part of the political infrastructure was that of NATO Senior Civilian Representative in Afghanistan. This office became operational on August 24, 2006, and Daan W. Everts from the Netherlands was its first occupant. There was also an office called First Representative, and that secondary position went to Hikmet Cetin from Turkey (NATO 2007e). The main focus of these two offices was the nonmilitary part of the ISAF mission. Selected important concerns of these two representatives were the secure delivery of goods, improvements in the police force, better courts, and enhanced border control with Pakistan. This new NATO machinery could build on the foundation of political development achieved by ISAF alone in the previous five years. They had achieved successes in the areas of education/employment for women, improved schools, and tools of democracy such as an elected Parliament (NATO 2007f).

The UN continued to be a significant part of the political process in Afghanistan. For example, on January 31, 2006, the UN assisted in creation of the Afghanistan Compact *United Nations Assistance Mission in Afghanistan* (UNAMA). This compact included the UN, the Afghan government, and the international community represented eventually by NATO. A main concern of this new organization in 2007 was the factional infighting within the police. In addition, the Afghan Compact played a role in development of plans for new networks of highways as well as construction of clinics. They would also take up the touchy issue of those provinces that permitted high poppy production and enticed drug traffickers (NATO 2007g). All of these worthwhile projects came under the heading of political development and added needed institutional components to that process. These endeavors constituted vital supplements to the military effort on the ground and in the air.

Policy Issues, Decisions, and Visions

The Rome Conference of July 2007 offers a useful summary of the policy issues on the table in Afghanistan for both the UN and NATO. The participants at that meeting listed six issues that needed goals and solutions. First, lack of political development was a major problem that needed attention. Growth of participatory institutions and effective governing structures were equal necessities. A second issue was the set of problems that afflicted the Afghan army and police. Training by the allies was one key method for defusing this particular issue. Third, there was a need to maintain an international military presence for an indefinite time period. By passing the baton of leadership to NATO in 2006, those involved had addressed that issue. Fourth, there was a need for steps to reduce the loss of civilian lives and property. This would be difficult in light of the increased number of casualties in 2007, especially in the summer and early fall. Fifth, there was a clear need to include Pakistan in planning and discussions, given the porous nature of the Afghan-Pakistan border. Stability of the Musharaff government in Pakistan was a question that affected planning in that issue area. Sixth, lack of effective coordination between the military and civilian sectors was a real challenge to mission effectiveness. With the arrival of NATO officially into the arena, planned additional infrastructure would address that issue (NATO 2007h). Thus, the Rome meeting both displayed the range of current issues and implicitly pointed the way to concrete steps that would address them.

The above array of issues did parallel a limited number of decisions in the early period after the NATO take-over of ISAF. A summer 2007 meeting of NATO Defense Ministers in Brussels resolved to supply more funds to equip the Afghan Army, to more strictly enforce rules of engagement in order to reduce civilian casualties, and to provide relief funds to families and communities that had been harmed (NATO 2007i). Another set of decisions that accompanied the transition to NATO control centered on the extent of military operations in the country itself. At the June 2004 Summit in Istanbul, NATO had committed itself to spread the campaign gradually to the entire country. In the middle of 2006, they had established a presence in the entire, conflicted southern region, and by the fall they had become more active in the east (Ministry of Foreign Affairs of Germany 2007c). Thus, the 2006 changes were simply an extension of early NATO activities.

A highly interesting issue about usage of allied troops had percolated for several years and needed attention, once NATO took formal charge of the military effort. A number of nations had limited the movement and activities of their troops, based on the fear of casualties and corresponding reactions from public opinion back home. At the Riga Summit in November 2006, NATO asked members to consider lifting the so-called caveats on the activities of their troops. Several alliance partners agreed with this request, and improvements took place. Based on one estimate, the commitments ensured that 26,000 of the 32,000 troops were more usable in genuine areas of need than they had been before (NATO's Riga Summit Confirms Present Commitments and Looks Ahead 2007, 4).

In fact, one could look at the formation of the Afghan Compact in early 2007 as a decision of sorts. The Compact itself announced three types of decisions. All 26 NATO partners would contribute a total of 30,000 troops to Afghanistan. A new Senior Civilian Representative would promote the political-military goals of the alliance. NATO would engage in liaison efforts with ISAF, the Afghan government, other international organizations, and neighboring countries (Ministry of Foreign Affairs of the Czech Republic 2007a). Each of these three goals implied a series of subsequent decisions by other parties and somewhat changed the direction of general activities.

Visions for the future were an additional patch in the overall fabric of NATO operations in the host nation. A British specialist (Sky 2007) called for a vision that centered on the pragmatic goal of assisting the Afghan military in holding ungoverned spaces and containing the insurgency. This snapshot of the future was a stark contrast to the dream of others that NATO should be endorsing primarily and promoting a liberal democratic model as the only basis for stability. Karel Schwartzenberg, the Czech Defense Minister (2007, 43–5) offered a forward-looking, somewhat futuristic vision for the joint operation. First, open the door for further assistance to new NATO membership for countries in the Western Balkans. Second, cement partnerships with non-NATO countries that shared alliance values. He mentioned Israel, Australia, New Zealand, and Japan. Third, strengthen and use the NATO Reaction Force (NRF) as a tool in situations that threatened to move to the emergency level. Such visionary thinking took strategists beyond the nuts and bolts of day-to-day activities in Afghanistan. That vision also suggested the possibilities for creation of a broader framework that could maintain some sort of stability, once most of the short-term goals had been achieved.

Contributions by the Member States

Breadth and Specialization of the NATO-led Coalition

As NATO began to play a larger role in the Afghan operation, a number of the alliance partners carved out their own special roles. For example, Germany provided 41 instructors to assist in training Afghan police officers. Especially important was their work with border police. Since Italy had experience in cleaning up its own corrupt legal system, they received special responsibilities in working with Afghan judicial personnel and offices. In fact, the Italians organized a Rule of Law in Afghanistan Conference. Britain assumed leadership of the counter-narcotics effort (McCain 2007, 29–33). Japan's role centered on disarming various armed groups, and the United States took the lead in building a national Afghan Army. This work of the United States included education at the Police Academy in Kabul, construction of seven regional training centers, and integration of women into the police force (Ministry of Foreign Affairs of Germany 2007d). All was not perfect harmony, however, for the European partners at times complained that the United States permitted them little influence over policy (Keohane 2006).

Contributions to the Afghanistan operation come from all 26 members. However, participation in the NATO mission was not confined to alliance members only. Several nations with PfP status also made contributions, and they included Sweden, Finland, and Austria. While the EU did not have a very visible presence in the country, only Malta and Cyprus among its members played no role at all (Rinkevics 2007, 29–30). In addition to all of those national players, Albania, Australia, Azerbaidjan, Macedonia, Croatia, Ireland, and Switzerland, and New Zealand chose to be involved in various ways (Ministry of Foreign Affairs of the Czech Republic 2007b). By early 2007, the total troop level was at 32,000, and later in the year it would hit 36,000. Of course, the Obama surge of 2009–10 would skyrocket those numbers.

In what kinds of activities did this array of NATO and non-NATO nations involve themselves? A selective picture can at least give a sense of the types of activities. One example was the contingent that operated in Helmand, in the conflicted southern part of Afghanistan. This had originally been a British contingent, but in the spring of 2007, a 35-member Czech contingent joined them. The job of the Czechs was to protect key British personalities and significant objects with military value (Ministry of Defense of the Czech Republic 2007a). In addition, there was a joint operation in the northeast area of Fayzabad, in the province of Badakshan. Danes, Czechs, and Germans were all part of that unit. They mainly provided protection to the base and to its transportation vehicles (Ministry of Defense of the Czech Republic 2007b, iDNES 2007b). Civilian workers at the base included those from the United States, Slovakia, Croatia, and Belgium. Activities were significant enough that the German Defense Minister Franz Josef Jung came for a visit in July (Ministry of Defense of the Czech Republic 2007c). Kandahar was a much troubled province, and the allies focused on "governance, economic development, and counter-narcotics" in addition to military operations. However, those actually engaging in battle with the Taliban included the United Kingdom, Canada, Netherlands, Australia, Romania, Estonia, Denmark, and the Afghan Army itself (Gates 2007, 36–9). During similar battles in the summer of 2006, they also received operational support from Portugal (Bush 2007, 5–10).

Dilemmas emerged for a number of the NATO allies during the first year of NATO-commanded military activities. For instance, in the early stages of "Operation Achilles" in June 2007, the Taliban kidnapped a British journalist (sueddeutsche 2007a). Several months later the British admitted that their troops were totally stretched out with activities in both Iraq and Afghanistan. They were considering a pull out of 5500 troops from Iraq in light of that pressure (SME 2007a). At the end of August the British actually suffered casualties from American bombs. The three deceased soldiers had been dragged into a battle with the Taliban in Helmand Province. The American bombing targeted the Taliban forces but ended up hitting British troops as well (DN 2007a). Finland had also lost a soldier in northwestern Afghanistan in May. A bomb had exploded while Finish and Norwegian soldiers were on patrol (DN 2007b). In May of 2007, Polish forces had become stirred up about the quality of their vehicles and actually carried out a formal protest. They claimed that the Hummers that the Americans provided them were inferior to the ones used by the Americans themselves (iDNES 2007c). A major problem emerged at about the same time in connection with South Korean Christians who were working with NGOs in Afghanistan. A group of 23 were captured, and two were killed before release was finally negotiated. It was unclear if the South Korean government had paid a large amount to the Taliban, but there was a suspicion that the government had paid a sum of around two million American dollars (iDNES 2007d).

A number of additional divisive issues plagued the alliance, even in its first year of operation. Civilian deaths were one of those main concerns. In May 2007, there was concern, especially from Germany, about the fact that operations by U.S. Special Forces had resulted in the deaths of 90 Afghan civilians. The German Defense Minister expected to talk with the U.S. leadership with an eye on exercising more restraint (USATODAY 2007b). The NATO Secretary-General cautioned that such casualties were at times unavoidable (latimes 2007a). By late summer the British were calling for a pullout of U.S. troops from the southern part of Afghanistan (sueddeutsche 2007b). In fact, in mid-October Afghan authorities shut down two private security firms in light of allegations of murder and robbery (USATODAY 2007c). Another complicating issue emerged in October 2007, when the Afghan government itself executed 15 prisoners, for the first time in three years. NATO allies opposed to capital punishment had mixed feelings about such an act in a country in which they had committed troops (USATODAY 2007d). Finally, continuing concerns developed over American plans to locate a radar site in the Czech Republic as well as antimissile capabilities in Poland. Although this was not on Afghan terrain, the logic of the emplacement was based on threats emanating from the Middle East. One of the main agenda items for NATO at its meeting of Defense Ministers in June was this controversial plan (iDNES 2007e).

Experiences of Selected Countries

At this point in the analysis, the spotlight shifts to the Afghan experiences of the new NATO partners. All ten have played some sort of role, although the level of the involvement is quite varied.

Bulgaria

Bulgaria had 540 troops in Afghanistan at the end of 2009 (NATO 2010d). Since July 2007, they had also sent 500 tons of weapons and ammunition as well as 70,000 Euros to fund humanitarian aid (Ministry of Foreign Affairs of Bulgaria 2010d). In the early period after 9/11 and the invasion of Afghanistan, they had worked with British troops to deploy a disinfecting bath/laundry complex. They had also provided to the United States "overflight, transit passage and stay" rights. In addition, Bulgaria made Sarafovo Airport in their own country available to troops that were part of the initial operation (Ministry of Defense of Bulgaria 2010b).

There were additional proposals that would push Bulgaria into the center of the battle against terrorism and thereby increase some risks to its territory and people. In July 2005 Uzbekistan evicted American personnel from Karshi-Khanabad Air Base. They had initially permitted American usage of the base soon after the 9/11 attacks. They reversed course four years later because the UN had airlifted over 400 refugees from their country to Romania, and Uzbekistan saw this as an insult. In order to compensate for the lost base, American leaders began to think about Bulgaria as one possible site for a new base. Potential choice of Bulgaria would be consistent with the logic that led to its admission to NATO in 2004. The country is closer to the area of conflict than most other alliance partners. Bulgaria could be an ideal staging ground for operations in the Middle East and Central Asia. Public opinion in the nation was supportive of such a venture, and the Bulgarian political leadership itself had enacted several related reforms. They included stronger civilian control over the military, some modernization of the armed forces, and increased transparency in military affairs (Cooley 2005, 79–92). In spite of the excitement in playing a more central role, addition of a base could make Bulgaria a more tempting target for a terrorist attack.

Czech Republic

Czech troops took on a large number of NATO-related activities, and thus they assumed a role of extensive involvement in Afghanistan relatively soon after joining the military alliance. In the spring of 2004, their meteorologists took on assignments at the Kabul airport. Part of their job was to provide weather reports for the Czech field hospital and chemical units that had been in the country since shortly after 9/11 (Ministry of Foreign Affairs of the Czech Republic 2010a). They also worked closely with others who were providing air transport and airport security. In addition, they provided forecasts that were linked to specific military activities, in particular along flight routes. This meteorological unit was particularly significant, since there were only twelve functioning stations in the country, and a number of them were only partly operational (Ministry of Defense of the Czech Republic 2007d).

A very different type of activity centered on inoculation of Afghan children against disease. Soldiers from the 5th contingent took the lead in this, but the Olivova Foundation assisted them. Orphanages in particular often had a lack of drinkable water, and so infections easily spread. Other NGOs supplemented this work by supplying the children with blankets, school supplies, and a new kitchen (Ministry of Defense of the Czech Republic 2007e).

Czech troops were also involved in work of a more military nature. For example, the 5th Contingent spent 86 days patrolling mountainous terrain in the Fajzabad area. Danish and German troops joined them in the effort. In addition, that contingent was involved in working with the local police, protecting several military bases, interacting with the Rapid Reaction Force, searching for explosives, building water tanks, and assisting the schools. After the 5th Contingent returned to its base in Pardubice, Czech Republic, the 6th Contingent based in Chrudimi replaced them. Thus, the Czechs had a continuing and diverse set of tasks as part of their overall work in provincial reconstruction (Ministry of Defense of the Czech Republic 2007f). Czech citizens almost became used to a regular rotation of units in and out of Afghanistan (Ministry of Defense of the Czech Republic 2007g). Czechs also played a role in HELI UNIT (Helicopter Unit) within Paktika Province in the southeast. Their 110 personnel included 20 who specialized in flying the helicopters (Ministry of Defense of the Czech Republic 2010c).

Further, Czechs contributed to other specialized types of activities. Interestingly, civilian workers went to the Afghan village of Itarchi. While there, they assisted at a school which provided education to boys in the morning and to girls in the afternoon. Only female members of the Czech team received permission to work with the girls. They also provided equipment to the school. During their stay, the Czechs learned to be sensitive to certain features of Afghan culture. For example, they had to cut out of their educational material illustrations of women in short European summer skirts, views of people from the back, and pictures of the traditional Czech beer (Ministry of Defense of the Czech Republic 2007h). Another contribution in the region was dispatch of a specialist team in 2005 to western Pakistan. After the earthquake there, there was a need for medical specialists and a 35-person trauma team (Ministry of Defense of the Czech Republic 2007i).

Risks to Czech personnel operating in Afghanistan provoked concern about the future of involvement there. In May the car of Czech chargé d'affaires Filip Velach received fire. Two body guards were injured, but the diplomat escaped unscathed (iDNES 2007f). During the same month, the first Czech soldier died in the area near Fajzabad, a region in which the Czech troops were part of PRT. In an accident of nature, he and five others had been buried in a landslide, while the others survived. This symbolic death led to a commemoration at the airport upon the return of his body. Both the Chief of Staff and Minister of Defense were present at the ceremony (iDNES 2007g). There was a moment of silence then and plans for another ceremony at the time of his burial (iDNES 2007h). Thus, the government treated his death as an event of national significance.

Some Czech units worked in quite dangerous terrain on a regular basis. Czech guards patrolled in the nearly inaccessible Badakshan mountain area of northeastern Afghanistan. They gathered information and also helped select sites for reconstruction projects (iDNES 2007i). They provided special assistance during the spring floods in that region (iDNES 2007j). Their highly respected field hospital worked continuously at the Kabul airport and helped airlift the wounded after treating them for their injuries. A predecessor field hospital unit had actually treated about 16,000 patients in the 2002–03, period (iDNES 2007k). A discussion also took place within the Czech Republic about the possibility of sending civilian experts into the theater of operations. They could help with transportation, health care, and agriculture. Dispatching them was a tough decision due to the fear that they could become obvious targets for attack (iDNES 2007l). The possibility of taking over the entire Logar province came up for discussion in late summer, a step that would add to Czech prestige but could cost as much as 650 million crowns each year. However, Czech firms might be involved in the reconstruction work, and so there would be an economic benefit to the Czech Republic. This proposal by the Czech government then became a subject for discussion in the legislature (iDNES 2007m). In the Logar PRT, Czechs had consistently contributed about 200 soldiers since March, 2004 (Ministry of Defense of the Czech Republic 2010d). As Czech soldiers also worked with Afghan police officers, they discovered that they had more impact if they dressed in local garb. Among other conclusions, they found that the Afghans responded well to award ceremonies, as they liked to be singled out (iDNES 2007n).

Overall, the Czechs played a role in Afghanistan that paralleled but was broader than some of its other NATO-related missions. While they had contributed in important ways in Bosnia, Kosovo, and Iraq, they had taken on significant positions of responsibility and authority in Afghanistan. This was particularly the case after the transfer of ISAF to NATO control in October 2006. By the end of 2009, they had 440 military personnel in the country (NATO 2010e).

Estonia

Estonian military forces played a role in a wide range of ISAF projects. Just prior to NATO's takeover of all operations in Afghanistan, Estonia took part with several other allies in a dangerous mission in Kandahar Province. At that time, in the summer of 2006, NATO in fact was already responsible for security in southern Afghanistan. Thus, Estonia at that time fought under the NATO umbrella. The precipitant to the crisis was the massing of Taliban-led forces in the area. The Afghan National Army plus additional allied forces repulsed that movement, and Estonia was one of the nations that offered operation support in that defensive effort (Bush 2007, 5–10).

By the end of 2009, they had 150 military personnel in the country (NATO 2010f), and they were operating under a parliamentary mandate that permitted as many as 170 soldiers to be in Afghanistan. Their activities over recent years included work with British and Danish troops in the dangerous Helmand Province, security assistance during the 2009 presidential election, and contributions to the war on drugs. Further, they also performed tasks at the Kabul and Kandahar airports as well as at ISAF Headquarters. In 2007, Estonia had also donated 4,000 AK assault weapons that were of high quality. Financial assistance by the Estonian government focused on the population and housing census, on construction of a new building for the Afghan Center at Kabul University, on creation of the Afghan National Archives, on creation of a pediatric ward at Helmand Central Hospital, and on development of a medical oxygen delivery system at Bost Hospital. In addition, Estonia provided two police officers and a political advisor to the EU Police Mission (Ministry of Foreign Affairs of Estonia 2010a).

Hungary

Hungary's military contribution to Afghanistan stood at 315 by the end of 2009 (NATO 2010g). A major contribution had been their leadership of the PRT in Baghlan, a role that began in 2006. Their own unit consisted of 210 military people, and their work centered both on improvement of living conditions in the area and work on infrastructure developmental projects. With increased civil-military cooperation as the hub of their concerns, they endeavored to pull in local workers to alliance-planned projects. They also donated five staff members to the police training operation that the EU managed (Ministry of Foreign Affairs of Hungary 2010d).

Latvia

It is also important to take a look at the perspectives of some of the new NATO partners with regard to the overall needs in Afghanistan. Edgar Rinkevics (2007, 29–30) offered several perspectives that include different angles on the needs in that military effort. In his view, NATO's main strength was its "common democratic values" rather than its military capabilities. However, the alliance was not at the moment designed to provide day-to-day management of a failed state. Thus, expansion of the organization to include troubled states like Georgia would help to increase alliance perspectives and strategies in dealing with failed or troubled states. He also recommended more use of the PfP members that could inject supplementary resources. For instance, the NATO Response Force could benefit from contributions that Sweden, Finland, and Austria are now making. Also, more NATO coordination with the EU would enable the work in Afghanistan to benefit from the capabilities of that all-European organization. Another writer expressed Latvian worries about the Russian factor and energy security. For that reason, he argued that Latvia always looked to NATO as the main pillar of its security. Further, in dealing with Islamic countries, Turkish membership in the organization was a positive factor and increased the relevance of the alliance (Pabriks 2007, 31–2). Such fresh perspectives from a new member state can offer new windows of opportunity to those who think about the military operation in more traditional ways.

Actual Latvian contributions numbered 175 troops at the end of 2009 (NATO, 2010h). Their contingent included regular military personnel, two state police officers, and one political advisor. In addition, they provided two employees from the Ministry of the Interior for the EU Police Mission (Ministry of Foreign Affairs of Latvia 2010c).

Lithuania

This nation had about 165 military personnel in Afghanistan at the close of 2009 (NATO 2010i). They had the important responsibility of heading a PRT in Ghor Province in the western part of Afghanistan. The goal of that PRT was to improve the environment for international organizations like the UN

(Ministry of Foreign Affairs of Lithuania 2010c). Lithuania also coordinated development projects in the province's capital city of Chagcharan. Successes included instruction of children about the dangers of land mines, rebuilding of important streets, creation of a Public Park, and founding of a library and internet reading room (Ministry of Defense of Lithuania 2010a).

Poland

With its large population and central leadership role in Iraq, Poland was a nation that could potentially provide valuable contributions in Afghanistan. In fact, by the end of 2009, 1,955 Polish soldiers made up its contingent in that country (NATO 2010j). Many of them had been assigned to the Multinational Corps North East (MNC NE), and protection of Kabul International Airport was an important project for them (Ministry of National Defense of Poland 2010a). One controversy connected with their involvement pertained to the involvement of Polish troops in the killing of Afghan civilians in August of 2007. In a battle between ISAF forces and the Taliban, a number of civilians had been caught in the middle and mistakenly killed. Among the innocent civilians were women and children. Poland recalled seven Polish soldiers from Iraq and decided to put them on trial. Polish citizens were divided on this matter, and sympathy for the soldiers prompted one individual to threaten to set himself on fire (iDNES 2007o). At another point the Polish government recalled six soldiers from the front because of their protest against inferior equipment provided to them. America had supplied Hummers to the Polish forces, but some protested that they were inferior to the vehicles that American forces used for themselves. American Hummers would provide defense against attacks with heavy weapons, while the vehicles supplied to the Poles would only fend off shots from hand guns. The soldiers recalled faced three years in prison for disobeying an order (iDNES 2007p). In sum, Poland's large contingent made them vulnerable to both the risk of becoming involved in causing civilian casualties and the threats of harm to their own individual troops.

Romania

Romanian troops were involved in at least one main battle with the Taliban. This was the above-noted conflict in summer 2006, and it took place in Kandahar Province. Its military forces took part with others in repulsing the surprise Taliban attack. Like Estonia, those troops mainly provided operational support (Gates 2007, 36–9). In addition, NATO planners looked to Romania, like Bulgaria, as a potential site for a new base. Again, this would partly offset the loss of a post-9/11 facility in Uzbekistan. The ready availability of Black Sea ports, airfields, and training ranges made a base in Romania an attractive possibility. Proximity to the tumultuous region was, of course, part of its appeal. As in the Bulgarian case, erection of such a base increased the risk of making Romania into a potential target of a terrorist attack, and so the base itself would require many layers of security. The economic value to Romania would not be much compensation for such an increased risk, for at most one thousand troops would be stationed there. In addition, a rather vigorous Romanian media would uncover any questionable activities that took place at the base (Cooley 2007, 79–92). Thus, there was some risk of lessened public support over time. At the same time, Romania had a full 940 troops in Afghanistan at the end of 2009 (NATO 2010k). In early 2010, the 280th Maneuver Battalion returned to Romania after a six-month stay in Afghanistan. This was their second successful operation in the nation (Ministry of Defense of Romania 2010c).

Slovakia

This small nation provided consistently a helpful level of troops for the ISAF operation, in spite of a governmental change that brought the critical socialists to power. They had campaigned on the promise to end Slovak involvement in Afghanistan sometime in 2008. Initially, in 2005, the government had made a decision to send troops to be part of the ISAF missions. One of their main functions was provision of airport security. For example, an engineering construction team of 40 Slovaks worked at the Bagram Airport, while another 17 were part of a demining unit at the international airport in Kabul. The activities of those engineers centered on reconstruction and repair of airstrips as well as demining of the airfields and their related communication routes (Ministry of Defense of Slovakia 2007a). In the summer of 2007, the Czechs requested the assistance of Slovak health specialists as part of its military field hospital in Kabul. It was expected that the Slovaks would provide material assistance as well (SME 2007b). It became clear that probably the Slovak presence in Afghanistan would not actually end in 2008, in spite of earlier election promises. In October they told Secretary of Defense Robert Gates that they would send 47 more troops to Uruzgan Province to work with Dutch troops in 2007.

They would increase their overall commitment in that province to 125 in 2008. In addition, they formed up plans to send 8 doctors to the previously mentioned field hospital (USATODAY 2007e). Finally, in early December, Minister of Defense František Kašický announced that peacekeeping missions in Afghanistan, Cyprus, and Kosovo would be the main priorities in the near future. This meant that they would send 55 professionals to replace existing military personnel in Kandahar (SME 2007c). If they had planned to withdraw totally in 2008, they would not have replaced that unit so late in the year. In fact, they were still there in early 2009, a year in which they sent a group of 50 soldiers to Camp Hadrian in Uruzgan Province in the central section of the country. They would be working with Czech military personnel to provide base security (SME 2009e). With this change in their plans to pull out, perhaps the principal risk would be to the incumbent party SMER in the hearts and minds of the voters. By the end of 2009, they had 240 military personnel in Afghanistan (NATO 2010l). At about the same time, their Defense Minister promised to increase that number but promised that they would not stay forever (Ministry of Foreign Affairs of Slovakia 2010c).

Slovenia

There were 70 military personnel from Slovenia in the country by the end of 2009, and this was the smallest contingent of any of the 10 new NATO partners (NATO 2010m).

Risks for NATO Partners

There are several strategic questions related to the new alliance partners that consistently preoccupy NATO planners. They include the matter of obtaining commitments from members for future years, changes in military tactics on the ground, evidence of involvement by outside powers such as Iran, and the huge challenge of bringing stability and control to the entire country, its rural as well as its urban areas.

Each fall, under the auspices of the UN, the alliance partners had committed troops for one more year of military activity and contributions. The Security Council extended the NATO mission again on October 13, 2007. At that time, the ISAF force consisted of 40,000 troops. That 2007 UN resolution called for contributions of personnel, equipment, and other resources (iDNES 2007q). So far, so good. However, each year more countries within the alliance have raised questions about the future direction of policy. Each year, more nations experienced casualties through violence. The increased number of violent acts there in recent years does not bode well for those whose publics are so doubtful about the need to be involved there. It may be wise to consider UN resolutions that last more than one year. If two-year commitments were passed, then NATO planners could have more flexibility in managing the whole operation in a way that had real prospects for success.

Danger of Disrupted Energy Supplies

With good reason, a number of the new NATO partners worried about the willingness of certain countries to shut off their energy sales in retaliation for participation in the Afghan operation. Richard Lugar (2007, 11–16) remarked on the importance of NATO's Article Five and its commitment to defend any member nation that came under threat. He suggested that the alliance should be a "refuge" for any of the member nations and should promise resupply if cut-offs occurred. He also offered a number of tactical steps that could help to guarantee such a "refuge." One was cultivation of Russia, and the other entailed revival of the Return of Forces to Germany (REFORGER) exercises to accomplish the resupply. In particular, he suspected Iran as a country that might utilize the punishment of energy politics as retaliation for support of American missions in the Middle East. On a related issue, Dan McNeill, the ISAF Commander, worried that Iran was exporting weapons that ended up in the hands of the Taliban in Afghanistan (iDNES 2007h). This could have been punishment to any number of countries for their role in the combined force.

The role of Russia on energy matters was also an unpredictable one. In the middle of 2007, the Russian parliament granted Gazprom and Transneft the right to form its own armed units. Their powers included possession of weapons similar to those used by interior ministry security guards (Lowe 2007). Given the past debacle of Soviet involvement in Afghanistan, one might expect that modern Russia would be sympathetic to the ISAF goals and motivation. Russia was supportive in the early months after 9/11 but then became quite critical of the occupation. Their higher profile activities in early 2007 were confined to support of Northern Afghan warlords who were creating obstacles to the Karzai central government in Kabul. Oil politics could enter the mix, for in the same year Russia signed an agreement with Kazakhstan and Turkmenistan to build the Pri-Caspian gas pipeline. This would provide an alternative to the western-backed Trans-Caspian gas pipeline (Baev 2007, 3–5). It is certainly the case that Russia would be happy enough to frustrate particularly NATO members in the Baltic Sea and Black Sea regions through oil politics, if their involvement in Afghanistan led to a scenario that clashed with important Russian interests.

Risks in the Central Asian Connection

Immediately following the al Qaeda attacks on the American targets, Central Asia became much more significant to American national interests. At first, strategic considerations drove this connection. The countries of the region provided landing and over-flight rights, and they also offered the use of air bases in Uzbekistan and Kyrgyzstan. If the United States could offer protection to those regimes against radicalized Muslim minorities, the Central Asian nations in return could promise to keep open the east-west energy corridor. However, any new Western energy dependence on those nations could result in bondage to the domestic situations in those countries. Turmoil and coups could result in negation of security and energy promises. Already, the United States had lost access to the base in Uzbekistan due to the changing domestic political power balance. If one or more Central Asian countries moved into the category of "failed" states, then those states ran the risk of falling into the hands of radical Islamic groups or warlords (Ispek 2007, 95–107). A new rogue regime might more easily succumb to the temptation to use oil politics as revenge for participation in the NATO operation in Afghanistan. In a very different way, Central Asian states could also use energy policy in order to gain more leverage over Russia (Baev 2007, 6). Increasingly, Russia needs Central Asian natural gas for itself, and an unpredictable leader in the latter region could use energy leverage to put Russia on its team in making ISAF nations pay a high price for their involvement in Afghanistan.

Budgetary Challenges

Involvement in peacekeeping missions like Afghanistan also imposed additional budgetary requirements on the member states of NATO. This was particularly difficult for the new NATO partners. A number of them were small and not able to commit sizeable amounts of money for new military involvements. Estonia and Slovenia are good examples, as neither had the capacity of Poland with its much larger population and tax base. Many of these postcommunist states had been through difficult times in the 1990s. Some like the Czechs had made the transition to capitalism through painful "shock therapy." Others like the Poles had elected leftist governments after early experimentation with the capitalist measures. Their publics had wanted to slow down the process and pain, but the postponement of difficult steps only made the transition last longer. All of these nations had been focusing on the admission process to the EU in the years leading up to 2004. Increased military spending had not been high on the list of that organization's priorities. Further, many EU leaders had been nudging the new nations to think in terms of contributions to an EU military force such as ESDP rather than to NATO. Once the same group of members joined NATO and became eligible for peacekeeping missions under the auspices of that alliance, new budgetary demands emerged. NATO expected each new member nation to contribute at least 2 percent of its GDP to defense (Lugar 2007, 11–16). For most new partners, this was unreachable or impractical. However, the demand for it continued to exert pressure on budgetary discussions within the new members and became a kind of risk to other emerging budgetary priorities.

Risk of Identification with Torture Techniques

Stories have emerged since 2001 about the use of torture techniques in the battle against al Qaeda-instigated terrorists. Civil Liberties groups as well as members of Congress have raised many questions about treatment of those incarcerated at Guantanamo. Others have issued stinging rebuttals of the implications of the Patriot Acts for those who question suspects in the war on terror. Reports of techniques such as "water boarding" always make the front page of European newspapers. In both Iraq and Afghanistan, the deaths of innocent civilians as a result of allied ground and air operations raise an outcry. Late 2007 reports of unnecessary deaths at the hands of Blackwater-type defense contractors compounded the concerns. How much risk do the NATO partners in Afghanistan run of implication in these suspicious and even sordid acts? One aspect of this crisis that has implicated some of the smaller alliance partners is the probable use by the Central Intelligence Agency (CIA) of their territory for questioning of terrorist suspects. Bulgaria has been one member state that has been implicated in this activity. Even though it is an older NATO partner, Norway experienced such an outcry and controversy in October 2007. Reports surfaced that Norwegian troops had been involved in handing over prisoners to the National Defense Strategy (NDS), an organization that had been reportedly involved in torture. Both Sweden and Denmark then began to explore and explain their role in similar situations (DN 2007c). Such moral quandaries bore the potential to tip public opinion in smaller nations in which doubts already existed about budgetary expenditures, energy cutoffs, and terrorist threats.

Overcoming the Risks

In early 2010, NATO was engaged in a general effort to supply allies with $350 million to enable them to fight more effectively the terrorist forces. They earmarked $50 million for 6 small countries that collectively had contributed about 1,300 troops to Afghanistan. The countries included Georgia plus new NATO partners Estonia (2004), Latvia (2004), Lithuania (2004), Croatia (2009), and Hungary (1999). Those troops would spend most of their allocation on equipment, but they would receive simultaneously training on detection of and countering of roadside bombs. Plans were in process to expand the allocation of this small program for Afghanistan (USATODAY 2010a). Although the amount of money was small, the nature of the program indicated alliance sensitivities to the doubts that many of the countries had about the increasing dangers of their Afghan commitment.

Continuing Issues

NATO also began to consider tactical changes on the ground as early as 2007. They considered providing smaller bombs to the geographic areas most subject to violence. The objective behind this proposed shift was to reduce the number of civilian casualties. Technically, this meant that planes would carry 250-kg bombs instead of 500-kg ones. This shift would lead to more precision bombing and a greater ability to hit the enemy with a lightning strike (sueddeutsche 2007c). Another change adopted at the same time switched responsibility for house searches from ISAF forces to Afghan troops. Both these reforms were directed at reduction of the number of civilian casualties, a much publicized issue in June when 90 civilians died (sueddeutsche 2007d).

The whole issue of Iranian involvement, which reared its head so noticeably in discussions about Iraq, also affected the assessment of future prospects in Afghanistan. In June, Secretary of Defense Robert M. Gates decried the flow of "illicit weapons" from sources in Iran to the Taliban fighters in Afghanistan. Other American officials voiced a concern that the Iranian government itself was fostering the movement of these weapons. A cloud of suspicion especially hung over the Iranian Revolutionary Guard Corps command (Shankar 2007). This discussion brought into the picture the larger issue of NATO/U.S. relations with Iran. Progress on talks between those two hostile parties would have a powerful effect on prospects for containing the influx of outside destabilizing capabilities into Afghanistan. However, both the unpredictability of the Iranian regime and their pursuit of nuclear capabilities erected huge barriers to the prospects for such talks.

The challenges both of penetrating NATO influence throughout the whole country and of bringing stability to all areas of Afghanistan are continuing ones. A number of informed observers maintained that NATO and the Afghan Army were doing a reasonable job of holding the cities in 2007. At the same time, the Taliban had penetrated its influence deep into the rural areas. With 75 percent of the population living in those rural areas, Taliban and al Qaeda were free to wage vigorous information campaigns. It is also true that allied control differed from region to region. The highest levels of stability existed in the north, west, and center regions. However, there was tough fighting going on much of the time in the east and south. Provision of stability to the whole nation depended not only on commitments, tactics, and outside influence, but it also depended on levels of troop commitments. In one study, Research and Development (RAND) analysts concluded that security personnel needed to constitute at least 2 percent of the population to have a fighting chance in Afghanistan. However, the percent in mid-2007 was less than half of 1 percent (Godges, 2007). Such data underlined the vital significance of the NATO role. They also drove home the importance of maintaining allied commitments at existing levels and beyond. Finally, they pointed to the need to improve planning capacities by lengthening the commitments of allied forces beyond the one year extensions regularly in place.

During 2008–09, the war in Afghanistan threatened to spin out of control, at just the time when more stability was beginning to characterize the situation in Iraq. Secretary of Defense Robert Gates encouraged the allies to contribute more due to the urgency of the situation. For example, he made such a plea in Macedonia at a meeting of the Southeast European Defense Ministerial. That group consists of 11 members and had 5,100 troops in Afghanistan at the time (USATODAY 2008b). As the American presidential transition approached, the Secretary called for a review of goals in the troubled nation. He de-emphasized democracy-building and placed the emphasis clearly on making sure that al Qaeda did not have a haven there (Barnes 2009a). Secretary Gates also had to plan in the general atmosphere of the global economic crisis and budgetary restrictions. It would be possible to retool some equipment and weaponry from Iraq, but it would not be possible to purchase all that was required (Borak 2009). At the same time, Pakistan became a problematic part of the picture. Control over areas in its Federally Administered Tribal Areas and North-West Frontier Province became a hotbed of al Qaeda activity (Rubin 2009, 18–19). As a result, Pakistan needed continuous attention, and there was a need to find new routes for mainlining supplies into Afghanistan. In February, Kazakhstan's leaders announced that they would permit transfer of nonmilitary supplies through its territory, and Tadzhikistan had made such an announcement earlier (SME 2009f).

Newly inaugurated President Obama ordered 17,000 more troops to Afghanistan in 2009, in his first action that related to troop commitments (USATODAY 2009e). Even with that announcement, General McKiernan feared that the 55,000 American troops that would be located there after the build-up would be insufficient. He indicated that he would be requesting more troops very soon (USATODAY 2009f). However, discussions were not confined to the military and Defense Department leadership. Secretary of State Hillary Clinton soon called for a UN-sponsored international conference on Afghanistan and considered inviting both Pakistan and Iran. She made the proposal at a NATO Foreign Ministers meeting in Brussels, but the alliance partners did not immediately give her a response that indicated their level of interest (USATODAY 2009g). Public support in the United States fell sharply in the first few months of the year. For example, the proportion of persons who called that war a mistake rose drastically from 30 percent in February to 42 percent in March (USATODAY 2009h). The Taliban played on these uncertain conditions by announcing at the end of the month plans for a major offensive against U.S. troops (sueddeutsche 2009a).

The search for extra help in the situation took a number of interesting turns at that time. Richard Holbrooke, the Special Ambassador for Afghanistan and Pakistan, actually got support from Iranian counterparts to assist in the reconstruction of Afghanistan and in the effort to suppress the drug trade (sueddeutsche 2009b). France did not promise to increase its 3,300 troop contingent, but that nation did say that it would quadruple its aid for the benefit of schools and nonmilitary institutions (USATODAY 2009i). General McKiernan increased the pressure on NATO allies by pointing out how much they could assist in training the police force (USATODAY 2009j). When NATO held its sixtieth anniversary celebration in Germany and France in April 2009, the allies promised 5,000 additional "troops, trainers and mentors" (USATODAY 2009k).

Replacement of General McKiernan by General Stanley McChrystal in May was coupled with endorsement of a new strategy. The new commander had been the "architect" of Special Operations in Iraq and had a reputation as a counterinsurgency expert. Protection of cities from insurgent attacks was the core of the new approach (Barnes 2009b), and it offered a change from the more offensive-minded counter-terrorist strategy of the recent past. These priorities dovetailed with the views and experiences of General David Petraeus, leader of the U.S. Central Command, and commander in Iraq at the time of the successful surge in 2007–08 (MacQuarrie 2009). The occasion of the anniversary of the liberation of Europe in 1944–45 gave the Secretary of Defense an opportunity to evoke strong symbolism. He appealed for the same kind of unity in the current war in Afghanistan that allies had displayed during World War II (USATODAY 2009l). Unity would be difficult to achieve, for the increase in terrorist activity affected some of the American partners as well. Germany lost three soldiers on patrol southwest of Kundus in a tough fight (sueddeutsche 2009c). Even Sweden, a non-NATO ally, worried as attacks came very close to its ISAF contingent in the southern part of the country (DN 2009b). One positive managerial change in the Pentagon, in light of all this turmoil and violence, was creation of a Pakistan-Afghanistan Coordination Cell within the Pentagon. This was the creature of Joint Chiefs of Staff (JCS) Chair Michael Mullen and offered hope for improved coordination of all of the players in this increasingly complicated struggle (Barnes 2009c).

In the fall of the year, debate about both tactics and strategy moved from the circle of the strategists into the public eye. Through a leak, General McChrystal made clear his view that an additional 40,000 troops would be needed to implement the new counter-insurgency strategy. This public request surprised and embarrassed President Obama, and a vigorous discussion ensued about the appropriateness of going outside regular channels of discussion (Rogin 2009). At about the same time, the Obama Administration announced objectives for Afghanistan and Pakistan, and they stated that clear metrics would be used in measuring progress toward the established targets (USATODAY 2009m). This was another step toward organizational coherence, and it provided a framework for making rational decisions about both future strategy and troop commitments.

In the background also was the matter of the Afghan elections held on August 20, for a UN-backed commission reported suspicions of widespread abuse and corruption (USATODAY 2009n). As the weeks unfolded, President Hamid Karzai on paper held a commanding lead with more than 50 percent of the vote, the threshold that would prevent the need for a runoff with second place finisher Abdullah Abdullah. After much pressure from the Obama Administration as well as from European partners, President Karzai called in late October for a new election to be scheduled on November 7. In fact, this election issue coincided with both uncertainty of the Obama Administration on the troop increase numbers and the related explicit switch to a counterinsurgency strategy. Some of the smaller NATO partners expressed a willingness to commit more troops, but they would do so only after the November elections were successfully held and after President Obama made clear his choice of strategy. For example, the Netherlands would thereafter send 2,160 more troops, while Denmark would send another 690.

Surge for Afghanistan

By the end of 2009, there was intensification of the new strategy on a number of fronts, and increasingly there were references made to the success of General Petraeus' "surge" in Iraq in 2007–08. A high water mark of the Afghan surge was surely introduction of 80,000 allied troops into the Marjah area of Helmand Province in February, 2010. There was talk as well of a parallel use of massive force in neighboring Kandahar Province in the middle of 2010. However, this period of heightened activity and focus had several additional components to it. For example, an important tactical change was the decision in March 2010, to pull nearly all of the U.S. troops in Afghanistan under the NATO umbrella. This was aimed at integrating units under one command, and the net result was that approximately 20,000 U.S. troops moved from American to NATO command (USATODAY 2010b).

Pakistan increasingly became a center of attention, as NATO leadership sought to convince that government to take a firmer hand in getting control of the Taliban forces who operated seemingly at will in the western areas. In early November, 2009, Pakistani troops were successful in getting control of Kaniguram in South Waziristan (SME 2009g). Within Afghanistan, there was great concern about the controversy over the presidential election. After the withdrawal of candidate Abdullah Abdullah, the Afghan Election Commission declared Hamid Karzai to have won his reelection bid (sueddeutsche 2009d). At the same time, western leaders like British Prime Minister Gordon Brown made the continued presence of British soldiers in Afghanistan contingent on introduction of measures by President Karzai to combat and root out corruption (sueddeutsche 2009e). Other reforms within Afghanistan were welcome as well. For example, education of women became an issue as a key to creating a more equal society, for only 10–20 percent of girls were able to read. With education often ending after three years, reformers pushed for at least a fourth year and preferably 4–7 total years of education (DN 2009c). An additional concept included use of foreign aid funds to encourage local villages to form their own militias to struggle against local cells of Taliban operatives (Michaels 2009).

Of course, a major debate preceded the decision of President Obama to approve commitment of an additional 30,000 U.S. troops to Afghanistan, in addition to the 21,000 extra that he had sent in the spring (Bumiller and Sanger 2009). This surge of forces was accompanied by increased pressure on all NATO allies to raise the level of their own military forces in the nation as well (Cowell 2009). Slovaks responded quickly by indicating that they would double their contingent to nearly 500 (USATODAY 2009o; SME 2009h). Prime Minister Brown promised an additional 500 troops, and this would bring the U.K. total to 9,500 (USATODAY 2009p). Germany experienced a vigorous debate over the matter of additional troops. The opposition Social Democratic Party (SDP) opposed an increase in troops (sueddeutsche 2010a), but the Merkel government called for 500 more personnel (IZVESTIYA 2010b). A bit later, they upped the increase by 350 more under a flexible plan to help with special events such as elections (USATODAY 2010c). Overall, the partners were willing to contribute an additional 7,000 troops to go along with the 30,000 that were part of Obama's "surge" strategy (USATODAY 2009q). Length of stay of the troops was also a key issue in these negotiations with the allies. Although there was a promise to pull out some troops by July 2011, Secretary of Defense Robert Gates continued to speak of a continued troop presence for 2–4 more years (USATODAY 2009r).

Surprisingly, NATO Secretary General Fogh Rasmussen even went to Russia with a proposal for their assistance in the fight against narcotics trafficking (IZVESTIYA 2009j). Even after this proposal, Russia continued to register concern about the failure of NATO to fight heroin smuggling with sufficient vigor. Her envoy to the alliance Dmitry Rogozin depicted the situation as a grim one in which the number of addicted persons in Russia was escalating beyond control. Even the new counterinsurgency strategy of General McCrystal may have encouraged a more hands-off approach to farmers, and they were becoming freer to tend to the crops that produced the heroin (USATODAY 2010d).

The world conference on Afghanistan in London held center stage at the end of January, 2010. This one-day conference solidified plans for the increased numbers of troops that so many members were going to inject. The conference also nailed down a timetable for turning over security duties to Afghan personnel at the end of 2010 and beginning of 2011. In addition, the countries at the conference committed funds to support a vague and general plan to convince Taliban units to renounce violence as a tool (USATODAY 2010e). Very touchy additional discussions centered on the idea of actually paying Taliban forces to put down their weapons and consider becoming part of the legal political process. Secretary General Rasmussen actually endorsed discussion of this provocative idea (SME 2010b).

Richard Holbrooke, the American special envoy for Pakistan and Afghanistan, sought extra help also in Central Asia, the region that had been supportive of U.S. efforts during the liberation of Afghanistan from Taliban rule in 2001–02. He spoke with heads of state in Tajikistan, Kyrgyzstan, Uzbekistan, and Kazakhstan. Transit rights for logistics material and humanitarian aid was one objective of these talks, as the route through troubled Pakistan had become untenable. Cooperation on a tighter electricity network was also a matter for discussion. However, the switch in routes did make conditions in the formerly quieter north of Afghanistan more problematic. As the new supply corridor became more useful, it also became a target of terrorist attacks. Thereby, allied forces such as the Germans who had been stationed there increasingly came under attack. In March 2010, German troops engaged in bridge-building and mine-clearing came under attack south of Kunduz city. In the ensuing engagement at night, their soldiers killed six Afghan soldiers. This served as a reminder that German airstrikes on tanker trucks in the region had resulted in the deaths of 142 persons, mainly civilians, in September 2009 (USATODAY 2010f). Chancellor Merkel apologized to the President Karzai of Afghanistan, and Minister of Defense Karl-Theodor zu Guttenberg expressed his sorrow to Afghan Minister of Defense Abdul Rahim Wardak. Guttenberg also suggested that Germans face up to the fact that they were involved now in what they ought to "colloquially" call a "war" (sueddeutsche 2010b; USATODAY 2010g). Due to restrictions in the German Constitution, terms such as "stabilization mission" and "armed conflict" had been used. Such violence in unexpected areas would undermine the confidence of the allies who had made commitments with the tacit promise that they would not be near any conflict. The new supply route through Central Asia did avoid the Pakistan conflict that afflicted the main route but then itself became a tempting target for the terrorists.

Debates continued after the conference about the types of new units to be dispatched to Afghanistan in conjunction with the changed strategy. The Czech Government discussed the possibility of sending another 55 military personnel to protect a Polish base in Ghazni Province. They would utilize capabilities with the radar system Arthur to provide that protection. However, the opposition CSSD opposed the new plan (iDNES 2010b). Controversy brewed in neighboring Slovakia as well, for the Slovak Communist Party began to send around a petition that called for the pull out of all Slovak troops from Afghanistan (SME 2010c). Even Sweden decided to send a new 30-soldier platoon to supplement the 410 troops it already had in Afghanistan (DN 2010). Probably, the most drastic outcome occurred in Holland, the home of the previous Secretary-General of NATO, Jaap de Hoop Scheffer. The Dutch had nearly 2000 troops in Afghanistan, and the Labor Party left the government over the matter of whether to extend that mission. Labor contended that the government had promised that there would be no more extensions after the last one, and thus it had violated its promise (USATODAY 2010h). Uruzgan was the southern province in which 1,600 Dutch soldiers were supposed to be stationed until August, 2010, and so that commitment became problematic (Kulish 2010). Prime Minister Balkenende eventually stated that this domestic political crisis probably meant that all Dutch troops would be withdrawn by the end of 2010 (IZVESTIYA 2010c).

An additional matter of upcoming urgency was adequate training of Afghan Police. Many NATO partners, including several of the newest members, participated in this training operation. However, the Department of Defense IG (Inspector General) reported that there was a lack of standardization in this process (Novak 2010). Controversy also centered on DynCorps, the major Texas-based provider of police training programs in Afghanistan. Investigations pointed to State Department failure to provide effective oversight of the private company (Chatterjee 2010). These issues connected with police training cried out for solution in light of the staged withdrawal process being planned by so many NATO allies.

Matching Capabilities to Objectives

By early 2010, the American involvement in Afghanistan had already exceeded the length of its stay in Southeast Asia in the 1960s and 1970s. One abiding lesson of that earlier war had been the importance of matching capabilities to objectives in future wars. In fact, that impelling necessity was a cardinal point on the list of both the Weinberger and Powell Doctrines for military engagements in which the United States might become involved down the road. In Afghanistan, the amount of force that the allies used in the early years appeared to be commensurate with the objective of both defeating the Taliban and keeping them from returning to power. However, by 2007, doubts began to emerge that the allied capability extended to Afghanistan did not meet the objective of containing the terrorist threat. The high number of casualties that the NATO partners took during the next two years reinforced the veracity of that lesson. Therefore, the debate centered on increasing the capabilities to a level that would be sufficient to achieve some sort of stability, if not a victory.

Accompanying the injection of far more troops was a change in military strategy as well. All NATO partners felt the pressure of this new commitment, and that accounts for the difficult discussions in so many of the old and new alliance members. No doubt, publics in the newer members had not expected that membership in the alliance would mean lingering concern, year after year, about the safety of their family members and fellow citizens in such a far off place. These doubts may have made the expanded capability more tenuous and fragile, but consistent support by a host of governmental leaders provided some confidence that objectives were reachable. In March 2010, the American leadership decided to bring under the NATO umbrella most of its 20,000 troops that had been operating separately from the alliance. A few prison guards and Special Forces components would be the only exceptions. One motivation for this shift was better insurance that military operations would avoid civilian casualties. Communications between the United States and its allies would also potentially be smoother (Innes, 2010). In this one way, the NATO leader made an effort to reconfigure its capabilities so that they would better fit developing objectives connected with the new counter-insurgency strategy.

CHAPTER NINE

The War in Iraq Shakes NATO Capabilities

In a sense, the Iraq War was like a cue ball whose force upon impact sent many other billiard balls rocketing in unanticipated directions. This chapter will focus on five of those billiard balls, each of which constitutes one component of NATO capabilities. Although the battle in Iraq was not a NATO project, its results had an enormous impact of the alliance. First, the War in Iraq weakened the capacity of the United States to lead effectively the alliance. Leadership capacity drained away particularly after the series of controversial decisions made by U.S. leaders in the first year after the initially announced end of the mission on May 1, 2003. In the years to follow, huge commitments of money, personnel, casualties, and equipment further weakened the leadership capabilities of the United States. Second, the Iraq War diluted NATO unity and undermined the will-power behind its significant post-Cold War military structure. This was true even though NATO had chosen not to supervise and oversee the war itself. Divisions within NATO became apparent in the lead-up to the war and continued for its duration. Third, the War opened the door to Russian ambitions at a time when increasing oil prices made it possible for that ambitious nation, under the strong leadership of President Putin, to flex its economic muscles in various parts of its own region and even the wider world. NATO capabilities indirectly suffered, for planning once again need to focus in part on containing Russian aggressiveness and its renewed search for greatness.

Fourth, the Iraq War diminished the ability of NATO to contribute to political stability in countries in which it had taken on official responsibilities. Those nations included Afghanistan, Kosovo, and Bosnia. In each of those nations the NATO role had been in flux, but the alliance always had a portion of the responsibilities. The controversy over a missile defense shield against nations like Iran and North Korea also fits into this picture of decreased capabilities. For the most part, the alliance had enough preoccupations that it threw this political football into the lap of the United States. Fifth, the War in Iraq weakened the ability of key NATO partners to do effective strategic planning in 2007–08, a time in which both the surge and effective military leadership on the ground had significantly reduced the level of violence in the nation. Effective overall alliance planning might have taken place had the discord that had accompanied the war not continued to simmer. In addition, the preoccupation of the United States with its own presidential election cycle magnified the planning weaknesses in 2008. There was a great need to pull the scattered billiard balls back into some sort of coherent pattern.

Weakening of the U.S. Leadership Capability

Confusion over the original goals of the war initially undermined America's leadership posture in general. In the early days of the war, there was a preoccupation with the search for weapons of mass destruction. Failure to locate such evidence reflected badly on the structure of intelligence gathering that include the CIA, Department of State, and Department of Defense. In addition, the American military had struck earlier than planned in an unsuccessful effort to knock out Saddam Hussein himself. There was also a decision made to begin the ground invasion before Air Force bombardment had sufficiently softened up the Iraqi military. Additional faulty assumptions were apparent to many international observers in the early weeks of the war. U.S. leaders expected that Shiites would joyfully welcome the Americans and be thankful for their deposal of the hated Saddam. Similarly, there was a belief that civilians would welcome the American Army as a liberator and even cast flowers in their path. Prewar build-up conveyed the expectation that the invasion could be accomplished with a minimum of casualties. Further, the prevailing assumption was that the Iraqi social order was soft, and thus any resistance would quickly fade away (Pelletière 2007, 6–25). These mistaken assumptions weakened the American leadership image in the world in the early days of the war.

From the spring of 2003 until the summer of 2004, American administrators managed political and economic life within the country in preparation for resumption of Iraqi control. Paul Bremer was the symbol of that leadership group and in fact the guiding force within it. A number of assumptions and decisions made in that year turned out also to be faulty and contributed to the growing negative view of American leadership. First, looking to Afghanistan as a parallel, the American leadership on the ground assumed that tribal leaders held power in Iraq. Thus, working with them alone would solve many problems. In reality, the Ba'thists under Saddam had already broken the power of these chieftains. Second, the decision was made to disband Saddam's army and send most of them home, as it was expected that they would be disloyal to any new Shiite-dominated regime. In fact, this put them out of work and created a large group of disgruntled former military members who then were tempted to join the resistance to the Americans. Third, de-Ba'thification became the hallmark of policy. It was assumed that the Ba'thist Party members were exclusively Sunni and should be kicked out of major positions in government and education. In fact, many Kurds and Shiites had joined the Ba'thist Party in order to obtain employment. Thus, de-Ba'thification was a policy that alienated members of each major ethnic group and drove some into opposition to the Americans (Pelletière 2007, 56-77). In these ways, America's image as an effective planning agent in the post-Cold War period became tarnished.

Certain American political decisions about governance in Iraq in the period before its January 2005, elections also went against the grain of actual ethnic and political conditions. For example, since the local leaders connected with the Ba'thists were all suspects, attention turned to seven Iraqi expatriates as those more deserving of leadership positions. Thus, the formerly U.S.-based Chalabi became an early favorite of the America for an Iraqi leadership position. Similarly, Kurd leaders with Iranian connections like Talabani and Barzani also became popular with the American team. Bremer also replaced former administrator Jay Garner's plan for an Iraqi-based Provisional Government with an American-Based Governmental Authority. These arrangements would last until the January 2005 elections generated locally based leadership. Basically, the seven expatriates would rule in that interim period in conjunction with a 25-member Council. That Council would include 13 Shiites, 5 Sunnis, 1 Kurd, 1 Turkoman, and 1 woman (Pelletière 2007, 78-103). All of these plans emphasized American control rather than Iraqi. In addition, the makeup of the Council reinforced ethnic divisions instead of creating frameworks in which members of several ethnic groups would have to work together.

All of the above evidence from the 2003-04 period of American intervention and management of Iraq creates a collective picture of American confusion. As such, the leadership capability of America as NATO's main player came into question. Another, quite different blow to American capabilities was the enormous expense connected with the war. As the United States increased the deficit in order to finance the war, its leadership stature became even more diminished. Further, money spent in Iraq was unavailable for other defense, collective security, and alliance projects. It is only possible here to focus on selected evidence, as the dimensions are so many. In all stages of the war, defense spending continued to climb. For example, it jumped between 2004 and 2007 from $405 billion to $524 billion per year (Pease 2008, 268).

Then, in 2007, President Bush announced his new strategy of surge. After all of the expense in Iraq, the situation earlier in 2006 had become very grim. Terrorist incidents multiplied, and both Iraqi and allied casualties mounted. However successful the surge eventually turned out to be, it certainly drained financial resources away from other defense projects, at exactly the time when Afghanistan was becoming a much more explosive terrain. The surge that was announced called for five more brigades that included deployment of another 21,500 troops. In spite of this commitment of new troops, the next summer was a time of a very high number of American casualties in the war. In June 2007, 126 American soldiers lost their lives, and it went into the record books as the second worst month for U.S. forces in the war. By that month, allied military capabilities in Iraq were at extremely high levels. Those military capabilities included 70 bases, 38 supply depots, 18 fuel-storage centers, and 10 ammunition dumps (Simon 2008, 57). If those physical capabilities could not generate more positive results after four continuing years of war, then doubts about the outcome continued to skyrocket. As they did, confidence in American leadership capacities of NATO continued to erode.

Although plans in 2008 solidified for an eventual date for U.S. withdrawal from Iraq, still major new capabilities continued to receive attention and budgetary commitments. One such project was the Joint Improvised Explosive Device Defeat Organization (JIEDDO). The new equipment offered the benefit of jamming communications devices and thus reducing the number of deaths through improvised explosive devices (IEDs). This program would be a significant contribution in light of the fact that 70 percent of the combat deaths in Iraq resulted from the IEDs. Costs, however, were very high. The total budget for such devices in FY 2009 was $4.5 billion, but $16 billion was actually spent. Planning for FY 2010 centered on a figure of $3.5 billion (Anonymous, 2008).

The figures cited above are, of course, very selective. However, they demonstrate the enormous increase in overall defense funding at critical points in the war, some of the costs associated with the "surge," and an illustration of one current new program that would require funding as long as American troops remained on the ground in Iraq, and probably after their departure as well. All of these projects demonstrated a strengthening of U.S. capabilities in Iraq itself. However, they seriously denied budgetary resources for other arenas and thereby drew the attention of the NATO leader away from growing alliance needs on other fronts.

Dilution of NATO Unity

From the outset, the War in Iraq has countered the efforts of the alliance to integrate effectively and harmoniously the ten new members admitted between 1999 and 2004. At the same time, dissension among the senior NATO partners continued to bubble from 2002 through the end of 2008.

As early as January 29, 2002, leaders of NATO became critical of American intentions towards Iraq. On that date, President Bush first used the "Axis of Evil" label for Iraq, Iran, and North Korea during his annual State of the Union message. Germany, France, and the United Kingdom immediately expressed disagreement with the utility or applicability of such a descriptive phrase (Thompson 2004, 135). In fact, that disagreement reflected a more longstanding set of differences over American labels. The U.S. State Department had earlier listed six states as sponsors of terrorism. They included Iraq, Iran, North Korea, Cuba, Syria, and Libya. The department added Sudan to the list in 1993. European alliance partners had expressed discontent with that list and even with the demonization of the targets as "rogue states," or later "states of concern" (Rees 2004, 172).

Tensions within the NATO structure also emerged over the issue of obtaining a UN Resolution to sanction the war itself. Initially, the United States endeavored to get the UN to firmly enforce its own earlier resolutions on Iraq's continuing military buildup. In his speech to the UN on September 12, 2002, President Bush told the body that they risked irrelevance if they failed to enforce those earlier resolutions. After much persuasion, the UN finally did pass a "tough new disarmament mandate for Iraq." At the Prague NATO Summit during the next month, the UN Resolution received support from that alliance as well. President Bush then asked NATO to provide military assistance in support of an invasion of Iraq. While the military organization had been willing to play a role in the Afghanistan War, they chose not to make such a commitment to the upcoming war against Iraq (Thompson 2004, 141).

However, when the time for war approached, the United States was unable to obtain support of the UN for it. This made all the difference for NATO partners who were at the time considering whether to grant their support for such an operation. Many senior alliance partners were unwilling to back a war that did not have the sanction of the UN behind it. In fact, one poll done in Europe in late 2002 revealed that there was majority support for such a war that had the backing of the UN but majority opposition if it did not (Thompson 2004, 137). The result of all the politics in this heated, tense period was further alienation of much of Europe from the United States.

An additional consequence was reinforcement of the inclinations of the Bush Administration to adopt a unilateralist policy.

Additional tension within the alliance developed over the Turkish issue at the beginning of the war. The Bush Administration hoped to convince Turkey to permit its territory to be used for an invasion of Iraq from the north. However, Turkish leaders worried understandably about the very real possibility of an Iraqi retaliation. This issue led to a vigorous debate within NATO, an alliance in which Turkey itself was a member. At one point Bush lobbied European leaders to consider earlier Turkish admission to the EU as a reward for becoming part of the Iraqi invasion path (Thompson 2004, 141). On February 10, 2003, Turkey itself invoked NATO's Article 4 that called for consultations in case of perceived threats against the "territorial integrity, political independence, or security of any ally." They were interested in obtaining a show of support for themselves, if Iraq attacked them in response to provision of their territorial corridor to the allies. When phrased in those terms, France, Germany, and Belgium all said no. Thus, invocation of Article 4 to protect Turkey was dead through use of the veto (Terzuolo 2006, 119). One analyst (Michta 2006, 111) described this veto as a blocking action that "effectively paralyzed NATO and was a shot across the bow of the alliance."

The split within NATO over the Iraq War became popularized as a division between the "old" and "new" Europe. Poland, one of the "new" European alliance partners, accepted major responsibility for oversight of an occupation zone south of Baghdad. In doing so, they sent 2,400 of their own troops to the conflict. By the end of 2004, they had sent a total of three rotations to the combat zone. One positive result for them was modernization of their military. They also had received a crash course in working under NATO procedures (Michta 2006, 37). Surprisingly, the country that provided the second highest number of troops in the Polish administered zone was Ukraine, a non-NATO country. Czech military police played a key role at the United Kingdom's Al Shaiba base near Basra from December 2003 until November 2006. The Czechs trained more than 12,000 Iraqi police officers in areas such as self-defense and border patrol, (Velinger 2006). That Czech mission included 100 members, and they worked alongside British and Danish units (iDNES 2006e). "New" NATO members that also provided assistance in that zone included Bulgaria, Hungary, Latvia, Lithuania, Romania, and Slovakia. Additional assistance came from Spain, Denmark, Kazakhstan, Netherlands, Norway, and the United States (Terzuolo 2006, 121). In general, however, the "old" European nations such as Italy, Spain, Denmark, and the Netherlands preferred to confine their primary assistance to training new Iraqi police units (Thompson 2004, 141).

German opposition to the war was forceful and continuing. In late 2002, that opposition was partly linked to the reelection needs of the Schröder governing coalition. However, there were deeply rooted philosophical differences behind German opposition as well. German leaders were very skeptical about the inclusion of Iraq in the antiterrorist campaign. In their view, the U.S. unilateral decision to switch from a war on terrorism to a war on Iraq "has caused major tensions with its European allies." They were not even certain that acquisition of nuclear weapons by Iraq would pose a substantial security threat to the United States (Rees 2004, 176, 181, 212). As the tensions between the "old" and "new" NATO members continued to bubble, President Chirac of France chided and berated the smaller nations who supported the United States and who really would not technically enter NATO until 2004 (Michta 2006, 111). However, their path to NATO membership was on course during 2003. Therefore, his threats bore more meaning about the likelihood of completing their membership process for the EU. As Germany and France pulled back from the embrace of the War in Iraq demonstrated by the "new" Europe, they began to speculate about the day when the EU's ESDPwould become a real alternative to NATO (McGuigan 2007, 158).

As the Iraq War became more and more of "an all-out test of NATO's internal consensus" (Michta 2006, 110), the threat to alliance capabilities became more and more real. A number of serious observers began to wonder if internal alliance conflicts over Iraq would permeate other areas of NATO cooperation. For example, would there be any damage to "intelligence sharing, force transformation, and small counter-terrorism operations." These were significant considerations, for all of Europe felt much more vulnerable in light of the original 9/11 attacks. On the threat from al Qaeda, the alliance was united, and the need for cooperation in transforming defensive capabilities was paramount. However, the Iraq War was another matter entirely, and it eroded the harmony that had developed in the late fall of 2001.

Encouragement of Russian Ambitions

As the twenty-first century dawned, Russia was struggling to catch up. The final years under Yeltsin had been riddled with problems. They included the economic breakdown of 1998 and the Second War in Chechnya that would last until 2001. However, as the baton passed to President Putin in 2000, the leadership for a more active and vigorous role was in place. While Russia expressed sincere sympathy and firm support for the United States after 9/11, its approaches on the Afghanistan and Iraq components of the battle against terror were very different. For example, Russia raised no objections when the United States sought to use the "stans" as launch pads for the invasion of Afghanistan. President Putin saw Russia's enemy in Chechnya as very similar to the American enemy in Afghanistan. It was even possible for Kyrgyzstan and Uzbekistan to permit American usage of bases at, respectively, Manas and Karsi-Khanabad. In addition, the other Central Asian players were willing to grant over flight rights. In contrast, Russia joined the German-French opposition to the War in Iraq. Thereby, they hoped to help make Russia and the EU into more powerful global actors. As President Putin watched the United States make use of its enormous hard power in Iraq, he also resolved to increase the same ingredients of power in Russia (Newton 2007, 192, 198).

It was also true that American preoccupation with Iraq gave Russia an opening to bid again for great power status (McGuigan 2007, 163). As the price of oil increased in the years after the beginning of the Iraq War, Russian leaders began to dream and plan about a larger role for themselves in world politics. They became increasingly critical of western policy on issues such as Kosovo, NATO expansion, the possibility of any American bases in Central Europe, Kaliningrad, and nuclear strategy and policy (Hesli 2007, 252–4). One analyst (Baev 2008, 160) thought that Russia might exploit the vacuum left by American leadership to take more forceful action on its border in an effort to protect Russian minorities. Baev had Georgia in mind, and that proved to be prophetic in light of the brief war of August 2008. However, action on behalf of the Transdniestrian Russians in Moldova was another possibility. Demonstrations of Russian Air Force power in the Baltic region also fit into this picture, as the plight of Russian minorities and symbols in the three Baltic nations was a principal concern.

Overall, the American preoccupation with Iraq offered Russia an unexpected opportunity to expand the power of the state at home as well as the scope of its influence in the "Near Abroad." Such an opening for Russia, of course, coincided with the unique leadership of President Putin, a man who at times seemed bent on restoring Russian greatness. This thrust matched the sentiments of many Russian citizens who had felt a clear sense of letdown in the wake of the Cold War. In a way, there is a certain parallel to the Vietnam Era. During that war the United States was also bogged down in a far off place. The Soviet Union, which had been humiliated during the Cuban Missile Crisis in 1962, resolved to catch up to the United States in nuclear capabilities. As American defense capabilities were drained away to support the air and guerilla conflict in southeast Asia, Soviet spending was free to flow to its nuclear arsenal. President Nixon acknowledged as much early in his first term when he asserted that the nuclear balance had become one of "equivalence" and the goal for the future "parity." Finally, the emergence of Leonid Brezhnev as a strong leader after the Czechoslovak crisis of 1968, is another striking parallel to Russian leadership under Putin in the early twenty-first century. In both historical situations, both NATO and the United States were left in weakened positions.

Diminished NATO Capabilities for other Missions

The NATO partners were not only preoccupied with difficult questions regarding participation in the War in Iraq. They also had taken on a number of other missions prior to that war, and at least one new major initiative sprung up several years after the start of the war. First, beginning in the fall of 2001, the alliance began to play a principal role in the war and stabilization of Afghanistan. For several years, NATO had supervisory responsibility for various regions of Afghanistan. However, in 2006, the organization took over management of operations in the entire country. The only exception included a portion of the American contingent that worked on its own. Second, at the start of the Iraq War, NATO still had major responsibilities, along with the UN, in Bosnia. The Dayton Accords of 1995 called for them to administer the peacemaking process. In 2004, the alliance handed off those responsibilities to the EU, but NATO members were of course still deeply involved in the EU mission. Third, duties in Kosovo were vital as well, for NATO, the UN, and the EU jointly managed most matters in that republic after the 1999 bombing campaign. Even after the declaration of Kosovo independence on February 17, 2008, that tri-polar administration continued. Fourth, a new issue that emerged after several years of war in Iraq was the American-proposed missile shield initiative for Europe. While this was not a NATO project, it did command much time and discussion from the strongest alliance partner. In addition, there were discussions about making it a NATO program after several years. Involvement in the Iraq War was thus costly in terms of the attention, commitment, and capabilities that alliance partners could devote to those four important initiatives and missions.

Heightened Costs of Iraq to NATO in 2008

Throughout 2008 especially, it was possible to see very clearly how the involvement in Iraq worked at cross purposes to other NATO commitments and strategic planning. In January and February, military officers and Department of Defense officials warned about the dangers of troop cuts in Iraq. Both General Petraeus and Secretary Gates warned that it would be wise to postpone any troop cuts until later in the summer. They were concerned that Iraqi violence might heat up again, after the surge that started in early 2007 had considerably calmed the situation (USATODAY 2008c). Pressure also built up to do more in Afghanistan because of the increasing violence there. For example, the Canadian Parliament voted to extend the Canadian mission in Afghanistan until 2011, as long as NATO overall supplied more troops and equipment to support its forces in the flammable south of the nation (USATODAY 2008d).

Some of the NATO partners experienced increased risks in a number of theaters. For instance, NATO units in northern Kosovo received enemy fire exactly one month after the declaration of independence (ČTK 2008). Demonstrators took over temporarily a UN courthouse, and there were many injuries and burned automobiles (DPA/AP/Reuters 2008). On the same day, a Czech soldier lost his life in an attack on a convoy in Kandahar Province in Afghanistan (SME 2008c). Ironically, the next day the first of 3,200 marines committed to the south of the country began to arrive. A full 2,300 of those would be based in Kandahar Province itself. In part, this deployment was a response to calls like the one noted above from Canada for more assistance, as a condition for continuing their own mission (USATODAY 2008e).

All of these developments made NATO's critical April 2008 Summit in Bucharest of great importance. From the American perspective, the top priority would be obtaining more commitments from the alliance partners for Afghanistan. At the previous Riga Summit in fall 2007, the United States had asked for 3,000 additional troops from the partners. The inability of alliance members to come through on that request was the event that led America to put another 3,200 troops in the southern part of the country. At the time of the Bucharest meeting, only the French had promised to commit another 1,000 troops (USATODAY 2008f). The conference also endorsed the U.S. missile shield proposal and outlined a scenario in which it could be linked to additional missile shields elsewhere (AP 2008). However, clearly the Bush Administration was disappointed that the allies were not willing or able to do more. That may have caused Secretary Gates to suggest that American forces might take over more authority in situations where they were currently under NATO command (Washingtonpost 2008b). At that point in time, the United States had 14,000 troops operating under its own command and 17,000 under the supervision of NATO.

Concerns at the Bucharest spring conclave were on target, for the following summer was very violent in Afghanistan. On one occasion, nine American troops lost their lives in an extremely bold attack on their base in northern Afghanistan (Wall Street Journal 2008a). The death of a Danish soldier in the same month hit that nation hard, as he was the 16th military person of that nationality to lose his life in the Afghan conflict. Perhaps, the fact that the NATO Secretary-General was the Dutchman Jaap de Hoop Scheffer kept that country from talking about a pullback of troops (DN 2008a). In part, the United States blamed some of the increased violence on al Qaeda forces operating out of western Pakistan and thereby increased its attacks there (Wall Street Journal 2008b).

At the end of 2008, it was apparent that the uncontrolled situation in Afghanistan was the primary current example of the costs of the extended and enormous commitment to Iraq. Much of the postelection defense policy discussion in America centered on striking a balance between gradual withdrawal from Iraq and steadily increased commitments to Afghanistan. Maintaining stability and strength in both arenas was indeed a dicey proposition.

Role of the New NATO Partners

The alliance members who had joined in recent years took part in two aspects of the military activity in Iraq. Some were part of the coalition of the willing and played a role in the early period after March 2003. As mentioned above, Poland took over a huge swath of territory south of Baghdad in the planning after May 2003. The other operation that involved the new members was NTM-I, a project that commenced on December, 2004. The UN had originally asked the alliance to set up this project (NATO 2010n). In fact, the training mission was preceded by NATO Training Implementation Mission—Iraq (NTIM-I) that was active between August 14 and December 16, 2004. The Iraqi Government had requested this training mission, and it turned out to be one in which they made key decisions, while the alliance offered help and advice. Accomplishments included training and advice to groups of headquarters military personnel, establishment of a military academy, planning of contributions of military equipment and training from other nations, and help in setting up an Iraqi Training Command. At its high water mark, the unit included 60 officers and noncommissioned officers (NCOs) from 12 NATO countries (NATO 2005a).

Bulgaria

During NTM-I, the leaders of Bulgaria were willing to train Iraqi security forces at military schools in Bulgaria. They also provided funds for additional training of Iraqi forces in other locations outside the theater of operations (Ministry of Foreign Affairs of Bulgaria 2010e).

Hungary

From August 2003 to the very end of 2004, Hungary had a 300 person battalion operational in Iraq. The nation then took part in NTM-I for an additional two years, but it was also willing to continue activities after expansion of the operation announced at the Riga Summit in November, 2006. In fact, Hungary took over the leadership of Military Advice and Liaison Team (MALT) in the 2007–08 period. They trained Iraqi forces and also served as a monitoring and authenticating unit. In fact, Hungary made the second largest commitment to this operation (Ministry of Foreign Affairs of Hungary 2010e).

Latvia

During the initial invasion of Iraq, Latvia played a role with 125 military personnel. Then, during NTIM-I, they funded training of security forces and essential equipment. They also made financial contributions to NTM-I in the next few years. In the summer of 2006, Latvian personnel trained two Iraqi specialists in neutralizing undetected munitions (Ministry of Foreign Affairs of Latvia 2010d).

Lithuania

Under the auspices of NTM-I, Lithuania assisted at various NATO schools and training centers in the training of high level Iraqi security forces (Ministry of Foreign Affairs of Lithuania 2010d).

Romania

General involvement by Romanian forces in NTM-I after December 2004, was the principal contribution of Romania (Ministry of Foreign Affairs of Romania 2010a).

Slovakia

Slovak contributions included dispatch of 70 soldiers in 2003–04, in order to monitor radiation, chemical, and biological risks. They also provided four men who actually went on patrols and engaged in surveillance. A Slovak Engineer Company of 105 military personnel worked in the Polish sector of Iraq as a stabilizing force. They worked on demining and also liquidation of arms and munitions (Ministry of Foreign Affairs of Slovakia 2010d).

Challenge for NATO and Renewal of Capabilities

The opening section of this chapter presented the image of a pool table on which Iraq was a cue ball that had struck other billiard balls forcefully and sent them rocketing in many directions. In effect, the primary focus of this chapter has been on the direction of eight of those affected balls. All of them are central to NATO's strength and future possibilities. The Iraq War weakened American leadership capabilities of the alliance, diluted the unity of the alliance itself, and encouraged Russian ambitions and willingness to exploit the alliance's weaknesses. Involvement in Iraq also compromised and weakened four other NATO or NATO-related projects. The situation in Afghanistan threatened to spin out of control in 2007–08. Smaller alliance partners found it difficult to keep up more than a decade of contributions to stability in Bosnia, in light of so many other cross-pressures. Kosovo declared independence early in 2008, and that set off a round of repercussions and fears. American leaders had little time or resources for effectively managing the controversy over the proposed missile shield in light of all the other commitments. Finally, the 2008 discussion about reassessment of strategy was complicated by the considerable costs that the Iraq War had already incurred.

The challenge for NATO and American leadership will be to restore some sense of a pattern to those scattered billiard balls. There is a clear need to create a mosaic out of them that has order, coherence, plausibility, and even appeal. While this impelling need challenges the Obama Administration, it also becomes a mandate for all of the NATO partners. The lack of strategic planning that incorporated the impact of the Iraq War with these other priorities became an enormous drain on both the alliance and its designated national leader, and for a time both of them floundered and even seemed on the verge of spinning into disarray. The strategic review that took place in Iraq in 2007–08 as well as the rethinking that occurred in a parallel way in Afghanistan in 2009–10, offered a renewed possibility for meshing objectives and capabilities in the future. Such an eventuality would stabilize the involvement of the new NATO partners and also make more likely the containment of the terrorist challenge in a number of significant locations.

CHAPTER TEN

European Security, East and West

Introduction

At the end of the first decade of the twenty-first century, the weaknesses of the governments to Europe's east are glaringly apparent. President Ahmadinijad won a second term as President of Iran in a highly divisive and controversial election. Continuing protests by the opposition movement demonstrate that his popular mandate is a very thin reed. Similarly, President Karzai won a new term as President of Afghanistan in very troubling circumstances that included evidence of corruption in the elections and a surprising pullout from the race by his principal opponent. President Zardari had become President of Pakistan only because he held the halo of his spouse Benazir Bhutto, who had died at an assassin's hand in the most recent election. Calls both to weaken the presidential powers that he inherited and to force his resignation mounted with the violence in the ungoverned western areas of the country. In Iraq, retaliatory attacks against the Sunni Awakening Councils increased in number as the 2010 elections neared. While the Bush Administration had partly justified American military involvement in the region on the basis of building outposts and models of democracy in the region, it appeared as if the opposite had occurred. In light of this extended sheet of thin ice to the East, security linkages between Europe and its transatlantic partner to the West may have offered the best option. There was a pressing need for realistic, workable, concrete security blueprints that could buttress European's defenses through an extended period in which the thin ice to the east could either thicken in positive ways or breakup with much more negative consequences. Whether the spotlight shifts to Europe itself, to its eastern neighborhood, or to its western alliance partner, the linkage between democracy and security has rarely been so striking.

Missile Shield Proposal

What exactly was the nature of the missile shield proposal that preoccupied the American, Czech, and Polish governments in 2007–09? In what sense did that project have the potential to underpin the security of Europe by addressing the dangers to the east through reliance on a proposal from the superpower in the west? It is important to clarify this matter before undertaking discussion of its origin, political ramifications, and policy implications. Basically, the missile shield would have extended protection across an arc of countries, stretching from much of the eastern Atlantic Ocean into the western part of the Pacific Ocean. The new protection would have covered part of western Africa and nearly all of Europe. Both the western and eastern parts of Russia would as well have come under the umbrella. However, the arc of protection would only have stretched north through western Russia to the Arctic Circle, and then it would have bent down into eastern Siberia. The vast middle of Russia would not have been covered, and neither would Central/South Asia or the Gulf states (Ministry of Foreign Affairs of the Czech Republic 2009a). The partial coverage of Russia enabled the advocates of the shield to argue that the program did not really threaten or aim at Russia.

While ten antimissile interceptors would have been based in Poland, the accompanying radar detection site would have been located in the Czech Republic in Brdo, southeast of Prague. Ideally, the Czech-based radar would have detected incoming ballistic missiles in time for the Polish-based interceptors to shoot them down. Presumably, the capability would have extended to both the middle and later stages of a missile attack against one of the protected partners. The whole system would have become part of the existing American Ground-Based Midcourse Defense (GMD).

Critics of the system raised important concerns that affected the political debate over it. Some criticisms paralleled the Cold War debate over the capacity of missile defense systems. For example, Garwin (2008, 41) argues that radar systems could not distinguish between dangerous warheads and aluminum covered balloons, if all were painted the same color. This factor puts pressure on those who manage the defense system to deploy far more interceptors than the number of incoming missiles. Lewis and Postol (2008, 38) point out that the enemy could complicate matters further by enclosing the missile itself in a balloon that mimics all of the other decoys. Precision measurements were also a factor in the doubts of some of these critics. It would be one thing for the radar to detect a single incoming missile. However, it would be a far greater challenge for the defense system to develop strong enough infrared sensors that could distinguish an incoming warhead from other objects. The enemy could also create a dense "cloud of targets" with small wires less than 2 cm long each. The resulting "chaff" would make it impossible to decide if reflections emanated from the warhead itself or from a piece of wire.

Such technical considerations merged with political and strategic issues to make the debate over the missile shield complex and challenging to both Czech and American national security leadership. Such significant details played some role in the decision of the Obama Administration to cancel the proposed program in fall 2009. However, it is important to understand the mix of considerations that led to all the work on this project that offered one method for enhancing the security of Europe on both its western and eastern flanks.

American Security Goals in Central Europe

The security goals of the United States in Central Europe since the end of the Cold War have centered on a number of key objectives. In part, the goal has been to nurture the growth of capitalist economies in the former countries of the communist bloc with an eye on development of strong partnerships with countries in the West. Stimulation of the democratic process has been an additional target of concern, in light of the four decades under autocratic control. Both of these initial processes offered the promise of a more dependable integration into the West. In addition, stability has been a principal value whose importance the chaotic Balkan Wars of the 1990s underlined. A further goal throughout the period has been expansion of NATO to include these postcommunist nations into a cohesive military alliance. Finally, creation of a buffer against post-9/11 terrorism has been a pressing and urgent need early in the twenty-first century. Taken as a whole, this set of five American security goals sets the table for presentation of two important conclusions. First, it was the previously noted mix of objectives that generated the decision to advocate creation of the missile shield. Second, as this web of pressures tugged on the Czech Republic, substantial questions about Czech autonomy emerged in a glaring way.

First, in the early years after the 1989 revolutions in Central Europe, American policy supported the conversion to capitalist economies. In part, this meant the fostering of connections between western companies and their counterparts in Central Europe. For example, the Czechs entered into a cooperative arrangement with French companies to rebuild their main airport in Prague. Injection of western financial resources and know-how was directed at restarting the economies that had labored under communist-controlled central planning and quotas for so many decades. In part, the policy of the United States was to encourage the move to free market capitalism within a reasonable period of time. For Romania, this meant a prolonged process that stretched into the late 1990s (Gledhill and King 2008, 326–7).

For the Hungarians it meant a moderately paced transition, while for the Poles it entailed "shock therapy" for several years (Argentieri 2008, 225–7). American policy also supported the exchange of economic specialists. Central European economists came to western universities to learn of the most advanced techniques, while American and West European academics traveled to Central Europe to share their expertise. In these ways, American policy more or less engaged with the economic transition in the region. Thereby, an economic base could potentially underpin a sense of security in the region rather than a vacuum that could invite trouble.

Second, stoking of the fires of democracy has been another security-related goal of American policy in the region. One motivation for creation of democracy is simply that it has been a NATO entry requirement. NATO and eventually EU required basic establishment of democratic procedures prior to entry. The logic of such a requirement is the necessity of extending a long-standing security alliance on the basis of common values. In addition, the idea of the "democratic peace" received much attention in the 1990s. Countries that established functioning democracies seemed safer and less prone to provocative attacks on their neighbors that led to continuing battles with one another (Jentleson 2007, 519–25). In contrast, those countries that hung on to autocratic forms were more suspect and more likely to lash out militarily against border countries. Variations in the region were apparent. On the one hand, the Baltic nations were quick to enact democratic reforms after 1991. All three simply restored the Constitutions that had governed them in the 1920s and 1930s, prior to their absorption into the Soviet Union in 1940 (Eglitis 2008, 241). Admission to NATO and the EU ensued for all three as a partial consequence in 2004. On the other hand, several of the Yugoslav successor states were reluctant to yield communist era autocratic political patterns, and thus their fate was quite different. Serbia loomed as a NATO enemy in the Bosnian War and Kosovo crisis, while Croatia produced a nationalist leadership whose features for some years bore striking resemblance to those of its communist predecessors (Baskin and Pickering 2008, 295–8). Overall, under American leadership, the West integrated new democracies into its security structures more quickly than it did unchanging, authoritarian regimes.

Third, promotion of a stable region is implicit in the previously mentioned American objectives, but such a goal is also a separate part of a larger historical tapestry. After World War I, Central Europe became a political vacuum. Collapse of the old empires resulted in creation of fledgling democracies. Most of those systems gave way to more authoritarian variants within a decade (Wolchik and Curry 2008, 10–11). As a result, Nazi ambitions capitalized on that vacuum and moved in to dominate the region for the duration of World War II. This pattern of vulnerability repeated itself after World War II. This time it was the Soviet Union that exploited the lack of effective political governance. In such a highly volatile and unstable atmosphere, the region fell under communist influence for a full four decades (Hesli 2007, 49, 245). It certainly seemed apparent that the post-1989 situation was a less dangerous one for the region. However, the rise of rogue leadership in the Balkans and nearby Middle East made the risk of another vacuum further to the north too great. While Central Europe was no longer the primary theater that it had been during the Cold War, its strategic location required priority treatment.

It is clear that the American plan for emplacement of a radar station in the Czech Republic fitted into this priority of increased stability. For example, President Bush visited Prague in June, 2007, while Secretary of Defense Robert Gates followed up with a visit in October. Both emphasized the importance of such a facility in the strengthening regional security in light of threats further to the east (iDNES 2007r). NATO Jaap de Hoop Scheffer underlined the regional security theme on a visit to Romania in the fall of 2007. He stated that the principle of security was indivisible and that the missile shield capability should protect equally each NATO partner (iDNES 2007s). Even if Iran stopped its work on a nuclear program, security against conventional weapons would also be advanced by the radar system (iDNES 2007t). By the end of 2007, arguments by Minister of Foreign Affairs Karel Schwarzenberg in defense of the missile shield emphasized its ability to protect both Western and Central Europe (iDNES 2007u). His American counterpart Condoleezza Rice expanded the application of the shield to the entire Euro-Atlantic region (iDNES 2008b). Thus, the Czech component of the missile shield was an important device for furthering the security of Central Europe as well as its immediate environs.

Fourth, expansion of NATO to include many of the postcommunist nations also included the goal of buttressing regional security in important ways. The Clinton Administration offered observer status through the PfP Plan to qualified postcommunist states by the middle of the 1990s. In the immediate aftermath of the first Persian Gulf War, and at the time of the tragic Bosnian War, a widened military alliance made much sense. By 1999, just months before the NATO bombing campaign in Kosovo, NATO admitted three nations ready for full membership. As that military campaign began, the alliance security network was thus broader. Admission of seven more nations in 2004 was closely tied to the security threat that 9/11 posed for so many western nations. With ten Central European nations anchored within the alliance by 2004, a potential vacuum was filled and west-east security thereby broadened. The decision to bring in the three Baltic nations had been a particularly difficult security concern. As they became part of this western military alliance, their potential to provoke Russian reactions was very real (Michta 2006, 18). However, over time Russian reactions to the admission of all ten softened. Instead of opposing NATO expansion per se, Putin became more selective and reacted mainly to issues that engaged Russian interests (Webber 2007, 270–3). The proposed missile shield was certainly one of those.

Fifth, American security interests also incorporate a view of Central Europe as a buffer against hostile regimes and terrorist groups that emanate from the east. For example, the 2002 NATO Summit approved the Prague Capabilities Commitment. That document in part focused on creation of a common barrier against a potential threat from chemical, biological, radiological, and nuclear (CBRN) threats. The Summit participants also agreed on four categories of action to counteract future terrorist acts. Further, they laid plans for eventual creation of a Terrorist Threat Intelligence Unit (TTIU) (Terzuolo 2006, 107–10). Changes in intelligence procedures included common projects in four distinct areas. Those areas consisted of firmer airline security, barriers against terrorist funding, border controls, and exchange of intelligence itself (Rees 2004, 178–9). Of course, the Central European nations would share in those projects, and the missile shield proposal would contribute to creation of the needed buffer.

In the end, Iran came to be a central figure in the threats that American leaders used to justify the missile shield project. President Bush estimated, in a speech at the National Defense University, that Iran might possess the ability to strike a number of European allies by 2015 (USATODAY 2007f). Concerns about Russian reactions were always simultaneously on the table. For example, Secretary of Defense Robert Gates followed up the Bush speech with comments intended to reassure Russia. He indicated at one point that, with the agreement of the Czech leadership, Russia might obtain an invitation to inspect the military sites that were part of the missile shield (iDNES 2007u). Thus, the security plans of the United States included a vision of Central Europe as a key player in the double effort to fend off terrorism and to reassure Russia that its interests would not be sacrificed.

Czech Security Goals in Relation to American Objectives

Czech goals in defense policy meshed with American objectives in a number of important respects. Participation in the broad transatlantic partnership was beneficial to most nations on the European continent, particularly the Czechs. At critical points in the history of Czechoslovakia, particularly in 1918 and then again during the World War II era, America provided key assistance in development of the nation. Further, in 1999, membership in NATO also brought the two closer together and created in the Czech leadership a conviction that they should take the new alliance obligations seriously. Then, following the catastrophe of the 9/11 attacks, Czechs perceived the common linkage with the American effort to combat the global, intensified terrorist threat.

Czechs understood that Europe as a whole shared common values with the United States. One such set of values consisted of building a framework of stability, democracy, and attention to nations in the developing world. Economic goals were also similar across the Atlantic partnership. Steady economic growth, low inflation, full employment, growth of the market economy, and development of the world market were high on that agenda. It is also true that these transatlantic partners had a similar view of emerging global threats. Combating the spread of terrorism and weapons of mass destruction (WMD) was a top priority on the list of anxious concerns. Both containing regional conflicts and checking rogue states also entered into common views about coping with threat perceptions. Joint work to stabilize the Middle East was a major topic of concern. Finally, the historic transatlantic partnership had a value of its own that required protection and nurturing (Černíková 2008, 41–3).

Another writer perceived American-European friendship as a significant national interest of the Czech Republic. Even though the United States was not a European state, in some sense it was a European power. In contrast to other powers, the United States had never made claims to European territory. When one European power historically had threatened the rest, the United States had been there to help contain such ambitions. The simple fact of the heavy U.S. economic and military involvement in Europe served as a sort of deterrent to non-European powers which might have had designs on European interests or even territory. While many Europeans became alienated from the United States after the invasion of Iraq in 2003, there were risks attendant on excessive anti-Americanism. A reversion by the United States to isolationism would not be in the interests of Europe more broadly or more specifically of the Czech Republic (Joch 2007, 1–20). Such observations reinforced Czech participation in NATO and also Czech receptiveness to American initiatives such as the missile shield proposal.

Historical links between the Czech Republic and America were important in knitting the two together on common twenty-first-century projects. In 1918,

President Woodrow Wilson had played an important role in the founding of the Czechoslovak state. Of course the entire West had let Czechoslovakia down by signing the Munich Pact in 1938. However, the United States was unique in its unwillingness to recognize the Munich appeasement of the Hitler Regime. During the World War II period, America had been the most consistent supporter of Czechoslovak independence. Again, in 1945 at Yalta the entire West sold out the Czechs and Slovaks. However, America's participation in the concessions to Stalin was no more extensive than that of the West European nations, and the United States did offer Marshall Plan aid. Thus, the American request for Czech participation in the missile shield was rooted in deep historical connections. While Russian hostility to the proposed Czech radar site was an immense problem, it made sense to cast the lot with the Americans rather than with those who had betrayed or occupied the country (Klaban 2007, 19–21). In sum, historical connections made acceptance of the radar site a natural step rather than an unusual policy initiative with no precedent in the nation's experience.

With regard to the new NATO linkage and the emerging terrorist threats, some Czechs perceived the old link to the United States to be the best bet for the future. In fact, the sense of security for Czechs in the post-9/11 world was no greater than it had been during the Cold War. Although terrorists had not hit the Czech Republic yet, it was true that terrorists tended to strike nations that underestimated regional insecurity and chose to live in a false state of security. The Czech nation was additionally unprepared to cope by itself with this threat due to its long-standing suspicion of the military. Occupation by Warsaw Pact forces after 1968 reinforced an ingrown skepticism about permitting growth of a powerful military of their own in postcommunist times. For these reasons, there was a strong argument for the Czech Republic to rely in the near future on American leadership of the NATO alliance. The United States had demonstrated a willingness to take on responsibility in major crises, while the EU was only slowly developing its CFSP (Vondra 2006, 16–19). Therefore, there was a significant set of Czech leadership attitudes and conclusions that sought to build on the historic transatlantic partnership. From that point of view, participation in the radar site was a logical outgrowth of NATO membership, reliance on the tested senior partner of that alliance, and acute awareness of the potential impact of the emergent terrorist movements on Czech territory and its population.

External/Internal Politics and the Radar Site Proposal

In the ideal world of the rational actor model, the intersection of American and Czech security goals would be unaffected by old-fashioned politics.

In fact, both global and domestic political pressure impinged on the policy process. Russian reactions to the proposal constituted the key international political pressure. Even though the new system would be directed against rogue states such as Iran and perhaps North Korea, the Russian leadership interpreted it as potentially useable against their nation. Thus, they raised many objections both to the U.S. proposal as well as to Polish and Czech receptivity to it. Domestic pressures also flowed from contrasting stands of the Czech political parties. The Czech and Moravian Communist Party (KSČM), a party that was seeking to cut the losses in its generally strong public support, hopped on the bandwagon of opposition to the radar site. The ČSSD was opposed to it as well. Public opinion polls taken throughout the period of consideration of the plan typically showed strong majority preference to defeat the plan. In addition, protests in the area around Brdo, the radar site, occurred on a number of occasions. A key question would consistently be how successful the coalition leadership would be in navigating through these tricky political waters.

The Politics of Russian Attitudes

Russian opposition was forceful and frequent. Some have suggested that Russia has recently been flexing its military muscle in an effort to restore its great power status. Part of that effort to strengthen its military posture entailed a public relations campaign that would renew emphasis on the nuclear component of national security. The public relations focus had become a more immediate priority after Russian leaders observed the role nuclear weapons played in the U.S. decision to invade Iraq in 2003. Instability in nations on its border that were proximate to potential nuclear powers in the Middle East reinforced the logic of renewed emphasis on the nuclear equation (Baev 2008, 83–5). For example, the 2003 Rose Revolution in Georgia and the 2005 Tulip Revolution in Kyrgyzstan certainly shocked Russia and made its leaders more aware of the soft conditions in the buffer between its own territory and that of the more troublesome nations further south. The 2004 Orange Revolution in Ukraine touched the same nerves but involved a geopolitical location a bit further from that center of trouble but closer to Central Europe. This overall perspective both about the direction of Russian foreign policy and about the link between its nuclear priority and search for international greatness offers a useful backdrop to consideration of its responses to the radar site proposal. The American plan for a missile shield in Central Europe basically put a dagger in the heart of Russian efforts to expand their global impact through elevation of the nuclear component of their military capability.

Russian reactions became part of the Czech political calculations right away. Some in the Czech Republic were concerned that Russia might react by trying itself to provide more assistance to Iran. On the one hand, a future scenario might be one in which Iran's growing regional power approximated that of Pakistan, India, and China. A potential, although less likely, prospect was an expanded Iran that included a breakaway Shiite sector of Iraq. On the other hand, Russian persuasive powers might convince Iran to back down in its nuclear ambitions. This eventuality could lead to a situation in which Russia itself would gain diplomatic stature as a world power (Suja 2008, 32–5). Neither the emergence of Iran as a regional power nor the rise of Russia in global political respect would benefit Czech security interests.

Other Czech analysts concluded that Russia overstated its own vulnerability and hence the threat posed by the missile shield. Those scholars doubted that Russia was trailing that badly in the global balance of power. Suchý (2007, 4–6) presented the following data in support of his contention that Russian fears were overstated (See Table 1).

Table 1. *Comparison of Russian and American Strategic Power* (2007)

Category of Weapons	Russia's Strategic Power (2007)	America's Strategic Power (2007)
ICBMs	489	500
ICBM Warheads	1788	1050
SLBMs	173	336
SLBM Warheads	609	2016
Strategic Bombers	79	115
Strategic Warheads	884	1955

Although the United States maintained a lead of 951 to 741 in the total number of strategic weapons and a lead of 5021 to 3281 in total warheads, still Russia was a strong nuclear power. Its numerical capabilities certainly offered a degree of protection that undermined the credibility of its seemingly nervous concerns about the missile shield.

At one point in the missile shield debate, Russia had also come up with a proposal to locate the missile shield at the Gabala site in Azerbaijan. Placement of a shield there would take care of the potential Iranian problem and could increase Russian leverage on regional politics. Of course, this Putin proposal was predicated on the assumption that the Czech-Polish system would then no longer be necessary. In Suchý's estimation, one result might be increased leverage by Azerbaijan over Russian policy. He averred that a Russian site such as Gabala should supplement rather than replace the American proposal for Central Europe. Again, he concluded that there was no pressing need to overestimate Russian pressure or to react to each of their provocative statements (Suchý 2007, 4-6).

In light of increased tension on the issue, American and Russian leaders developed initiatives to defuse the growing tension. For example, in May 2007, America and Russia agreed to hold a joint meeting of their defense and foreign ministers (iDNES 2007v). One month later Russian Minister of Foreign Affairs Sergei Lavrov suggested that the NATO-Russia Council was the best vehicle for discussion of the issues that divided the two. The proximity of the proposed site to the Russian border was the factor that activated Russian concern at that time. Lavrov contended that it was natural for Russia to apply pressure against that extension of American influence into Central Europe (iDNES 2007w). Russia may also have feared that its own radar defense capabilities would not match the ones proposed for Poland and the Czech Republic. In fact, later in the summer of 2007, Russia apparently dismantled two aging, Cold War radar stations in Ukraine (SME 2007d). On the anniversary day of the Warsaw Pact invasion of Czechoslovakia in 1968, the Chief of the Russian Army Jurij Balujevskij called upon the Czechs to postpone their decision about the missile site until after the American elections at the end of 2008. Ironically, even American politics were entering the discussion about the Brdo site. The Russian commander also threatened to aim Russian ballistic missiles at points in the Czech Republic, if the radar site plans materialized (iDNES 2007x). It was obviously very difficult to keep tension out of any discussions about these sites.

The American side also sent up trial balloons on occasions. In late October 2007, Defense Secretary Robert Gates seemed to be considering the possibility of constructing the sites but delaying their "activation" until Iran made its missiles a more definitive threat. Simultaneously, he presented a plan to Russia to permit them physical access to the bases. Czech willingness to accept the presence again of Russian troops on its soil was problematic (USATODAY 2007g). However, Moscow rejected that concession as unacceptable; the Czech Defense Minister Vlasta Parkanová was skeptical as she recalled serving on the parliamentary commission that oversaw the departure of Soviet troops after 1989; and an American Defense spokesperson backed off from Gates' earlier comments to say that they had only constituted thoughts rather than a concrete proposal (iDNES 2007y). In fact, Russia escalated the rhetoric one month later by including Belarus in retaliatory plans. For some time, Belarus had desired to strengthen its army with the Russian rocket Iskander (iDNES 2007z). Nearly a year later, Belarus again entered the dialogue by making an agreement with Russia for a joint space defense system as a reaction against agreements signed by NATO states. This agreement would build on the Customs Union that they formed earlier in 1997 (SME 2008d).

At the end of the year, Russia decided to retaliate in another way, by pulling out of the 1990 Conventional Forces Agreement/Europe (CFE). The status of that existing agreement was somewhat unusual, for Russia had updated it in 1999, in order to take account of the breakup of the Soviet Union. However, Russia was the only country that signed the 1999 modification. All NATO nations refused to sign, because they disagreed with the continued presence of Russian soldiers in both Moldova and Georgia. In any event, Russia justified its abrogation of that agreement on the basis of American plans to build the missile shield (SME 2007e).

In early 2008, Czech Prime Minister Mirek Topolánek continued to work on plans with the American government with an eye on signing the radar agreement sometime in the middle of the year. President Putin continued to protest that emplacement of such a system so close to the Russian border would destabilize the European balance of power. In fact, he compared the project to the Cuban Missile Crisis in reverse (iDNES 2008c). In the spring of the year, the matter of a physical Russian presence at the base surfaced again as an issue. Secretary of Defense Robert Gates clarified the American proposal to mean that Russian personnel could be present at the sites in both Poland and the Czech Republic, but he suggested that their stay there would not be a continuous one (USATODAY 2008g). Moscow's clear preference was for a permanent presence at those two sites. Minister of Defense Sergej Lavrov was agitated that the written agreement seemed to be at odds with the verbal promises made by the Americans. He had heard talk of a permanent presence on the sites, but the written agreement outlined a situation in which Russians would be located at the embassies in Prague and Warsaw. On occasion, they would have the right to visit the bases (iDNES 2008d).

Russian signals continued to be mixed in the fall of 2008, even after the Americans had signed the agreements with the Czechs and Poles. On the one hand, Nikolaj Solovcov, Commander of Russian Rocket Forces, seemed somewhat calmer about the proposed missile shield. He said that he was reconciled to the existing program, as long as no expansion or spreading of it occurred. He acknowledged the force of the argument that the proposed system could not really threaten hundreds of Russian rockets with multiple warheads. At the same time, he could not help but point out that there was still a possibility of aiming Russian rockets at Poland and the Czech Republic (iDNES 2008e). On the other hand, Dmitrij Rogozin, Russian Ambassador to NATO, spoke in more ominous tones. In his view, the Czechs were in the process of selling out the security of their people on behalf of a new game. He did not see any difference between defensive and offensive weapons. Russia needed to assume the worst, when it confronted strengthened defenses in suspect countries (iDNES 2008f). In the midst of all of this discussion, Russia tested a new guided missile called Bulava. It was designed to evade the type of missile shield being planned for Central Europe (DN 2008b). This test served as a reminder of Russian capabilities. When rumors about Russian soldiers in the area around Brdo surfaced at about the same time, more suspicions on both sides were fueled (iDNES 2008g).

Clearly, there was no way of predicting or guessing what the Russian reactions would be on a given day. Their attitudes over time combined bold posturing, anxious defensiveness, and rational argument. In all situations they remained a potent factor influencing both the dialogue and the decision-making process.

Czech Party Politics

Domestic politics in the Czech Republic also influenced the conversation about the proposed joint military project. In control of the government, the ODS took the lead in support of the proposal. Prime Minister Topolánek strongly favored the new system. He sometimes spoke in dramatic terms. Inattention to a country's defense could result in a threat to civilization. In his view, Europe slumbered into a rosy dream after the end of the Cold War. He could not comprehend how the events of 9/11 and the Madrid bombings did not have the capability to awaken the Europeans from that slumber (iDNES 2007aa). At the same time, he held firm to the belief that America should foot the bill for the entire project. He also expressed concern for popular anxiety that the radar itself might jeopardize public health (iDNES 2007bb). President Klaus also offered his thoughts about the agreement on occasion. For example, in the summer of 2007, he said he would give consideration to such opposition proposals as the call for a referendum on the matter. However, he simultaneously warned against the danger of stirring up "cheap populism" through referendum campaigns (iDNES 2007cc). One issue that opposition leaders continually brought up was the possibility of hooking the new facility to NATO rather than to the United States. Karel Schwarzenberg, Minister of Foreign Affairs, agreed that the facility should be incorporated into NATO. However, he pointed out that Americans should still possess control over usage of the system. In particular, his speech stirred up the Green Party that was part of the government coalition. They saw him as departing too much from their own party platforms (iDNES 2007dd).

Czech politicians became quite animated when American leaders offered the surprising conclusion that their intelligence indicated that Iran stopped work on its nuclear facilities in 2003. Opposition leader Jiří Paroubek immediately called for termination of the radar site proposal (iDNES 2007ee.). The ČSSD leader followed up a few months later by writing a letter to the Prime Minister. He called upon the Prime Minister to cancel his trip to the United States and any plans to sign the agreement. In his letter he asked whether the radar site would strengthen or weaken Czech security. Might the plans worsen Czech relations with other European countries? In his view, the Czech nation needed to have the right to vote on the radar site via a referendum (iDNES 2008h). Prior to Poland's acceptance of the American plans for their portion of the missile shield project, there was a minor debate in the Czech Republic over the meaning of potential Polish rejection of the ten interceptors. Minister of Defense Vlasta Parkanová quickly suggested that Polish rejection would send plans back to the drawing board. Prime Minister Topolánek thought that her statement was courageous but premature. A spokesman for the Minister of Foreign Affairs countered that the radar system by itself would strengthen Czech security (iDNES 2008i). Czechs should not be concerned about what the Poles were doing.

Former President Václav Havel brought another factor to the discussion table, one that supported the American initiative. He took the long historical perspective by observing that the Americans had supported Czechs in the founding of their state in 1918, during World War II, and then at the time of the fall of the Iron Curtain. For the first time America was asking something of the Czechs, and the nation had an opportunity to repay its obligation to the United States. He compared the pacifists who opposed the project to those who called for doing nothing against Hitler prior to the Munich Agreement of 1938 (iDNES 2008j).

One additional political issue that appeared was linking the signing of the radar site accord with ratification of the Lisbon Treaty that was a special project of the EU. Opposition political leaders in the Czech Republic threatened to take the radar agreement to the Constitutional Court for a ruling on its legality. If that happened, key ODS members of the Senate threatened to take the Lisbon Treaty also to the courts for consideration. Thus, there was an attempt by the government to make the Lisbon Treaty a hostage of the decision on the radar base. In fact, it was the Communists (KSČM) who had the most interest in taking the radar agreement to the courts. Without the support of the Social Democrats (ČSSD), however, they would not have had enough legislative votes to meet the threshold required for submission to the Court (iDNES 2008k).

As the prospect of elections loomed upon the horizon, party platforms became a more significant factor. The 2009 Election Program of the ČSSD stated that location of the radar site should depend on expression of the majority of citizens, most probably in a referendum (cssd 2009). The Communist Party was much more scathing in its official statements. Even after the inauguration of President Obama, their leaders continued to point to citizen opposition and to the fact that the system was virtually untested. They also argued that the huge investment in the shield made no sense at a time of economic crisis. In their view, American lobbying interests and the military-industrial complex were driving the new policy (kscm 2009).

Thus, all the key political forces presented views about how to handle this controversial issue. There was no possibility of reconciling all of those points of view. However, the range of issues demonstrates how extensive the discussion continued to be.

Political Role of the Public

Public opinion polls in the Czech Republic were another key factor in the political process. As early as December 2006, one key poll (Ivan Gabal Analysis & Consulting) revealed that a majority of Czechs favored the system if it included only the radar component. However, if missiles were connected with the radar, then a majority opposed construction or approval. The poll also revealed that those who supported NATO in general were more approving of the radar site than those whose trust in the alliance was small. In addition, support and opposition to a referendum about the site was about equal. In general, Czechs did see nuclear activity by Iran and North Korea as dangerous, but mostly they preferred economic and diplomatic pressure to military solutions (iDNES 2006f). By the middle of 2007, however, public opposition to the project had grown. The Center for Research on Public Opinion's (CVVM) research revealed that two-thirds of Czech respondents were in opposition by that time, and the opponents were beginning to fasten on the referendum as a logical next step in the discussion. Perhaps another expression of public opinion was a study done by Czech experts with information provided by the Americans. They concluded that the base would not endanger the health of persons living near the site (iDNES 2007ff). The impact of such a study on the population was uncertain.

Protests at the Brdo site were another occasional expression of one segment of opinion about the missile shield proposal. In September 2007, the protestors carried out a symbolic blockade of fourteen villages near Brdo. The plan was to send five protestors to each village with the objective of talking with citizens and distributing leaflets. They were also going to present a document to a meeting at which the leader of the Communist Party Vojtěch Filip would be in attendance (iDNES 2007gg). Iniciativa NE Základnám was one Czech interest group that had overwhelmingly opposed the new base. However, they dismissed the planned protest as the work of only the communists (iDNES 2007hh). Another group called the Humanist Party called for a boycott of American goods, in the tradition of Gandhi and Martin Luther King. Its leader Jan Tamáš called for a series of concerts, festivals, and meetings with prominent personalities in order to magnify the opposition (iDNES 2007ii).

By the spring of 2008, the protests had increased in size. In May, several hundred people protested in Prague against the radar site. This time Iniciativa NE Základnám organized the demonstrations. Iniciativa also supported the movement Greenpeace which had already been at Brdo for a week. About the same time, SC & C did another public opinion survey that reinforced the conclusion that a majority of Czechs opposed the base. That survey discovered that the typical supporter of the base was a male with a high school education who lived in a city of more than 100,000 inhabitants. In contrast, the typical opponent was a woman over 60 years of age with only a lower school education (iDNES 2008l).

Protests continued even into July, the month of both the signing ceremony and the visit by American Secretary of State Condoleezza Rice. Iniciativa NE Základnám set up a tent on Wenceslaus Square and planned at least one demonstration. Visitors to their tent would be able to vote on a virtual referendum on the radar plan. Greenpeace was also planning to organize a demonstration (iDNES 2008m). Some wondered if threatening global events might throw public opinion back toward support for the base. However, there was no evidence of that. CVVM did a survey of opinion one month after the Russian invasion of Georgia, an event that most interpreted as threatening in many ways. Still, opposition to the base by Czech citizens amounted to 67 percent. It was expected that such controversy would continue and that politics would not cease on this controversial proposal iDNES 2008n).

At Last, the Signing Ceremony

A number of NATO Summit Meetings of Heads of State had given some discussion to the proposed missile shield. For example, the Prague Summit in 2002 listed such a project of antimissile defense as one of its main priorities (iDNES 2006g). In November 2006, the leaders had put the missile shield proposal on their agenda at their Riga Summit. They decided to give further study to its feasibility. In preparations for the Bucharest Summit in April 2008, there was a much higher priority placed on that project. Earlier, in the fall of 2007, NATO Secretary-General Jaap de Hoop Scheffer observed that the antimissile system would be one of the main themes at the upcoming April Summit (iDNES 2007jj). In fact, it was at that summit that Czech Minister of Foreign Affairs Karel Schwarzenberg announced both that the Czechs had accepted the American proposal and that they were planning the official signing ceremony. Alliance leaders noted further that they supported the project and expected that in the future it would actually become a NATO system. This semiofficial NATO support for the system was a surprising summit result for the Czechs. However, some issues were still hanging in suspension. One was the so-called Status of Forces Agreement (SOFA), which pertained to the movement of American soldiers on Czech soil. Another was a tougher upcoming discussion about controls over potential Russian officers and experts in the area of the radar base (iDNES 2008o).

Planning for the actual signing ceremony intensified soon after conclusion of the Bucharest Summit. Initial plans focused on an invitation to American Secretary of State Rice for a May signing. Eventually, the ceremony would be postponed until the month of July. At the time of these preparations, the political landscape and political party divisions were clear. Public opinion polls still demonstrated that a majority of Czechs opposed the plans. Both the opposition Social Democrats and the Communists were opposed and demanded the holding of a referendum. Within the governing coalition, the ODS led the support for the radar base. Part of the Green coalition partner was supportive, and part was opposed. The Lidovci, the other coalition party, were still registering misgivings about the new plans (iDNES 2008p).

There was a minor setback for the project in the time frame between the Bucharest Summit in April and the official signing ceremony in July. Leaders of the EU nations held their summit in Slovenia, and they considered the question of support for the missile shield. In the end, they voted "no" and commented that the matter really fell within the competence of NATO (SME 2008e).

In early July, the signing ceremony finally took place, and Secretary of State Condoleezza Rice traveled to Prague for the occasion. In spite of the finality of this ceremony, many unfinished issues lingered in the atmosphere. The Poles had not yet signed their agreement to accept the ten antimissile interceptors. The SOFA Agreement on movement of American troops was not yet ready, and plans for inspections by Russian troops were not close to being in final form. Also, the parliamentary vote had not yet been scheduled (iDNES 2008q). In spite of those unresolved matters, Prime Minister Topolánek was forceful in defending the project. He did not see the threat of ballistic missiles as an imaginary one, and he warned his countrymen and countrywomen not to repeat the earlier Czechoslovak failure to accept Marshall Plan aid after World War II (iDNES 2008r). Minister of Foreign Affairs Schwarzenberg pointed out that the missile shield would protect not only the Czech Republic but also Europe and the whole euroatlantic sector (iDNES 2008s). President Klaus, a recovering surgery patient, expressed no doubts and stated that he would sign the agreement, as long as the legislature first approved it. In his view, the Czech Republic needed to stand on two legs, the American and the European (iDNES 2008t).

Another piece of the puzzle fell into place in September, when the parties finally signed the SOFA Agreement. One important condition of that agreement that permitted American soldiers to operate on the base was the proviso that the land and physical property on the base remain in Czech hands. Czechs would be responsible for security outside the station and the Americans for security within it. That signing ceremony was planned for September 19th, on the occasion of a meeting of NATO Ministers of Defense in London. American Secretary of Defense Robert Gates and Czech Minister of Defense Vlasta Parkanová were the cabinet officials who ended up signing that document (iDNES 2008u.). On the American side, the defense bill that President Bush had sent to Congress at that time included $466 million to develop the entire missile shield system in both Poland and the Czech Republic (CQ Today 2008). One important footnote to these two agreements was an additional agreement that treated the process of actually building the base. The Czech Prime Minister proposed to the Cabinet an agreement that accorded Czech industry a primary role in construction of the facility. Czechs would benefit from participation in the research and development of the components of the site. In addition, the Czechs would learn from exchange of specialists between the two countries (iDNES 2008v).

In the end, such additional provisos made the details of the agreements much more concrete. It was initially unclear if revelation of these last agreements firmed up either the opposition to or the support for the base. Much depended on media interpretation and stands taken by the various political party leaders. For example, a *Lidové noviny* reporter commented that the base would give a "privileged position" to the "Czech Republic's relationship with the United States" (Palata 2008, 11). Other less positive interpretations entered the discussion as well.

Changes during the Obama Administration

In March of 2009, there was a flurry of discussion about possible new directions with regard to the missile site. During the campaign, Candidate Obama gave the impression that he was less committed to the project than had been President Bush. In early March, he sent a letter to President Dmitry Medvedev of Russia with the hint of a compromise. He requested from Russia assistance in solving the touchy issue of Iran's nuclear program. In exchange for such assistance, he suggested that he would be willing to consider sacrificing the missile shield in the Czech Republic and Poland. Reference to this letter appeared in the Russian newspaper *Kommersant,* and the source was unnamed. Officially, the American Administration had not yet spoken about this offer, and Czech Prime Minister Topolánek said that he had no information that the new American administration had yet made a decision on the matter (iDNES 2009b). A day later the media fleshed out the story further in stating that an American diplomat had delivered the letter to the Russian President three weeks earlier (DN 2009d).

Several weeks later President Medvedev made news with a surprise of his own. In 2011, Russia would throw itself into rearmament of its ground and naval forces. The factors that pushed them in this direction included the spread of global terrorism and the advance of NATO to Russia's doorstep. Another change in the Russian strategy would be the focus on purchasing totally new equipment. Since the end of the Cold War, he lamented that Russia had relied too much on repair of its older equipment. At the same time, he acknowledged that President Putin had made some improvements in Russia's military strength. In reality, former President Putin had been able to do this due to profits from the oil-inspired economic boom of the early twenty-first century (iDNES 2009c). Thus, the signals were very mixed on this brief spate of high level discussions. Were the Russians responding to President Obama, if he indeed had dispatched the diplomat with the above-noted letter? Or, were the Americans and Russians once again talking past one another?

Then, in the fall of 2009, it was President Obama's turn to bring surprising news. He cancelled the entire missile shield proposal and replaced it with a lower cost project that relied on existing sea- and land-based capabilities. This announcement to both Poles and Czechs came in the middle of the night of September 17, 2009 (iDNES 2009d). Reports from the Pentagon stated that their intelligence showed that Iran was no longer developing the type of long-range weapons against which the missile shield was designed (USATODAY 2009s). Current expectations were that Iran was working on short-range missiles that had a range of 5,000 miles and could be a threat against all of Europe. The American replacement plan would again center on Poland and the Czech Republic, as it would include components in the two (USATODAY 2009t). Technological problems with the missile shield had also factored into the calculus that led to this huge change in the Bush Administration's plan. For example, 5 of 13 tests of the missile had failed to hit targets, and planners had not figured out ways to overcome the problem of decoys (USATODAY 2009u).

Czech and Polish reactions were mixed. Czechs understood that the decision was the right of the Americans, and those who were connected with the antiradar movement rejoiced. On the one hand, ODS leader Miroslav Topolánek warned about increased threats to the Czech Republic. On the other hand, ČSSD Chair Jiří Paroubek called the new decision a "victory for the Czech people." President Václav Klaus simply said that he was not surprised (iDNES 2009e). At one point, the Czech President dismissed concerns about threats from Russia by commenting that he feared the EU more than he feared Russia (iDNES 2009f). In contrast, some Polish leaders were even more apprehensive, as they expressed concerns about the uncertainty of Russian intentions. Would cancellation invite more aggressiveness by that former enemy (IDNES 2009g)? President Lech Kaczynski worried publicly that Poland would now find itself in a precarious "gray zone" between West Europe and former Soviet space (Gera 2009). In fact, the Poles did not talk to President Obama until the day after the Czechs did. Either Prime Minister Tusk refused to accept the call, or phone communications broke down. Reactions from several other countries in the neighborhood emerged as well. Lithuania was not a site for location of any components of the missile shield project, but their reactions were similar to those of the Poles. The Lithuanian Foreign Minister described the American President's announcement as "not the best news" (IZVESTIYA 2009k).

Russia's reactions were not mixed. President Medvedev called Obama's decision a "responsible" one, and he was prepared to continue dialogue with the United States on a variety of issues (iDNES 2009h). Prime Minister Vladimir Putin expressed the hope that the United States might be willing to open the door to Russian membership in the World Trade Organization (DN 2009e). One positive step by Russia pertained to the Kaliningrad issue.

Deputy Defense Minister Vladimir Popovkin stated that planned deployment of the Iskander short-range missiles to Kaliningrad was now unnecessary (USATODAY 2009v). In fact, Russia's earlier concerns that the shield might be directed against them as well as Iran may have had some basis in fact. Secretary of Defense Robert Gates spoke with reporters after a formal presentation at the Air Force Association Convention. In those comments, he mentioned that the proposed Czech radar site could have monitored the Russian Intercontinental Ballistic Missile (ICBM) activity as well as missile-related activity in Iran. Previously, Pentagon officials had denied that the system had the potential to pick up activity in places as distant as the Caucasus Mountains (Pincus 2009).

At NATO headquarters, the new Secretary-General Anders Fogh Rasmussen attempted to put the new situation into a broader alliance-based framework. He asserted that there might be a future proposal that would link the United States, NATO, and Russia into a missile shield program. He compared such future cooperation to the links among all three in the global battle against terrorism (sueddeutsche 2009f). Hans Blix from Sweden, the former UN chief for nuclear arms inspections, greeted the Obama decision with the words "It was high time." He also contended that Russia would now feel a greater sense of security and could more confidently take part in arms control talks. Blix also welcomed Obama's intention to engage in discussions with Iran (DN 2009f).

Within a few weeks, the outlines of President Obama's replacement plan for the missile shield became public. Reliance would be principally on the Navy's SM-3 interceptor missiles. The cost would be $10,000,000 per copy in contrast to the previously planned interceptors that would have required $70,000,000 per copy. In late September 2009, the existing SM-3 missiles were carried on 18 Aegis cruisers. Incorporation of them into a new scaled-down missile shield program would require expansion of those outfitted cruisers from 18 to 67. The plan called also for 3 cruisers with 100 SM-3s each to be on patrol in the Mediterranean and North Seas by 2011. The land-based counterparts of this system would be erected between 2015 and 2020 (USATODAY 2009w). Confirmation that those new land-based interceptors would also be located in Poland came quickly (SME 2009i).

Official, high-level conversations about the new plan took place during Vice President Biden's visit to Europe, October 20–24, 2009. He visited Poland, Romania, and then the Czech Republic. In Poland, he discussed the possibility of introducing the SM-3 missiles after 2015, and Polish leaders were receptive. Prime Minster Donald Tusk labeled the new project interesting and indicated that his country would take part in it. Clearly, the government had rebounded from its disappointment during the surprise of the previous month. Vice President Biden reassured the Poles that the new project would be more effective than the previously planned one (IZVESTIYA 2009l). Czechs were prepared also to accept their prospective role as the site of the command post for the new missile shield system. Descriptions of the Czech role were a bit uncertain at the time of the visit. Prior to the Biden trip, Under Secretary of the U.S. State Department Ellen Tauscher had described how a command system for development and control of the components of the new system would be put in the Czech Republic (iDNES 2009i). However, the description changed somewhat during the Biden visit. Prime Minister Jan Fischer made a more general reference to Czech willingness to participate in a new architecture, and the specifics included creation of an office in the Czech Republic. In that office, presumably, Czechs and Americans would work together on the scientific and research aspects of the new system (iDNES 2009j).

Plans for increasing the military security of Europe may have shifted away from the Bush Administration's missile shield project, but security threats did not abate in the ensuing months. Iran, the main target of the cancelled project, continued to engage in a cat and mouse game over its intentions in regard to nuclear development. At times, they leaned toward cooperation with EU initiatives that set up a network of nations to process Iran's nuclear fuel to make certain that its uses would be for peaceful purposes. At other times, the Iranian leadership transformed nuclear discussions with the West into a political football whose leather always bore the imprint of the term "Iranian sovereignty." It was difficult for the nations of Europe to settle back into any sort of security comfort zone in that atmosphere.

Further, events further east continued to be very unsettling, even in the aftermath of the winding down of the Iraq War. De-escalation of violence in Iraq was accompanied by a sharp increase in terrorism in Afghanistan. NATO leaders and publics felt continued pressure to respond to American initiatives for some sort of Afghan parallel to the successful surge strategy of General Petreaus in Iraq. Requests for additional troops from the NATO partners were not just based on concerns about adequate contributions from them, but they were also rooted in the realization that Europe's psychological and emotional security depended as well on reduction of the power of the Taliban and al Qaeda immediately across the continent's eastern frontier. Intensification of the violence in Pakistan, especially in its Federally Administered Tribal Areas, compounded the worries and uncertainty in Europe. It was much more difficult for NATO to engage in forays into

Pakistan, and the alliance needed to depend on use of drones in combination with the willingness and ability of a weakened Pakistani government to have any effect at all.

A Renewed Focus on European Security

All of this turbulence drove home the need for new and effective plans that would ensure European security at the same time that it assured the people in the region. There was no luxury of time in the aftermath of the missile shield cancellation. Hesitation would be costly and the security of Europe would be thereby diminished.

Russia itself had proposed creation of a new framework for collective security in Europe in June 2008. One month later publication of the Foreign Policy Concept of Russia included similar references. Discussions would be aimed at a new Treaty on European (Collective) Security that would require signatures by all countries in the "Euro-Atlantic space." In effect, such a treaty would rule out the continuing need for NATO and the OSCE. In the Russian view, this proposal would be superior to preservation of the status quo, expansion of the scope of existing organizations on security questions, creation of a series of special treaties on concrete policy questions, or Russian admission to NATO. No one state or organization would have a monopoly on solving security questions, if the Russia option were adopted. An additional value of the treaty would be that it would be the first piece in creation of a new and more stable "Euro-Atlantic security architecture" (RIA NOVOSTI 2009). Russian President Dmitry Medvedev innovatively used a very broad definition of Europe as stretching from Vancouver to Vladivostok. Even former Soviet President Mikhail Gorbachev supported the new Russian concept in light of the "crisis of all the models used previously" (Lukyanov Interview with Mikhail Gorbachev 2009).

Initially, informal western reactions were critical of the Russian concept and continued to point in different directions. There was a concern that the Russian-proposed treaty did not pay enough attention to "soft power" challenges such as humanitarian problems, lack of human rights, and absence of democracy (RIA NOVOSTI 2009). Some alliance partners also pushed the Obama Administration toward goals that clearly conflicted with the Russian plan. For example, the Polish Foreign Minister Radoslav Sikorsky used a visit to Washington to call for the introduction of NATO military units on the territory of selected Central European nations (IZVESTIYA 2009m). American Secretary of Defense Robert Gates mentioned that discussions were taking place with Turkey about a new role for them in NATO's antimissile defense

(IZVESTIYA 2010d). There was also new discussion of locating components of the defense system on Romanian territory and discussion centered on location of up to 24 antimissile rockets (IZVESTIYA 2010e). Such comments continued to stir up Russian leaders. For example, Prime Minster Vladimir Putin commented that Russia might need to develop new offensive weapons, if the west did not give up on its hopes to establish some sort of successor to the cancelled missile shield program (SME 2009j).

Key western leaders also made official, formal comments that were quite critical of the Russian proposal. For instance, NATO Secretary-General Rasmussen described the Russian concept as unrealistic and bankrupt. From his point of view, the proposed treaty made it seem as if NATO was an enemy of Russia. In Rasmussen's view, all of this undermined the joint effort to build strategic partnership between the military alliance and Russia (IZVESTIYA 2010f). American Secretary of State Hillary Clinton also stated that the United States was not interested in the proposed new European security architecture. She expressed the belief that both NATO and the EU had brought a stability and progress to the European continent that had benefitted even Russia. In her view, European security was indivisible, and the OSCE and NATO-Russia Council were sufficient tools for eventually achieving it. Further, the United States was serious in its offer to work with Russia to develop a missile defense system that would include and cover all of Europe. The need to prevent Iran from developing a nuclear bomb should draw all parties together behind a common program (sueddeutsche 2010c).

On a more optimistic note, some voices in Russia defended their treaty by using the language of reciprocity that suggested the possibility of reciprocal understanding and progress in the future. Constantin Kosachev, chair of the Duma Committee for Foreign Affairs, spoke of a confluence of values between Russia and NATO that could be a foundation for future agreements. He averred that Russia was no longer pursuing ideological goals but simply new forms of reciprocity with the West. All such efforts were aimed at getting beyond the baggage from the Cold War (IZVESTIYA 2010g). The tone of these kinds of observations paralleled the attitudes of western leaders and offered hope for eventual agreements to buttress European security, both east and west.

Symbolically, Prague became the location for the signing of the nuclear arms agreement that was a successor for Strategic Arms Reduction Talks I (START I), a treaty that had been in effect from 1991 to late 2009. Both President Obama and President Medvedev came to the "Golden City" for this momentous event. In Prague, one year earlier, President Obama had pointed to the urgency of nuclear disarmament in a highly publicized speech.

It is possible that the scheduling of the event was also related to the cancellation of the Czech radar component of the Bush Administration's Missile Shield Program. There were some Czech leaders who still remembered that unexpected cancellation with some bitterness. For example, Senate Chair Přemysl Sobotka commented that the 2010 signing ceremony pleased him but that President Obama's earlier cancellation did not (iDNES 2010c). Veronika Kuchyňová Smiglová, an ambassador to the OSCE, both recalled that Obama's cancellation was not done in the best way and that the new treaty to be signed would not bring anything new (USATODAY 2010h). At the time of cancellation, there had been vague discussion about incorporating the Czech Republic in important future defense projects. If the 2010 ceremony was fulfillment of one of those promises, then the contributions of the new NATO partners was still central in building essential structures of European security, both East and West.

CHAPTER ELEVEN

The Coasts of NATO, North and South

Both the Baltic Sea and the Black Sea lap at the shores of the NATO alliance in the extreme North and the distant South. Actual NATO members located on the Baltic Sea include Denmark, Estonia, Germany, Latvia, Lithuania, and Poland. Non-NATO members include Finland, Russia, and Sweden. The fact that the Russian Republic of Kaliningrad is surrounded by NATO territory accentuates the tension in the region. Alliance-related issues that pertain to those nations often include Russian provocations, in particular toward the three former Republics in the Soviet Union. Deepening links among those three and the neighboring Scandinavian nations provide a supplement to NATO capabilities in responding to threats and intimidation. On the Black Sea there are three actual alliance partners, and they include Bulgaria, Romania, and Turkey. Ukraine and Georgia have been engaged in negotiations with NATO over possible future membership, and Russia keeps an ear cocked to the entire process.

Baltic Sea as the Northern Coast

Russian Concerns

Russia has stated an overall strategy for dealing in a positive way with the Baltic region as a whole. That strategy includes both a set of broad policy goals and a willingness to work with some of the organizations that operate in the region. One key policy intention entails promotion of the economic progress of the area. Further, Russian foreign policy goals stress the need for "sustainable development" that is sensitive to the multitude of social and economic factors in the individual countries. The Russian leadership also calls for development that is sensitive to the need to protect the environment as well as to the role of indigenous peoples. Russian assertions also include a willingness to work with the Northern Dimension, the Arctic Council, the Council of the Baltic Sea States, and the Nordic Council of Ministers (Ministry of Foreign Affairs of the Russian Federation 2008a). Russia itself is a member of the first three of those organizations but not of the last named one. It is easy to be skeptical of such noble policy goals, in light of the Soviet/Russian record on environmental values and on protection of minority rights. However, such a list of policy goals and organizations does give an overall purpose and direction to Russian decisions about the area.

Close proximity of the Baltic nations to Russian territory makes some of the region's issues very critical, and Russia has paid attention to a few of those. For example, Russia and Latvia had not ratified an agreement that made official the post-Soviet borders between the two countries for a full 15 years after the 1991 breakup of the state. However, on March 27, 2007, the Russian Prime Minister Michail Fradkov and his Latvian counterpart Aigars Kalvitis finally signed an agreement. A key concession by Latvia was the Pskov Oblast, a territory that had been part of Latvia prior to World War II (SME 2007f). The concession by Latvia was understandable in light of the temporary decision made by Transneft in February 2003, to shut off all oil supplies to Latvia (Europe 2003, 42). Perhaps an agreement would make future threats less likely. Similarly, Russia had a strong incentive to create some sort of viable framework for joint projects with Estonia. Since Estonia is only 160 km from St. Petersburg, Russia, pursuit of common political and economic interests was important (Politics 2004, 1).

At the same time, provocative acts took place that created tension between Russia and its immediate region. In the summer of 2007, Lithuania closed down its only remaining Russian TV news show. The Lithuanian leadership contended that the ratings of the program had fallen to 1 percent. However, the Russians countered that 16.6 percent of the Lithuanian population spoke Russian and would be poorly served by such a decision (IZVESTIYA 2007a). A few days later, the Russians dispatched two Tu-95 bombers over the North Sea in a show of force. They flew in an unusual pattern to an area between Norway and Scotland, and it is possible that the real target may have been British complaints about the murder of a former KGB agent (SME 2007g). Given the small area and close proximity of the various northern nations, this overflight cast a shadow over the rest as well. What were Russian intentions and tactics for the entire region?

Russian tensions with Estonia peaked in the spring of the same year. Estonian leaders decided to relocate a bronze statue of a Soviet soldier who had assisted in the liberation of the region during World War II. They transferred it from the center of Tallinn to a military cemetery outside of town. Russian leaders issued sharp complaints and threatened to cut exports of oil-based products, coal, and metal to Estonia by one half. Many of those products were slated for transit to additional nations of West Europe (iDNES 2007kk). In late summer, Russia warned about further dangerous influences in Estonia. They noted that a fascist group called "Erna" was holding exercises in the Estonian forests, with sponsorship from the Estonia Ministry of Defense. In their view, the fascists were recreating events from July 1941, a time when the Third Reich attacked Soviet troops (IZVESTIYA 2007b). In the fall, the Russian media sought to downplay another issue from the World War II era. In response to Estonian anger about the deportation and killing of many of its citizens by the Soviet Union in the 1940-53, period, the media spotlighted a recent book entitled "Myth of Genocide," written by a young Russian historian named Alexander Djukov (IZVESTIYA 2007c). Thus, the events of World War II made their way into Russian-Estonian relations on a number of fronts. Another event that engendered even further tensions was the discussion of Estonia about putting on trial four men who had sought to defend the bronze Soviet soldier (IZVESTIYA 2008).

An additional vexing issue from the Russian perspective was the fate of Kaliningrad, the Russian enclave separated from Russia by Lithuania and Belarus. Russia's regional governments have taken a great interest in border definition, and they have voiced concerns about the lines of division among the CIS, about the plight of the Russian minorities living in the Baltic nations, and also about Kaliningrad (Busygina 2007, 79). With Lithuania in the EU, the Schengen Regime of that organization applied to the new border with Russia. Russians who desired to go to Kaliningrad needed visas in order to transit Lithuania (White and Light 2007, 45-9). In addition, the fact that Kaliningrad was now surrounded by NATO both increased its sense of vulnerability and provoked Russia into proposed reconfiguration of its North-West Force (Averre 2007, 93). In February 2008, Russia revealed its ability to make use of Kaliningrad as a pawn during discussions about the American plan to build a radar station in the Czech Republic as well as antimissile interceptors in Poland. At that time, they threatened to respond by deploying missiles in the Baltic Sea region of Kaliningrad (USATODAY 2008h).

In 2002, Russia negotiated a promising Facilitated Transit Document (FTD) with the EU and Lithuania, and the agreement went into effect the following year (Averre 2007, 123-4). An accompanying Facilitated Railway Transit Document (FRTD) also went into effect. Together, the two agreements offered some hope of stable relations in the future. Russian citizens traveling to Kaliningrad would need both of these documents, but the EU agreed to finance them. After 2004, Russians would need to carry a passport as well. This new thrust was based on admission of both Lithuania and Poland to the EU in that year. Poles and citizens of Kaliningrad would also need visas when they moved back and forth, but there would be no cost for those visas (Michta 2007, 82-6).

It is difficult to overstate the significance of the Kaliningrad conflict in Baltic-Russian relations. Since the expansion of the EU in 2004, trade patterns of the enclave have dramatically shifted. Prior to 2004, a majority of Kaliningrad's trade was with the EU, but 40 percent was still with Russia. In the years after 2004, the percent of trade with Russia declined, while the proportion of trade with the EU shot up to 75 percent. There was some logic in attaching Kaliningrad to Lithuania itself, but the continuing Russian military presence in the enclave made that a difficult move. Russia clearly wants to maintain its bases there, as they provide key logistical support to its Baltic Fleet. Further, Baltiysk Base in Kaliningrad is Russia's best intelligence gathering station in the region. Russian leverage in the Baltic Sea and Gulf of Finland rely heavily on that base (Michta 2007, 78–82).

Overall, it is apparent that the optimistic goals that the Russian Ministry of Foreign Affairs presents do not square with the reality of continuing tension between Russia and the Baltic states. It is hard to anticipate much progress on the overall Russian strategy while both sides are provocative. Russia can always stir emotions with its demonstrations of military power in the area. Individual Baltic countries are very able to jangle Russian nerves and sensitivities both through policies directed at the Russian minorities within their borders and through manipulation of World War II symbols that still have meaning to Russian leaders. At the same time, Russian responses on both types of issues are powerful and often equally provocative.

Perspectives of the Baltic States

Certainly, a significant experience for the individual Baltic nations was the NATO admission process in the aftermath of the breakup of the Soviet Union. At the Prague Summit in 2002, NATO announced plans that would eventually include seven more nations, and the three Baltic countries all entered the alliance officially two years later. Similarly, in 2004, they also entered the EU, an organization that had announced creation of a European Security and Defense (ESDF) at its St. Malo meeting in December, 1998 (Michta 2007, 99–104). Thus, by the end of 2004, Estonia, Latvia, and Lithuania were all part of two organizations that had created an infrastructure for collective security.

Although small, the three Baltic nations do share perspectives about the priorities for NATO and the EU. For example, they have prodded the EU to upgrade the issue of Russia on its agenda. In fact, the Baltic nations have at times depicted Russia as the most important EU agenda item. Their perspectives are not the same as those of Germany, which has periodically been more interested in cultivating relations with Russia than in confronting it (Michta 2007, 28). The three have also been very interested in the role of the eastern neighbors of the EU. They have prompted the EU to place a high priority on the democratic reform process in Ukraine, Moldova, and Georgia (Newton 2007, 216–19). With respect to NATO, the Baltic nations have clearly turned away from the nonalignment option that was one possibility in the immediate aftermath of independence in 1991. With NATO assistance they have created their own military forces from the ground up (Michta 2007, 18–19). In these ways, they have sought to use their two new organizational memberships to increase the security and stability of their own neighborhood.

Of course, the Baltic nations are not a monolith or carbon copies of one another. Each one has somewhat different needs and views about security and stability. For instance, NATO decided to locate its air space patrol for the region in Lithuania. Lockheed-Martin sent some of its F-165s, and they were located in Lithuania to assist in the project (New NATO Nations 2004, 1). Lithuania's vulnerability became apparent the next year, as a Russian fighter crashed on its territory. That nation had been frustrated for some time by the tendency of Russian planes to fly very close to the Russian-Lithuanian border. As a result, a minor crisis occurred when Lithuania decided to hold the plane for awhile, instead of returning it to Russia (Europe 2005, 39). At the same time, the Lithuanian legislature began consideration of potential participation in the American anti-rocket system. Finally, in mid-2008, Lithuania provoked the Russians by banning the use of the hammer and sickle symbol throughout the nation. After Russian reactions broke out, Lithuanian politicians explained that the proposed law was directed at extremists rather than explicitly at communists (iDNES 2008w).

In spite of this tempest with Russia, in some ways Lithuania has the basis for building some common links with Russia. Its capacity in that regard may exceed the abilities of the other two. For instance, Lithuania has embraced radical market reforms more slowly than the other two. As a result, they have more large Soviet-style industries that were characteristic of the communist era past. Only one-twelfth of their population is ethnic Russian, and so the issue of treatment of the Russian minority is less divisive than it is for Latvia. Occasionally, Lithuania chooses not to goad Russia when the other two Baltic countries are provocative. For example, in 2005, Lithuania was the only Baltic country that sent representatives to celebrate the sixtieth anniversary of V-E Day in Moscow (Paulikas 2005, 27).

In some ways, Latvia has a more tempestuous relationship with Russia than Lithuania does, and this makes its security situation more unstable. World War II actions by the Soviet Union still grate on the Latvian memory as Latvia still clamors for an apology by Russia for the 1940 annexation of the country. They also demand reparations payments for the damage and deportations that took place at the same time. From the vantage point of Russia, equally aggravating is the policy of Latvia toward the Russian minority, a substantial 40 percent of the population. Russia resents the parades that former SS Latvians occasionally conduct. They also are angered by Latvian education and citizenship reforms. For example, Latvia has required that ethnic Russian teachers deliver their classes in the Latvian language. In addition, they have created tests in the Latvian language and history that are prerequisites for citizenship (O'Flynn 2005, 45). On the other hand, finally in late 2007, Latvia and Russia signed a treaty that clarified their border. American leaders commented positively on this treaty as a step toward more Baltic stability (State Department Issues 2007).

Estonian-Russian tensions create few grounds for optimism about future stability. In 2004, Estonia moved firmly into the NATO structure and contributed key capabilities. These included Special Forces units, demining squads, and nuclear/biological/chemical forces. NATO offered to provide air cover so that Estonia and the others would not need to purchase expensive fighter jets (New NATO Nations 2004, 1). The previously mentioned decision by Estonia to move the Soviet bronze soldier clearly did severe additional damage to any prospects for Estonian-Russia cooperation. The move of the statue was rooted in a law passed in February 2007. That bill prohibited monuments that might have celebrated the occupation of Estonia. Its legal justification was based on a law passed the previous month that sought to protect war graves from damage or deterioration. While Russians looked at the bronze soldier as a symbol of liberation from fascism, Estonians saw the statue as a reminder of Soviet repression (Boryk 2008, 1–4).

Russia responded with cyber-attacks against Estonia. This was particularly harmful to that nation, for Estonia had become quite advanced with conversion of voting and banking largely to online service systems (USATODAY, 2007h). In fact, the Minister of Defense of Estonia stated that Russia had become more dangerous through this crisis. Further, in the fall of 2007, he warned that the West in general underestimated the new higher level of the Russian threat (SME 2007h). In early 2008, the Estonian Prime Minister Andrus Ansip added another wrinkle to the danger. He noted that Russia had created obstacles to the work of the British Council in Estonia. This was a real problem, for that Council had been involved in teaching

English to members of both the Estonian and Russian ethnic groups. The overall effort of Estonia to cement itself in western institutions hinged in part on increased facility of its people in the English language (Estonia 2008). It is clear that the spiral of antagonistic statements and acts by the two nations had not yet died down or been resolved.

Thus, it is possible to glean both common themes and differences among the three Baltic partners. All have joined western alliances that can provide a modicum of security in light of the risks to them. However, a number of issues make the security situation of each different. With the highest proportion of Russian speakers, Latvia risks the most in terms of its Russian relationship when it creates reform legislation in that issue area. The single provocative act of relocating the bronze statue of the Russian soldier led to an unending round of hostile, accusatory actions by both Estonia and Russia. Perhaps Lithuania bore the most potential for creating a stable relationship with Russia. In spite of the overflight issue, Lithuania's economic situation and ethnic makeup may have provided the foundation for the most understanding between a Baltic nation and Russia.

Scandinavian Responses

Regional organizational patterns in NATO and the EU for the Scandinavian nations are more varied than they are for the three Baltic nations. Whereas all the Baltic nations now have several years of common membership experiences in both NATO and the EU, the historical membership patterns of the key Scandinavian countries present some differences. Finland and Sweden have not opted for membership in NATO, while Norway continues to keep its distance from the EU. However, all four have a common concern about Russian intentions and ambitions in the region. Thus, they have all provided assistance to help modernize the Baltic military forces (Michta 2007, 7–9). In addition, since early 2005, the Baltic nations have been members of the Scandinavian Investment Bank. This is unusual in two respects. It is the first time that the Bank has offered membership to nations outside of Scandinavia, and it is the first experience that the Baltic countries have had in being part of a Scandinavian organization. This admission enabled the Baltic nations to borrow money on better terms as well as to share in the Bank's profits. Common membership of all the Baltic countries and three of the Scandinavian nations in the EU has enabled this institutional activity to take place (Ministry of Foreign Affairs of Sweden 2008a). Such military and financial bridges between Scandinavia and the Baltic nations help anchor the latter in western institutions and also offer the promise of increased future stability.

It is also useful to look at the overtures made by the individual Scandinavian nations toward the Baltic partners, as there are some differences among the nations. Finland had closer relations with the Soviet Union during the Cold War than did the other Scandinavian nations. They are now keenly aware of the significance of energy imports from Russia and thus have made their own proposal to engage Russia on a variety of fronts. Under prodding from NATO, they also issued a Defense Reform Report in 2004. That report calls for upgrading their military equipment and spotlights Northern Europe as a very high priority area for NATO. In contrast, Norway is geographically more distant from Russia. Its geopolitical position leads its leaders to think in more Atlanticist terms. While NATO membership leads them to rate Russia as a major concern, their western location within Scandinavia suggests to them that the Baltic lands are less important. Denmark is different in that it has played a central role in NATO, and so for them its projects are of great importance. Denmark actually took part in the 1999 Kosovo operation, has helped create the NATO Response Force, and has supported the United States on the Iraq War. In overall planning toward the Baltic nations, each Scandinavian nation has taken on a special obligation in the area of defense reform. Finland has provided special assistance to Estonia, while Norway has focused on Latvia, and Denmark has developed special ties with Lithuania (Michta 2007, 52–68).

In its defense policy, Sweden has been evolving away from its historic pattern of neutrality in the early part of the twentieth century through World War II era "military nonalignment" to a post-Cold War strategy of "nonparticipation in military alliances." The last theme explains the Swedes' lack of interest in NATO membership. At the same time, the phrase does open the door to cooperative activity in selected international operations. For example, Swedes have participated in creation of the EU Rapid Reaction Force and have also contributed to various UN peacekeeping operations. In terms of the Baltic region, Sweden has provided assistance in creating new military forces, in building civil defense capabilities, in improving coast guard systems, and in border control (Michta 2007, 49–52). Specifically, Sweden has also pushed for development of an EU Baltic Sea strategy. Cornerstones of that strategy, from the Swedish perspective, include environmental protection and economic growth. Sweden also chaired a key EU committee on the Baltic nations in 2009, and so were responsible for development of an agenda (Ministry of Foreign Affairs of Sweden 2008b). Much of Sweden's work with the Baltic nations rests on Country Strategies that they developed with each in 2002.

Perspectives and goals included in that strategy parallel in several ways in Sweden's strategies for Central and East Europe (Ministry of Foreign Affairs of Sweden 2008c).

Part and parcel of the work of the Scandinavian countries with the Baltic nations is concern with the Russian factor. On the one hand, there has been some outreach by Russia toward the area to its immediate west. The northwestern Russian republics have signed transborder agreements with Norway, Finland, Lithuania, and also Poland. In particular, the Karelian Republic has established agreements with Finland in order to smooth out border ambiguities and also to increase contacts in the areas of culture and tourism. Those republics have also taken part in some of the regional organizations that have been created to serve the needs of the area as a whole (Busygina 2007, 82–6). In addition, some of the Scandinavian nations have reached out to Russia in hopes of increasing stability in the Baltic Sea area. Sweden has established solid contacts with Russia at the local, regional, and national levels. Strikingly, trade between the two nations doubled between 2005 and 2008. As a member of the EU, Sweden has taken steps to improve relations between that organization and Russia. While both the EU and Sweden support Russia's aspiration to join the World Trade Organization (WTO), they have been careful to include in the dialogue contentious issues such as Chechnya, human rights, and individual freedoms (Ministry of Foreign Affairs of Sweden 2008d).

All is not tranquil, however, in the three-part formula of Russia, the Baltic nations, and Scandinavia. In July, 2007, Norway became quite aroused by two separate incidents involving flights by Russian bombers. First, two Russian Tu-95 bombers flew south along the Norwegian coast in international airspace. Second, a few days later, two Tu-160 bombers flew near Norwegian air space over the Barents Sea. These Russian bomber flights penetrated further south along the coast than normal and may have been related to the clash between Russia and the United Kingdom over the Litvinenko killing in Britain and Russia's refusal to turn over the main suspect to London (USATODAY 2007i). Lingering concerns about Russian intentions continued into the fall. Norwegian Minister of Defense Sverre Diesen worried publicly that Norway could not count on much help from NATO if a real crisis that involved Russia took place. He reasoned that the military alliance's preoccupation with the war on terrorism in locations such as Afghanistan sapped its capabilities as well as its ability to put the spotlight on threats in other parts of the world such as the Baltic region (DN 2007d).

In 2008, both Sweden and Finland were angered by Russian reactions to Estonia's relocation of the bronze Soviet soldier. Russia's cyber attacks on

Estonia were nettlesome, but so was the blockade of Estonia's embassy in Moscow. One incident in the blockade was an attack on the Swedish ambassador's automobile, and thereby Swedish interests were engaged. Sweden was also concerned about expansion of the Russian fleet in the Baltic Sea. As Russia made plans to build a gas pipeline to Germany across the Baltic seabed, it would seem obvious that Russia would increase its military presence in order to protect the new pipeline. Finland's proximity to Russia made their complaints less vigorous (Europe 2007, 50). Obviously, Russia casts a military shadow over its immediate northwest. Military movements in that region counter some of the work done by the Scandinavian nations to build bridges to Russia.

In sum, Scandinavian nations have become quite involved in the process of rebuilding both the military and economic capabilities of the three Baltic nations. In the process, they have created goodwill and nurtured both stability and a presence that can prevent the emergence of a dangerous vacuum in the area. In addition, the individual Scandinavian nations have looked further east toward Russia. They have intended both to ease some of Russia's anxieties and to nurture its relationship with the EU. Expanded trade with Russia can provide all concerned with a stake in the stability of the area. At the same time, Russian military moves and overreactions have heightened anxieties within the Baltic countries and also in Scandinavia. Bomber overflights and cyber attacks have made the target countries wary again of Russian intentions. They have also created setbacks to Russian interests in the stability of the Baltic Sea area.

Organizational Links

Of course, NATO and the EU are vital organizations that include the three Baltic nations and some of the Scandinavian countries. Each organization interacts frequently with Russia, sometimes in a cooperative framework and at other times in a tension-filled one. In addition, at least seven other organizations have sprung up to deal with pieces of the Baltic puzzle, and they supplement the work of the security goals of NATO. A number of them do not include Russia, and those organizations are the Nordic Council of Ministers, BALTNET, and BALTBAT. Others do include Russia, and those are the Council of Baltic Sea States, the Barents Euro-Arctic Council (BEAC), the Arctic Council, and the Northern Dimension. Each of these nine organizations has unique features and can potentially contribute to stability and continuing dialogue among the various national actors.

Organizations that do not Include Russia

The Nordic Council of Ministers includes the Prime Ministers of the individual Scandinavian nations. They have met on a regular basis since the organization's founding in 1971. The Chair position rotates among the five key nations. Members include Denmark, Finland, Iceland, Norway, and Sweden. In addition, the Åland Islands, Faroe Islands, and Greenland are technically members as well but do not share in the leadership responsibility (NORDEN 2008).

BALTNET is the acronym for the Baltic Air Surveillance Network. The member nations created this organization in 2000, and it works closely with NATO. The organization coordinates the radar-based surveillance of the various partners and also pools information that is acquired. The individual countries share air pictures with each other and with NATO leadership. The center is in Lithuania, and the United States has provided much of the funding. U.S.-based Lockheed-Martin originally installed a number of the surveillance centers. One advantage of this structure is that NATO standards become the common pattern for each of the Scandinavian and Baltic countries that take part in it. For example, Norway has assisted in setting up communication links. Estonia envisions BALTNET as a tool for developing its own Air Force. With BALTNET Estonia expects to achieve full control of its airspace in a shorter time (MIL 2008).

BALTBAT is an organization whose full title is Baltic Battalion, and its home base is Latvia (Michta 2007, 90). It was originally created as a peacekeeping unit in 1994. In April, 1999, the members signed a document entitled Political Guidance in an effort to raise the defense capabilities of the Baltic nations. The plan was to create infrastructure that would inevitably smooth the path of entry into NATO in the near future. Eventually, the battalion might be upgraded to a brigade (Kazocins 1999, 47–54). It's mission has undergone changes throughout its brief history. During Phase I, from 1994 to 1997, the emphasis was on provision of weapons for self-defense only. The militaries in the three Baltic nations received training and then held exercises. However, finances were limited, and thus Phase II was established in 1997. The individual militaries trained as a light infantry battalion that could provide support to peacekeeping operations. In theory, the BALTBAT Training Team was supposed to inject British tactics and doctrine into the exercises. However, the commanders were from the individual Baltic nations and preferred to follow their own patterns rather than the British model. A portion of the battalion joined the Danish contingent in Bosnia after 1998, but there continued to be an abiding need for more multilateral coordination (Møller 2000, 38–42).

Organizations that do Include Russia

The Council of the Baltic Sea States is an extensive organization that operates at national, regional, and local levels. The founders set it up in Copenhagen on March 5, 1992. This organization now includes the three Baltic nations, Denmark, Finland, Norway, Sweden, Germany, Poland, Russia, and a representative from the European Commission. For the last 10 years, the Permanent Secretariat has been located in Stockholm, Sweden. Policy concerns of the organization radiate in many directions. The Council is interested in lowering barriers to trade and investment. In addition, they focus on improved nuclear safety, on promotion of human rights and democracy, and on stimulating cross-border cooperation.

The Council also has a great interest in transformation of postsecondary education according to the Bologna Process. In the latter regard, they have been involved in curriculum and teaching reform at three universities in the individual Baltic nations (cbss 2008a). They also have had an impact on Kaliningrad, in particular through their focus on Immanuel Kant State University of Russia. Specifically, the Council's representatives helped revise that university's curriculum of Economics and Law Studies. Their assistance also led to creation of new Bachelor and Masters' Degrees in Economics. Under their tutelage, the university injected more student participation in classes and upgraded library/information technology capabilities. They made it possible for 100 instructors from Immanuel Kant to visit partner universities in foreign countries, and in turn 35 foreign lecturers came to Kaliningrad to offer classes. Student exchanges were also part of the plan, and a full 120 economics and law students attended partner institutions in foreign countries (cbss 2008b). Thus, the Council was involved in very concrete programs that would bring educational patterns in the northern region in tune with broader trends within the rest of the EU.

Security issues were also part of the work of this key organization. For instance, in terms of organizational structure, the Council plans the meetings of the member states' Ministers of Foreign Affairs. Each year the chair position rotates from country to country, and they publish a journal entitled *Baltinfo* twice per month. In 2006, the Council decided to grant observer status to France, Italy, Netherlands, Slovakia, Ukraine, the United Kingdom, and the United States. They also have engaged in joint work during the last few years with a number of Strategic Partners. Those Partners include the Baltic Development Forum, the Baltic Sea Chamber of Commerce Association, the Baltic Sea Forum, the Baltic Sea NGO Forum, the Baltic Sea Trade Union Network, the Helsinki Commission, and the Scan Belt (cbss 2008c). Thus, they have taken organizational steps to ensure as wide a discussion as possible, and thereby the security net becomes wider.

An additional priority of the Council is the nurturing of public administration and democracy at the local and regional levels (Ministry of Foreign Affairs of Sweden 2008e). For example, in 1993, the Council founded the Baltic Sea States Sub-Regional Co-operation organization in Stavanger, Norway. All Baltic Sea states are participants, and the main thrust is the economic development of subregions within the individual nations. In 2006–08, their key priorities included transportation, maritime policy, sustainable development, energy production/efficiency, quality of life, public health, and civil security. The Board that governs the organization includes two persons from each of the countries, and there is also a Chair and Secretariat.

Further, the Council has sponsored creation of a Union of the Baltic Cities. There are a full 103 cities that are part of this Union. Organizationally, they include a President, three Vice Presidents, a Secretariat, an Executive Board, and a General Conference that meets every other year. In addition to the policy concerns noted above for the Sub-Regional organization, the Union also places an emphasis on gender equality, the information society, sport, tourism, urban planning, and youth issues (Ministry of Foreign Affairs of Sweden 2008f). With such a significant array of issue concerns, the sweep of the Council's activities penetrates deeply into local communities. As urban connections strengthen and work on concrete projects multiplies, one possible result may somewhat lessen overall tension between the northwestern part of Russia and the small nations further west.

The BEAC is an additional piece of machinery available to assist with Baltic matters. Its founders set up the organization in 1993, and they included the five Scandinavian countries, Russia, and the European Commission. In fact, Russia served as the Chair in the 2007–09. In 2007, they set up an International Barents Secretariat with headquarters in Rovaniemi, Finland. The Secretariat provides technical support on behalf of this intergovernmental organization (beac 2008).

Additionally, an Arctic Council that is much broader in membership also exists. Its membership includes the five Scandinavian nations, Greenland, the Faroe Islands, Russia, and the United States. Inclusion of both the United States and Russia brings superpower considerations to the table, and its discussions, of course, center on purely Arctic Sea matters. Under the leadership of its Chair, Norway, the Arctic Council declared 2007–08 to be the International Polar Year (arctic-council 2008). While the Baltic nations were not formally part of this organization, they clearly had a stake in many of its discussions.

A final organization is the EU-sponsored Northern Dimension. The EU established this program in 1998, and in part its original intention was to defuse some of its tension with Russia over EU expansion matters (White and Light 2007, 49–50). Members include Iceland, Norway, Russia, and the entire EU. Since the whole EU is involved, the three Baltic nations, Sweden, Denmark, and Finland are members as well. Their policy thrusts include, among others, the situation of indigenous peoples, public health, external security, research, education, and culture (ec 2008). In addition, the Northern Dimension developed an e-dimension Action Plan (NeDAP), and the EU Commission funded it to the tune of twelve million euros. Both Baltic and Scandinavian countries can entertain the possibility of chairing this Northern Dimension. For instance, Sweden was the Chair from 2003 to 2005, and Lithuania then took over for the period 2005–07 (Ministry of Foreign Affairs of Sweden 2008g).

In sum, a full nine organizations are currently working to provide a framework of stability and security in Northern Europe. Each one is unique, and together they create a rich and interesting tapestry. They collectively contain a capability of dealing with a range of pressing and complicated defense and nondefense issues. Some of these organizations are partly designed to protect against Russian ambitions, while others include Russia in a very central way in the dialogue. Most of them are products of the post-Cold War period, and as such they offer promise of heightened security in an era when so many of the world's resources focus on the global war on terrorism in other places.

Implications for Collective Security

The thaw that ended the Cold War freed the three Baltic nations from the ice block of the Soviet Union and left them as ice floes in the region. Certainly, one conclusion of this chapter is that those floes have many possibilities for new connections. Each of the Scandinavian nations has reached out to them in helpful ways. At least nine organizations exist to provide meaningful partnerships into the future. Even Russia, with its occasionally provocative moves, could be a potential ally on certain kinds of issues. The Baltic nations do have a range of choices that could further their own development and potential. As they firm up ties with new allies and organizations, perhaps they build escape routes from the fate of being frozen into one bloc or of floating aimlessly in the Baltic Sea. They develop the capabilities to follow a third option that enables them more fully to plot their own course.

Russia's ability to help build more stability in the Baltic region has not yet come to fruition. Russian leaders have undercut their positive overtures to the region with very destabilizing actions and reactions. Understandably, they have a concern and interest in the fate of Kaliningrad, a piece of their territory that is now lodged to the west of the Baltic nations. However, their anxiousness to hang on to base rights in that enclave creates genuine fear among the smaller nations in the neighborhood. While it was Estonia that removed the bronze Soviet soldier from Tallinn, Russia did blow the issue out of proportion and angered the Swedes as well as the Estonians. Russian concerns about the plight of the ethnic Russian minorities, especially in Latvia, are legitimate ones. However, there is a case to be made that the ethnic Russians in those Baltic states should become proficient in the languages of their new countries, if they expect to progress in the education and economic arenas. Perhaps a good starting point for improved relations in the future would be confidence building measures adopted by the subregional and urban components of the Council of Baltic Sea States. City-to-city partnerships and region-to-region connections can bring Russia and the Baltic states into contact on concrete local problems and can perhaps avoid the higher level security conflicts at the national levels.

Collectively, the three Baltic nations have discovered new levels of security through their membership in NATO and the EU. At the same time, their membership in those organizations increased the wariness of Russia. Expansion of NATO to the Russian door step was the greatest challenge posed by the two new organizational links in the region. However, the expanded EU also raised new questions about its new neighborhood further east. The Baltic nations collectively were very interested in integrating some of the neighborhood countries like Ukraine into the EU framework, and that perspective clearly bothered Russia. In another sense, the security of each Baltic player rested on its own unique circumstances. Estonia is still dealing with the echo of the crisis over its relocation of the bronze Soviet soldier. Latvia is still evolving its policies toward the large Russian minority within. Lithuania is most centrally involved in the tensions over Kaliningrad and the accompanying matter of transit rights. Given the small size of the three Baltic nations, it is likely that they can best resolve these controversies by accepting the multifaceted offers of assistance from neighboring countries and regional organizations. For NATO, the concerns in this region center on intimidation and perhaps psychological terrorism. While the threats are not of the same level as they are further south, they still draw the attention of the alliance and force it to generate additional measures and possible solutions.

Black Sea as the Southern Coast

On a morning in late May, the Black Sea is a jewel with a riveting color of deep blue that is framed by the softer blue of the sky and the gentle green of nearby hills and fields. The entire panorama conjures up images of harmony between nature and surrounding communities. However, a central question is whether political and security realities beneath the surface also reflect the symmetry of images that meets the eye. Among the six nations that border the Black Sea are a host of critical issues and simmering conflicts. Russian activities in the area provoke concern on several fronts. The cutoff of natural gas to Ukraine impacted not only that nation but also Bulgaria and Romania. The war between Russia and Georgia reverberated into a number of nations in the area. Admission of Bulgaria and Romania to the EU offered a western link that also appealed to Georgia and Ukraine. Turkey's concerns about tension flowing from its southern neighbors inevitably influence their conversations with other Baltic Sea partners. Further, a mix of ethnic and religious tensions within several of the littoral states bore the potential to undercut efforts to build regional stability. Contenders for the top of this list included Russian-Ukrainian dynamics within Ukraine, the history of animosity between Russian and Chechnya, and Georgia's two decades of conflict with Abkhazia and South Ossetia. While these dilemmas are not congruent with the symphony of visual beauty, there is still hope for shaping a community of nations that shares interests and values. Continued growth of an enriched community could also have the spillover benefit of bringing more collective security weight to bear on resolution of some of the conflicts between the Black Sea Six and their neighbors further away.

What sort of role does and can the NATO play in this region and process? NATO's concerns, of course, center primarily on matters of military strategy and security. The center of gravity of the military alliance is far to the west of the Black Sea. Further, political forces within the nations bordering the Black Sea are not particularly interested in inviting NATO to be a permanent guest at the table. At the same time, a western alliance cobbled together in the early Cold War years to defend Western Europe from further extension of Soviet influence possesses interests in the region. The concerns of Turkey, Bulgaria, and Romania enter the NATO dialogue due to their membership in the organization. Use of the Russian navy based in Sevastopol of Ukraine in the 2008 conflict with Georgia certainly caught the attention of alliance strategists. An extended period of stalemate in the Ukrainian government created the fear of a vacuum in this large country that also borders Belarus and Russia itself. The original applications of both Georgia and Ukraine for

NATO membership sealed the engagement of a sixty-year old alliance in this vibrant area. The eyes of both the military alliance and the Black Sea Six focus on each other, as gestures and overtures begin to forge links that may or may not include alliance membership.

The continuing battle against terrorism constitutes a significant part of the framework through which NATO looks at the region. Inclusion of Bulgaria and Romania into the military alliance in 2004 occurred partly because of their key geopolitical position and potential to act as buffers against extremism located further east. Concern about the situation of the long-standing Turkish partner has much to do with its soft southern border, a line that separates the nation from Syria, Iran, Iraq, as well as the Iraqi Kurds. Issues connected with terrorism continually flow from Iraq and Iran, in particular. While the Russia-Georgia conflict of August 2008 did not involve the battle against terrorism per se, the threat loomed in the background. Chechnya is nearby, and Russia had fought two wars in the last 15 years against the terrorism circulating within and from that Republic. In addition, in the early period after the 9/11 attack, the United States had actually sent a few military personnel to Georgia in light of fears that terrorists could find sanctuary there. Therefore, NATO's interests in the Black Sea Region were doubly rooted in overall matters of military strategy but also in the region's critical location in the ongoing struggle with terrorist extremists.

Systems Approach to the Black Sea Region

The systems approach developed by Easton and used with current applicability by writers such as Stillman offers an opportunity to develop a clear picture of interrelationships both within the region and between the region and NATO. An established theoretical framework is necessary, as this region is potentially more complicated and multidimensional than any others treated in this book. Easton depicted any political system as located within an environment but separated from it by a boundary. Events and developments within the environment are not technically part of the embedded political system, but some of them have the potential to cross the boundary and become stimuli within the system that was under the microscope. When factors cross that boundary, they then became external pressures with demands and supports on the system. As political issues emerge within the system, often those external pressures flowing in from the environment play significant roles as internal pressures that actually become part of the system itself, at least temporarily. Elected leaders and appointed managers within the system factor these demands and supports into the decision-making process itself. The resulting decision thus is partly a function of the chain reaction of environmental forces, external political pressures, and internal stimuli. As decisions emerge, they then constitute the outputs of the system and exist as formal policies. Finally, it is clear that policies are never final in a democracy. A feedback loop circulates them back into the environment of the system, and they have the power to ignite chain reactions that lead to policy adjustments or innovations (Wasby 1970, 108–13). It is critical that this interrelated set of variables stays in balance or remains at equilibrium. Like an airplane, a political system risks genuine disruption if one or more factors that impinge upon it become too powerful or too demanding.

Stillman (2004) has utilized this model in recent years in an effort to organize some of the vast literature on public administration. Similarly, systems theory has the potential to help clarify patterns and prospects in other areas such as the Black Sea Region. For purposes of this paper, the outside environment will include the general context of the end of the Cold War in the last 20 years, the emergence of an expanded EU, and the new role of a larger NATO. The definition of external pressures will center exclusively on the nations that border the Black Sea Six. In particular, attention will focus on those border nations that have deep problems or a history of tension with the Black Sea nation. Internal pressures will selectively entail NATO-related issues. Three Black Sea nations are members of the military alliance, while two others had actually sought membership for several years. With the sixth, Russia, NATO has had continuing tension on a host of issues in recent years. Outputs and policies will constitute the heart of the analysis. Analysis will focus on decisions that pertain to the relationship within the Black Sea Community itself, to the regional organizations that exist or could potentially exist within the area, and to the potential for a strengthened Black Sea community to assist the six in resolving some of the issues with their border states. Within the framework of the feedback loop, implications of policies that deal with these questions on the future stability of the Black Sea community will receive brief attention.

Outside Environment

The Black Sea region has been profoundly affected by the end of the Cold War. During the four decades of Cold War, three of the nations were republics in the Soviet Union. Russia was, of course, the principal player, but both Ukraine and Georgia contributed key leaders to the Politburo and to other Soviet leadership positions. Two of the nations were Soviet-bloc communist states with very different postures toward Moscow. Bulgaria was certainly one of the most reliable of the satellite states to the west of the USSR. In contrast, Romania was a principal challenger to Soviet leadership in the foreign policy area. Romania did not take part in the Warsaw Pact invasion of Czechoslovakia in 1968, received a visit from the American President Gerald Ford, sought to be an intermediary on Middle East issues, and flirted occasionally with China. Finally, Turkey has been a member of NATO itself from the earliest days and was a key linchpin in the military and security barrier against unpredictable events emanating from southeastern Europe.

In 1989 and 1991, that longstanding Cold War model exploded. With the implosion of the Soviet Union, three former republics emerged as nations with borders on the Black Sea. Anti-Russian nationalism had played a role in the Ukrainian and Georgian desires to break away, and those attitudes continued to burn for the next two decades. Bulgaria and Romania both took part in the anticommunist revolutions of 1989. However, the changes came much slower to those countries, and former communist personalities remained on the scene in differently named positions (Derleth 2000, 141–3). Turkey now was no longer the odd man out in the Black Sea region but soon confronted new challenges from a different brand of extremism circulating in nations to their south and east.

Inevitably, the lure of membership in western institutions became a magnetic force within the region. During the Clinton Administration of the 1990s, NATO's PfP Plan impacted the Black Sea Region as it did other pieces of the former communist empire. During the late 1990s the path to full NATO membership for these nations opened up, primarily due to their proximity to the troubled Balkan Wars. In 1999, it was clearly too early for the alliance to include formally any nations from the Black Sea area. However, in 2004, both Bulgaria and Romania entered NATO (Mahncke 2004, 60–7). Inclusion of them truly added a strengthened Black Sea dimension to the alliance. Subsequent addition of Croatia and Albania in 2009 even more deepened the presence of the military alliance in the area adjoining the Black Sea.

A similar pattern of eastward expansion characterized the EU in the first decade and one half after the end of the Cold War. In this process, the EU administrators in Brussels set up a checklist of 33 chapters that potential new members had to complete before they received consideration for full membership. After years of interactions between the interested nations and the EU bureaucracy, ten nations joined in 2004. They included again the three former Baltic Republics of the Soviet Union, the Czech Republic, Hungary, Poland, Slovakia, Slovenia, Cyprus, and Malta (Raik 2007, 209–16). By 2007, the EU was willing to follow NATO's example and offer membership to

Bulgaria and Romania. As a result, two Black Sea nations were members of that organization as well and could engage in its ESDP. In sum, the NATO expansion process added two Black Sea members besides Turkey, and EU expansion brought in the same two nations from that critical area of the world.

All of these activities made up the environmental configuration within which the Black Sea community carried on its activities and made its policy decisions. Clearly, all the above-noted sets of factors transcended the boundary that separated the Black Sea Six from Europe and the United States. While the collapse of communism did directly involve five of the six countries, the stimulus for that tremendous change in world politics lay much further to the north. NATO expansion circulated outwards from the United States with its security concerns, and thus that could be considered a transatlantic phenomenon. EU enlargement flowed from decisions made in Brussels, mainly by the nations of Western Europe. By 2004, definitely a watershed year, all three of these sets of pressures had entered the world of the Black Sea and begun to have a fire cracker effect on external pressures, internal dynamics, and political decisions themselves.

External Pressures from Border States on the Black Sea Six

While the collapse of communism, NATO enlargement, and EU expansion all generated pressures on the Black Sea region, for purposes of this portion of the study, the concrete focus here is the set of additional border pressures that impinge on each of the six countries under the microscope. Each nation faces not only the Black Sea and the countries on its border but also a series of problematic and challenging nations in its backyard, away from the Black Sea area.

Bulgaria shares a border with two such challenging states, and they include Serbia and Turkey. There has not been a history of strong antagonism between Bulgaria and Serbia, but the Balkan Wars of the 1990s took place very close to Bulgarian space. Bulgaria's need for an anchor became more pressing, as the Serbian leaders fought first against Croatia, then in a long war within Bosnia, and finally in Kosovo at the end of the century. In fact, Kosovo is geographically quite close to the Serbian border with Bulgaria. In contrast, the fact that Turkey shares a border with Bulgaria has meant even more pressing concerns along the dividing line between the two countries. Even during late communist times, Bulgaria's treatment of its Turkish minority created consternation in Turkey itself. Changing of place names in the Turkish neighborhoods rankled in both southern Bulgaria and in northern Turkey (Bell 1993, 96–8). The situation of Bulgaria was one in which external pressures flowed into the leadership's decision-making process from the constant wars in one adjoining nation and from the presence of an important minority that was ethnically linked to another country.

The Romanian border also has the potential to be a troubled one. Like Bulgaria, the Romanians are neighbors of Serbia, but they share a border with the northern part of that country. Romania is closer to Belgrade and not that far away from Bosnia, and so its proximity to the worst of the Balkan wars was greater than that of any other Black Sea state. Further, Moldova is a border nation with a unique history in relation to Romania. Historically, Moldova had shared space as Bessarabia with Romania but had ended up as a Republic in the Soviet Union after World War II. Initially, after the anti-communist revolution, there was speculation about the prospects for the two units merging (Ratesh 1991, 113–15). As a result, Romania's leaders keep a close eye on Moldovan policies, especially in light of the strong role played by the communist party in the latter. Election results in Moldova in 2009, and the protests against the outcome, were nettlesome for Romania to a greater extent than they were for other border nations.

With its enormous size, Ukraine's border bears the potential to keep a number of conflicts bubbling. To the north is located Belarus, a country which in the past has had much in common with Ukraine. However, Belarus and its leader President Lukashenko have become isolated and somewhat of a maverick in regional decision making. While no civil war or war of aggression has taken place, it constitutes a problematic state in the same category as Serbia. Ukraine also shares a very long border with Russia, and the two have battled over numerous contentious issues. The large Russian minority in eastern Ukraine and the Russian majority in Crimea are levers by which Russia seeks to manipulate developments within Ukraine (Balmaceda 2000, 231–5). Russian threats of a shutoff or reduction of natural gas supplies obviously destabilize the Ukrainian economy (Baev 2008, 122–8). In addition, the Russian naval presence at Sevastopol, the Russian invasion of Georgia in August 2008, and the residue of the Orange Revolution have kept the pot boiling.

Russia itself shares a vast border along which many potential problems exist. Belarus and Russia have negotiated and come to a handful of agreements, and yet Belarus is not the type of ally that does the giant to the east much good. As noted above, both Estonia and Latvia have both been in conflict with Russia in recent years. In 2007, Estonian leaders removed from Tallinn the bronze statue commemorating the World War II contributions of the Red Army. Latvian language and education restrictions on the sizeable

Russian minority have provoked outcries in Moscow. Lithuania does not share a border with Russia proper, but it lies to the east of the exclave of Kaliningrad. As such, tough issues of transit rights for Russian citizens across Lithuania have begged for attention and received it. Poland also shares a border with Kaliningrad, and its historic anti-Russianism bears the potential for border conflict. In effect, Kaliningrad is an island in the middle of an EU and NATO sea, and that enhances both its own sense of isolation and Russian's protectiveness (Michta 2006, 75–82). Ukraine is another troublesome border state, and Russian political figures and media sources are continually fond of pointing out the trouble and paralysis in that nation. Election of Viktor Yanukovych in early 2010 bore the potential to change those dynamics somewhat. Finally, the presence of North Korea on the eastern border parallels the position of Belarus to the West. North Korean leaders have made their nation into more of a pariah state internationally than have leaders in Belarus with regard to theirs. Russia is part of the six-nation group that seeks to inject stability into the situation, but nuclear saber rattling by Kim Jong Il provides no benefit to Russia's eastern policy.

For Georgia, Russia is the principal border opponent. Negative statements by Russian political and media sources are very similar to the kinds of statements made by Russia about politics in Ukraine prior to 2010 (Raik 2007, 220–2). Further, Russia's protectiveness about Abkhazia and South Ossetia is very similar to its attitudes about Kaliningrad. The difference is that the Georgian government provoked the hostilities to a new level in the summer of 2008. The strong Russian response and invasion compounded the animosity of Georgia toward Russia and caught the attention of NATO and the EU.

The list of problematic states on the Turkish border is a bit shorter than the Russian list, but potential conflicts may be even greater. Armenia and Turkey are working seriously toward a more stable relationship, but memories of the 1915 mass murders continue to provoke tension and protest marches. Tensions with Bulgaria over its treatment of the Turkish minority have abated somewhat, but memories still linger. With Greece, Turkey has had a long history of conflict, in particular centering on the island of Cyprus. It is often within the NATO setting that Greek-Turkish tensions emerge most fully. Countries to Turkey's south present a very different kind of problem. Iraq has been the scene of dictatorship and war for at least three decades. Importantly, the Kurd minority directly across the border acts as an irritant on many occasions and has led to considerable loss of life (Pelletière 2007, 94). Iran in the same 30 years has been a difficult nation for much of the rest of the world, no less Turkey. The secular Turkish regime has little in common with the Sharia based legal system in Iran, and the rise of conservative Islamic political extremists in Turkey has created more instability in the politics of that nation. Syria is certainly not in the category of Iran or Iraq, but suspicion of its links to Palestinian extremists or violent Sunni groups in Iraq raise further concerns within Turkey about its own neighborhood.

Thus, each of the six Black Sea nations possesses a number of difficult nations across its own more distant borders. If the Black Sea is the front door or front porch of the littoral nations, then these troubled nations are located out the back door or on the back porch of the region. Problems posed by those backyard nations include past conflicts with the Black Sea Six as well as a history of ethnic tensions and wars within them. From the vantage point of systems analysis, this wide array of external pressures was partly a product of the end of the Cold War, an environmental factor. Pressures that had been subordinated to superpower politics exploded. In addition, the expansiveness of NATO, and to a lesser extent that of the EU, constitute additional factors from the environment that passed across the imaginary boundary of systems theory and clearly jolted the external relationships between the Black Sea Six and some of their back porch neighbors.

Internal Pressures within the Black Sea Six

Among the Black Sea nations themselves, there is a whole array of internal problems and pressures. Those that will receive attention here are the ones that fit into the emerging picture of a systems analysis and pertain to security matters. In other words, the environmental factor of NATO resonates through many external factors and has become an internal issue within the Black Sea Community. To a lesser extent, the same has occurred with the EU.

Both NATO and the EU tug on their member nations in the Black Sea region. Bulgaria and Romania are members of both organizations, while Turkey is in NATO and has great interest in joining the EU. NATO obligations in particular loom large in the foreign policy considerations of all three states. The United States pressured Turkey to permit access to Iraq through its territory in 2003. Turkey ended up saying no to that petition, but still they cooperated with the American-led operation in other capacities. Admission of Bulgaria and Romania to the military alliance was partly conditioned on their potential to contribute as buffer states to the war on terrorism. Landing rights for the invading forces, communications, holding of prisoners, and maybe future bases would all have grown out of their recent membership in NATO. Work toward EU criteria had forced both states to strengthen their efforts to treat minorities fairly, move quickly toward capitalism, and confront corruption in the public sector. The tug from western-based organizations gradually became an internal variable within the Black Sea region.

In contrast, it is Ukraine and Georgia that have tugged at times on both western organizations. In particular, both were expectant about the 2008 Bucharest meeting of NATO. However, the military alliance turned them down at that point, with advice about inclusion at a later date. The invasion by Russia of Georgia a few months later led to second guessing about the earlier negative decision. Both countries are divided about the desirability of joining NATO. There are those who see it as a way to become more fully part of the west, but there are other political forces that worry about Russian responses. In addition, full membership would mean, at the least, more pressure to upgrade their role in Afghanistan. That upgraded role could come in the form of increased troops, a greater willingness to work in combat areas, or both.

Russia has been engaged in a tug of war with NATO and is not seeking membership in either the EU or NATO (McGuigan 2007, 158–63). However, the nation does have a special link through the Russia-NATO Council, and after its suspension in August 2008, it has now been reactivated. The tug of war includes issues such as Russian defensiveness about the eastward march of NATO to its border, anger over NATO perceptions of the war with Georgia in 2008, and concern about the plight of Russian minorities in Latvia, Ukraine, Moldova, and Georgia. Kaliningrad is in a different situation, but its plight does not contribute to a stable situation.

These three briefly outlined internal factors generate a decisional and policy agenda that constitutes the next step in systems analysis. How can all of these factors lead to the building of a rational set of policy objectives that could meet the needs of the Black Sea Six? Also, to what extent does and should NATO assist in shaping those policy initiatives?

Outputs and Policies: Rank-Ordering Priorities

Knitting Together the three NATO and three non-NATO Nations

The highest priority in terms of policy-making is knitting together the three NATO and three non-NATO nations within the region. It is on this type of issue that the military alliance can make a contribution, even if it chooses not to offer full membership status for some time. NATO-sponsored events and speeches can enable collaboration that might not otherwise take place.

For example, as early as 2001, Georgia hosted a military exercise that included eight full NATO members and some who were PfP. The latter consisted of the four Black Sea nations of Ukraine, Bulgaria, Romania, and

Georgia. Azerbaijan and Sweden also contributed to the operation. The exercise itself took place on the Black Sea and had the objective of developing "naval and amphibious interoperability" between NATO and PfP countries (Thompson 2004, 110). The Georgia–Russia War of August 2008 also drew the attention of the western military alliance. NATO welcomed the eventual agreement that was signed between the two but also tasked the North Atlantic Council "to develop with Georgia rapidly the modalities for a NATO-Georgia Commission." At the same time, they said that it was no longer possible to continue business as usual within the framework of the NATO-Russia Council that dated back to 2002 (NATO 2008e). A bit later NATO issued another warning to Russia after it extended recognition to South Ossetia and Abkhazia. The alliance saw that recognition as a violation of the six-principles agreement signed by President Saakashvili and President Medvedev (NATO 2008f). Interestingly, the NATO-Ukraine Commission chimed in with agreement in condemning Russian recognition of the two separatist regions of Georgia (NATO 2008g).

The Georgia-NATO link was even more evident by the end of 2008. Alliance leaders noted with satisfaction that Georgia was taking an active part in the ISAF and Operation Active Endeavor in the Mediterranean Sea. In December 2008, the military organization wrote an Annual National Program for Georgia and set up a NATO Liaison Office in the capital city of Tbilisi. Other important activities entailed the work of Georgian military troops in Kosovo in the 1999–2008 period and the participation of the nation in the Partnership Action Plan on Terrorism. In return, NATO partners and allies had assisted Georgia in demilitarizing ground-to-air defense and other missiles. Along with many former communist countries, NATO also realized the need to build more positive views about the alliance within the Georgian public (NATO 2008h).

NATO strengthened the Russian component of its Black Sea strategy in March of 2009. Allied Ministers, while meeting at the Strasbourg/Kehl Summit, decided on formal resumption of the NATO-Russia Council (NRC) sessions (NATO 2009k). One month later, the alliance made an agreement with the Cabinet of Ministers of Ukraine. As a result, transit of goods to the ISAF Operation in Afghanistan could follow a path through Ukraine (NATO 2009l). It may have been coincidental, but a few days later the Ukrainians requested something perhaps in return from the United States. They asked for financial assistance in order to liquidate what was left of the Soviet nuclear arsenal. The United States had provided such assistance from 1993 to 2003, but the money had stopped at that point, probably due to the heavy investment in the Iraq War (SME 2009k).

In late April 2009, another issue put a strain on NATO-Russian relations. The military alliance decided to hold military exercises on the territory of Georgia. The exercises would be held only 20 km from Tbilisi and would include 1,300 soldiers from 19 nations. While the Russians saw these exercises as a provocation that was a consequence of the August 2008 War, the Western Alliance argued that they had planned these operations well before the events of August (SME 2009l).

NATO Secretary-General Jaap de Hoop Scheffer gave a unique speech at the end of April in Bucharest. In a sense, his visit commemorated the Bucharest NATO Summit a year earlier. He mentioned the conclusion reached a year before that both Georgia and Ukraine would be welcomed into the alliance once they met its criteria. He also made pointed comments about the priority of the Black Sea region to NATO. In his view, admission of Romania to NATO in 2004 had significantly raised "the profile of the Black Sea area," and he further indicated that the alliance would soon be promoting regional initiatives that bore the potential to "contribute to greater cooperation among the Black Sea states" (Scheffer, 2009). A week later the Secretary-General supported Black Sea partner Turkey after a terrorist attack resulted in the deaths of nine Turkish soldiers in Diyarbakir Province (NATO 2009m). Both of these high-level statements constituted evidence of the higher profile the Black Sea region held in the eyes of alliance leaders.

A meeting of the NATO Military Committee in Brussels in early May led to additional comments on the Black Sea priority. The committee actually met with the Defense Ministers from Ukraine and Georgia. They encouraged the two to continue with bold military reforms in spite of the economic set-backs of the previous year. Admiral Di Paola singled out Ukraine for special praise by applauding its role as the first NATO partner to contribute to the NATO Response Force (NATO 2009n). These more-involved steps by the alliance did produce reactions on the east coast of the Black Sea. For example, Russia threatened both Ukraine and Bulgaria with a cut off of natural gas supplies if Ukraine did not pay for its May imports in a timely fashion (SME 2009m). It was difficult to judge whether these were serious Russian policy indicators or whether they were simply additional reactions to the continuing military exercises in Georgia.

Relying on Trans-National Regional Organizations

The second highest priority for the region includes use of existing and potential regional organizations in a more active way. This step is separate from

NATO initiatives, but progress in building more cooperation through these organizations would serve NATO objectives of increasing the security of the region as a whole.

A number of existing regional organizations are currently active and can contribute to goals of greater regional understanding. The BSEC has been in existence for over a decade. In addition to the Black Sea Six, the organization also includes Albania, Greece, Moldova, Armenia, and Azerbaijan. A second organization is the Black Sea Studies Center that is located in Athens. The focus is on completion of research studies and activation of academic institutions in the nations of its parent organization, the BSEC (Bremmer and Bailes 1998, 131–47). Parallel to the work of this organization is the emerging Constanta-based Black Sea Universities Network. Both Bulgaria and Romania also take part in a Black Sea NGO Network that could be expanded to include other Black Sea nations. Its focus is on "transparency and accountability of governments," civil society, and mass media.

Conferences are often held that pull together the nations of the region and focus on some aspect of future policy needs. In December, 2008, the Center for International and Regional Policy held a conference that emphasized the security needs and environment of the region. In late March, 2009, Harvard University was the site of a Black Sea Security Program that included 25 Black Sea officials and 20 from the United States. In April, Giresum University in Turkey hosted The Second Black Sea International Symposium that put the spotlight on strategy, energy, economics, defense, and security. In the United Kingdom, the University of Leicester put on a conference whose priority was EU policy in the region. Relevant topics were economic cooperation, energy security, conflict resolution, and democratization. In early May, the Southeast Europe Association organized a conference on regional cooperation in the Black Sea Region, in Berlin. One panel treated the region through the lenses of supranational actors, while another depicted the European Neighborhood Policy as an "anchor" for Black Sea cooperation. Yalta itself was the site of an important conference on "Power and Ethnicity" in the Black Sea Region, and it was the eighth workshop organized jointly by Tavrida University in Simferopol and the Norwegian Humanist Association. Greece hosted its Second Annual Black Sea Symposium in the summer at its International Center for Black Sea Studies. In the fall there were two more significant events. SMi planned its second annual International Port Security Conference at the end of September, while Harvard would team up in October with the Armenian International Policy Research Group to address common approaches to both Black Sea and Caspian Sea security needs (Photius 2009).

All of the above organizations and conferences share the goal of improved security and life for the nations and peoples of the Black Sea region. At this point, it is useful to mention models from other corners of the world that could spark new ideas for Black Sea cooperation. One is the Baltic Sea region in the north, and it is a region that shares a number of features in common with the Black Sea area. A second is the Mega-Region initiative of America 2050 in the United States. A brief review of each may seed the ground with new perceptions that might transfer to the Black Sea Six.

Several Baltic organizations mentioned above could be relevant to the Black Sea region. The Council of the Baltic Sea States has been in existence since 1992. They have a number of suborganizations, but two are particularly interesting for the Black Sea area. The Baltic Sea States Sub-Regional Co-operation Organization emphasizes mainly the economic development of the subregions within the ten Baltic Sea states. A second suborganization is the Union of Baltic Sea Cities that includes 103 urban areas scattered across the various nations of the region.

These two organizations are rich with implications for the Black Sea region. If politics often divides the national leaders from one another, practical policy issues at the local level can unite managers and politicians on concrete topics. Study of the varying power of regional units within each of the six can lead to important comparative conclusions. Further increased contacts among cities such as Sochi, Sukhumi, Poti, Batumi, Trabzon, Ordu, Samsun, Burgas, Varna, Constanta, Odesa, Yevpatoriia, Kerch, Novorossiysk, and others can be useful as well. As Sochi prepares for the 2014 Olympics, outreach to some of the other regional cities makes sense. Nations often share Olympic sites among several cities. Why could not cities in several Black Sea countries also share in some of the events? Sport can be divisive for teams but unifying for nations.

Within the United States, American 2050 is an organization that highlights the eleven fastest growing mega-regions in the United States. They are the ones with the biggest share of population at the moment and the greatest economic impact. However, each includes portions of several states. Thus, to be excited about the mega-region in the future is to place one's trust and focus on units broader than one's city or state. For example, in the southeast, the Atlantic-Piedmont Mega-Region stretches from Raleigh, North Carolina, through Atlanta, Georgia, to Birmingham, Alabama. Priorities for each comparable large unit include managed growth, environmental protection, social equity, infrastructure improvements, and global competitiveness (America2050, 2009). Again, this concept is replete with meaning for the Black Sea Community. Those five issues are policy concerns in all six Black

Sea States, and there is no reason for each to suffer alone in developing solutions to them.

Reaching out to the Border States of the Six

The last priority is one that resonates with the external pressures outlined above within systems theory. Could a strengthened Black Sea Partnership become a significant regional player in assisting individual Black Sea nations with solutions to some of the issues in their backyard? NATO has the capability to assist in this process as well.

In the spring of 2009, Secretary-General Scheffer expressed concern about the conflict that ensued after the April elections in Moldova (NATO 2009o). In fact, Moldova already had a two-year agreement with NATO entitled the Individual Partnership Action Plan. Moldova contributed helicopters to the UN mission in Afghanistan and would benefit from alliance assistance in removing Russian weapons and ammunition from Transdniestria (NATO 2009p). In addition, Armenia received a visit from the NATO Deputy Secretary General Claudio Bisogniero. The leaders discussed regional security, democratic institution building, and Armenian participation in KFOR in Kosovo (NATO 2009q). Further, Azerbaijan's President Ilham Aliyev visited NATO headquarters in the spring as well. Their discussions centered on the nation's role in ISAF, KFOR, civil reconstruction projects in Afghanistan, civil emergency planning, energy security, and environmental cleanup (Azerbaijan Diplomatic Academy 2009).

These three nations are only part of the vast puzzle outlined in the early pages under the heading of external pressures. However, the visits and discussions give a hint of the topics and settings that could bear fruit in a number of situations. Certainly, Black Sea nations such as Romania, Georgia, and Russia could be involved in some sort of cooperative framework that would take these discussions further.

Feedback Loop

How might decisions and policies that flesh out the three priorities discussed above feed back in a positive way into the Black Sea System? First, knitting together the six nations can make individual security decisions and the relations with NATO less troubled. Second, relying on regional organizations can create the habit of cooperation on small issues that can spill over into more complex ones. Third, reaching out to the border states of the six can bring the weight of an emerging Black Sea Community to bear on contentious territorial and historical differences. The dream for the future would be development of political, economic, and social partnerships that reflect, to a greater extent, the deep blue harmony of the gem that is the natural center of the region and that illuminates and touches the shores of each nation.

Simmering Controversies on the two Coasts

Irritants in the Baltic area of the north often included incidents at the border. For example, in mid-December 2009, the Russian authorities held up traffic that was attempting to enter Russia from Latvia. At two locations a total of 760 trucks were stopped and forced to endure delays of 49–78 hours. Latvia expressed the hope that the authorities in both countries could resolve the matter within the week. This action by Russia was a response to a demand earlier in the week by Latvia that the Russians change the way in which they inspected Latvian trucks. Russia had recently tightened customs controls on the Latvian vehicles. Russia talked of taking this EU-Russian issue to the European Commission (IZVESTIYA 2009n).

In the Black Sea area far to the south, a variety of issues continued to bubble, and they usually pertained to Russia in a direct or indirect way. For example, Polish President Lech Kaczynski went to Georgia to take part in an energy summit in late 2009. His stated purpose was to work on a plan to construct an oil pipeline from Odessa all the way to Gdansk. Discussions had begun in Krakow in 2007 on the issue of energy security, and these talks were a continuation of those (IZVESTIYA 2009o). At the same time, the Ukrainian Prime Minister Julia Tymoshenko announced that the nation planned to begin drilling on the shelf for oil and natural gas. This created pressure and potential conflict on the other Black Sea nations, for a means of dividing up the shelf resources did not yet exist (IZVESTIYA 2009p). Any plans that pertained to oil or gas brought up the hidden issue of Russia's control over supplies and ability to cut the flow of those resources, as it had for two weeks in January 2009.

In addition to economic conflicts, there were occasional struggles over symbols of meaning in the region as well. For example, the town of Dioknis destroyed a memorial to those who had died during World War II. A similar event had taken place in Kytais several days earlier. Such actions always seemed to Russia to be an attack on them that was coupled with failure to appreciate their sacrifices and contributions on behalf of the region in the 1940s, in light of the Nazi occupation. On the other hand, the election in

Ukraine of Viktor Yanukovych in early 2010 emboldened some citizens of Sevastopol to raise the Flag of St. Andrew in celebration of the victory of the Soviet Army in Crimea on February 23, 1945. That flag had been the compromise solution as a substitute for the Russian flag during the 1990s, after the fall of the Soviet Union. However, following the victory of Ukrainian nationalists during the Orange Revolution in 2004, no flag had been flown (IZVESTIYA 2010h). The visit of Yanukovych to Moscow on March 4, 2010, drove home the symbolism of the potential for improved relations between Ukraine and Russia even more (IZVESTIYA 2010i). Of course, this had the effect of embittering Ukrainian nationalists who sought to keep alive the memory of the Orange Revolution.

Memories of the 2008 Georgia war did not disappear from the region, after one and a half years. Georgian Vice Premier Temur Yakobashvili presented the nation's plan for reintegration of South Ossetia and Abkhazia to the UN in February, 2010. He had earlier presented his strategy to French leaders as well, and he had indicated that representatives of the Ministry of Defense would be included in the discussions (IZVESTIYA 2010j). A bit later, Russia's President Medvedev claimed that he had evidence that both NATO and the United States were arming Georgia to strengthen its ability to make good its claims to the contested enclaves (SME 2010d). At the end of March, Russia signed documents with the two enclaves that aimed at guaranteeing protection of their borders with Georgia. The parties to the agreement stated that the document was not directed against any third parties but rather against terrorism, movement of weapons of all sorts, and narcotics (IZVESTIYA 2010k).

While both of NATO's coasts were bedeviled with conflicts that were a heritage of the Cold War and that engaged primarily Russia, the potential for continuing conflict appeared to be greater in the Black Sea region than in the Baltic Sea community. As such, NATO leaders continued to put a strong spotlight on each critical or troubling new step on its southern coast.

CHAPTER TWELVE

NATO Missions Reshape the Battle against Terrorism

The seven alliance missions described in the preceding chapters would have been unimaginable during the Cold War. While not all of them contribute in the same way to the global struggle against terrorism, each one changes the configuration of that battle in some way. The seven missions include SFOR in Bosnia, OAF in Kosovo, ISAF in Afghanistan, NTM-I in Iraq, missile defense in Europe, Baltic Sea tensions, and emerging challenges in the Black Sea area. The agenda for NATO planners is integration of all seven of these pieces into a meaningful whole. Without that broad perspective and the ensuing search for a central theme, the battle against terrorism will remain a matter month-to-month adjustments to new crises. A fragmented perspective will always win out over a cohesive blueprint.

Within Bosnia, NATO still has a major stake, for EUFOR relies heavily on its experiences, members and capabilities. Under UN supervision, management of the three enclaves of Muslims, Serbs, and Croatians can be a model for solutions in other violence-prone countries that include a substantial Muslim population. How can a common state build links among formerly hostile groups in such a way that stability becomes an expected feature of the political landscape? Perhaps the consocational democracy model of Arend Lijphart (1980, 25–52) can offer insightful conclusions for Bosnia as well as for other countries in similar situations. Collaboration among the elites can preserve the peace while the roots of a common understanding penetrate down over time to the members of the various subgroups. Thereby, the shadows from the Cold War begin to shorten.

The NATO involvement in Kosovo had the unintended consequence of producing sovereignty and a qualified independence nearly a decade after completion of the bombing campaign itself. Even with that 2008 declaration of independence, NATO troops continue to make up two-thirds of the security forces there. From the point of view of the Kosovars, NATO's contribution was substantial enough that the capital city of Priština erected a statue to American President Bill Clinton in October 2009. Early action by NATO in 1999 may have prevented a catastrophe, and the alliance's demonstrated ability to act in a situation that required quick decisions can be useful in other theaters in which terrorism rages. As such, the lessons of inaction or late action in Bosnia cast a long shadow that protected Kosovo.

The tragedy in Afghanistan centers on the fact that 2001 defeat of the Taliban terrorists and their sometime accomplices al Qaeda was not permanent. Preoccupation with Iraq prevented a continued attentiveness to the struggle in Afghanistan, with the result that the violence flared up a half dozen years after the imagined victory. Failure to attend to the incredibly decentralized political system in that nation contributed to the misunderstandings and misperceptions. A permanent victory is not possible in such a state, if the exclusive political developmental focus is on creating a visible central government. Few in late 2001 would have believed that the decade would end with Afghanistan reemerging as the central theater of NATO's battle against terrorism. It is not a surprise that the debate at the end of the decade centered on the question of what level of additional NATO capabilities were needed to produce a satisfactory result.

Even though Afghanistan came to replace Iraq as the central battleground against terrorism, the latter nation contributed heavily to the learning process of how to organize the struggle against such a new type of enemy. Careful attention to existing dangers is mandatory before the commitment of troops. Establishment of achievable objectives is also a necessity. The mere presence of a major western military force in a predominately Muslim nation can become the magnet for an inflow of outside terrorist groups whose numbers may have initially been small. NATO partners who commit to missions that are not officially alliance commitments can run the risk of reducing the organization's ability to obtain results in more central battlegrounds. The experience in Iraq shook NATO capabilities and made the alliance weaker and disoriented in the search to locate the highest priority threats.

In fact, another distraction from the central conflict in Afghanistan was the disruption and tumult that characterized the Pakistani political landscape in the first decade of the twenty-first century. By the end of the decade, it was difficult to unravel the struggle with the Taliban and al Qaeda that was taking place in Afghanistan from the one occurring simultaneously in Pakistan. If Iraq was a drain on NATO resources that could have been riveted on Afghanistan, Pakistan became a psychological and emotional distraction from the escalating conflict in the southern part of Afghanistan. A key problem is the existence of an ungovernable area in the western part of Pakistan that adjoins Afghanistan. The extreme western portion is called the Federally Administered Tribal Areas, and the first two words in that description bear only a passing acquaintanceship with reality. Just to the east of that area is the North-West Frontier Province, and much violence occurs in its Swat Valley and environs.

Both Presidents Musharraf and Zardari, in succession, have been unable to impose the firm hand of the central government in Islamabad over those regions. In fact, there was an ongoing effort to transfer broad power from the office of President to the position of Prime Minster in an effort to create both more domestic stability and international credibility for this relatively new nuclear state (iDNES 2010d). As a result, the Pashtun militant groups protect al Qaeda in the region, while the Taliban looms in the background (Rubin 2009, 23–7). No reminder is necessary that this is the wild, mountainous area in which the religious schools trained al Qaeda operatives in the period just before and after 9/11. Bin Laden himself may have roamed and received protection in this region after the tragic events of September, 2001. In March 2010, a terrorist attack came very close to the American consulate in Peshawar, and the spokesman for the Pakistani Taliban Tehrik-i-Taliban Pakistan (TTP) claimed that the operation was an effort to extract revenge for the series of attacks from the air by American drones (SME 2010e).

European security against the nuclear threat from rogue state terrorists centered for several years on the Bush proposal for a missile shield whose components would be situated in several key nations of Central Europe. This initiative by NATO's most powerful partner and informal leader offered a hope by which the West could offer more military protection to the East. In particular, such a system could offer reassurance at a time of uncertainty about the intentions of Iran. Cancellation of the Bush proposal by President Obama did generate expectations of a substitute that would be equally useful. However, it also brought to the surface the role of public opinion in partner countries and presidential elections in leading NATO nations. At the same time, the continuing links between East and West on security matters related to terrorism were evident and powerful.

The northern coast of NATO is easy to overlook or ignore, for terrorist attacks and violence have typically been geographically located much further south. Also, the region is characterized by a number of seasoned democracies whose leaders have a reputation for rationality and a steady hand. In that sense, the area is the opposite of Bosnia during the war of the 1990s. In the latter case, the nations close by were themselves undergoing the process of deep change and transition. Older democracies further west stayed on the sidelines, until the end. In contrast, the Scandinavian nations in the Baltic region have been proactive in reaching out to the three former Soviet Republics in hopes of pulling them into a stable framework. At the same time, Russian provocations continue to echo periodically, and this reminds that the Russian factor is also consequential in all six battles against terrorism further south. Engagement of Russia on Baltic questions can help transform that key nation into a partnership that can benefit those other six struggles. NATO would benefit if its northern coast were less stormy at unpredictable and inopportune moments.

The southern coast of NATO will continue to demand the attentiveness of alliance planners and managers for some time to come. The nations and their political systems in the south bear the marks of more diversity than do the Baltic Sea states, and the Black Sea Six have not moved as far in building institutions across state lines. This coast is very close to the center of global terrorism, and a number of nations such as Georgia, Russia, and Turkey have felt its presence and pain. In contrast, Bulgaria and Romania are in part members of NATO because they offer a bulwark against the press of terrorist groups from the east. The problematic nature of the applications of both Georgia and Ukraine for alliance membership weakens temporarily construction of a Black Sea linchpin to assist in the struggle with terrorism. With its palm trees and warm summer sun, this shore can deceive by concealing the boiling controversies just below its blue surface.

In the end, each of these seven missions includes a NATO dimension. In Kosovo, Afghanistan, the Baltic Sea region, and the Black Sea area, the alliance is engaged through its members, promises, troops, and equipment. In Bosnia, NATO has yielded management of security to the EU, but the NATO partners provide substantially the capabilities for keeping the peace. In the case of both Iraq and European security, America as the lead power in the alliance has mainly called the shots and done the planning. However, in both cases NATO has offered perspectives, advice, and often considerable support. The abiding problem is that there is no mosaic into which all seven of the pieces fit. Each bears the marks of the struggle against terrorism and is a piece of it, while two of the involved countries remain key battlegrounds of the twenty-first century. An integrative view that envisions progress in one area as having a ripple effect in another is missing and needed. Construction of such a vision would better prepare NATO for unexpected challenges in both old and new theaters of operation. Current missions have already reshaped the alliance battle against terrorism in profound ways. Without the earlier and continuing expansion of the organization, NATO's transformed missions would lack the broad base that would enable its leaders to plan more effectively for future victories and finally defeat of the vicious threat of terrorism.

References

America2050. 2009. The Importance of Megaregions in the Global Economy. March 9. http://www.america2050.org/.
Anonymous. 2008. JIEDDO to Fold Funding Request into FY '10 Base Budget. *Defense Daily* 240(49). Accessed December 12, 2008.
AP. 2008. Bush says NATO Must Remain Open. April 3. http://www.associatedpress.com/.
arctic-council. 2008. Arctic Council. March 3. http://www.arctic-council.org/.
Argentieri, Federigo. 2008. Hungary: Dealing with the Past and Moving into the Present. In *Central & East European Politics: From Communism to Democracy*, ed. Sharon L. Wolchik & Jane L. Curry, 215–32. New York: Roman & Littlefield Publishers.
Ash, Timothy Garton. 1990. *The Magic Lantern: The Revolution of '89 Witnessed in Warsaw, Budapest, Berlin and Prague.* New York: Random House.
assembly-Kosovo. 2008. Constitution of the Republic of Kosovo. October 23. http://www.assembly-kosovo.org/.
Averre, Derek L. 2007. The Russian Military and European Security Cooperation. In *Russia and Europe in the Twenty-First Century: An Uneasy Partnership*, ed. Jackie Gower & Graham Timminst, 89–107. New York: Anthem Press.
Azerbaijan Diplomatic Academy. 2009. NATO-Azerbaijan: Assessing the Past, Looking into the Future. *Azerbaijan in the World* II(9): May 1.
Baev, Pavel K. 2008. *Russian Energy Policy and Military Power: Putin's Quest for Greatness.* New York: Routledge.
Balanzino, Sergio Silvio. 1995. Adapting the Alliance: Restructuring NATO after the Cold War. *Harvard International Review* 17(2): 34–8. http://proxygsu-val1.galileo.usg.ed/.
Balmaceda, Margarita M. 2000. The Ukrainian-Central European Borderland after NATO Expansion: Wall, Fortress, or Open Door? In *On the Edge: Ukrainian-Central European-Russian Security Triangle*, ed. Margarita M. Balmaceda, 231–60. Budapest: Central European University Press.
Banac, Ivo. 1984. *The National Question in Yugoslavia: Origins, History, Politics.* Ithaca: Cornell University Press.
Barnes, Julian E. 2009a. Gates Calls for Scaled-Back Goals in Afghanistan. *Los Angeles Times*, January 28.
— 2009b. A New U.S. Approach Expected in Afghanistan. *Los Angeles Times*, May 12.
— 2009c. Joint Chiefs Chairman Making His Influence Felt. *Los Angeles Times*, August 3.
Baskin, Mark and Paula Pickering. 2008. Former Yugoslavia and Its Successors. In *Central & East European Politics: From Communism to Democracy*, ed. Sharon L. Wolchek & Jane L. Curry. New York: Rowman & Littlefield Publishers, Inc., 281–315.
beac. 2008. Barents Euroarctic Council. March 4. http://www.beac.st/.

Bell, John D. 1993. Bulgaria. In *Developments in East European Politics*, ed. Stephen White, Judy Batt, & Paul G. Lewis, 83–97. Durham: Duke University Press.
Borak, Donna. 2009. Gates: DOD Faces 'Hard Choices' On Acquisitions. *Washingtonpost.com*, January 27.
Boryk, Jennifer. 2008. History does Matter: The Fate of the Bronze Soldier in Estonia. Paper presented at the annual meeting for the Southern Conference on Slavic Studies, March 27–9, in Atlanta, Georgia.
Bremmer, Jan and Alyson Bailes. 1998. Sub-Regionalism in the Newly Independent States. *International Affairs* 74(1): 131–47.
Brown, J.F. 1970. *Bulgaria Under Communist Rule*. New York: Praeger Publishers.
Brzezinski, Zbigniew. 2009. An Agenda for NATO: Toward a Global Security Web. *Foreign Affairs* 88(5): 2–20.
Bumiller, Elisabeth and David E. Sanger. 2009. Obama Wants Afghans and Pakistanis to Commit to War Plan, Officials Say. *New York Times*, November 11.
Bush, George. 2007. NATO Stands with the Forces of Freedom. *Hampton Roads International Security Quarterly* January 15, 2007: 5–10.
Busygina, Irina. 2007. Russia's Regions in Shaping National Policy. In *Russia and Europe in the Twenty-First Century: An Uneasy Partnership*, ed. Jackie Gower & Graham Timmins, 75–88. New York: Anthem Press.
cbss. 2008a, c. Council of the Baltic Sea States. March 4. http://www.cbss.st/.
— 2008b. Eurofaculty in Kaliningrad (2000–07). March 4. http://www.cbss.st/.
Černíková, Petra. 2008. Evropská unie a Spojené státy americké: politické vztahy Na počátku 21st století. *Mezinárodní Politika* XXXII (01): 41–3.
Chatterjee, Pratap. 2010. Afghan Police Still Out of Step. *Asia Times*, March 2.
Chittick, William O. 2006. *American Foreign Policy: A Framework for Analysis*. Washington, D.C.: CQ Press.
Cowell, Alan. 2009. British Prime Minister Presses Allies to Increase Their Troop Levels in Afghanistan. *New York Times*, November 14.
Cooley, Alexander. 2005. Base Politics. *Foreign Affairs* 84(6): 79–92.
CQ Today. 2008. Defense Policy Bill Nearly Ready for Bush. September 24. http://www.daniel.meyer@dodigmil/.
Csergo, Zsuzsa. 2008. Ethnicity, Nationalism, and the Expansion of Democracy. In *Central & East European Politics: From Communism to Democracy*, ed. Sharon L. Wolchik & Jane L. Curry. New York: Rowman & Littlefield Publishers.
cssd 2009. Volební program. March 17. http://www.cssd.cz/.
ČTK. 2008. Jednotky NATO v Kosovu pod silnou palbou. March 17. http://www.ceskenoviny.cz/.
Czech Radio 7, Radio Prague. 2006. Czechs hand training over to Iraqis at police academy. November 8. http://www.radio.cz/.
D'Arnieri, Paul. 2007. *Understanding Ukrainian Politics: Power Politics and Institutional Design*. Armonk, New York: M.W. Sharpe.
Declaration by the North Atlantic Treaty Organisation and the Islamic Republic of Afghanistan, September 6, 2007. Online Library, North Atlantic Treaty Organization.
De Nevers, Renee. 2007. The U.S., NATO, and the War on Terror: Sustaining the Security Community. Paper presented at the annual international meeting for the International Studies Association, 2007. http://proxygsu-val1.galileo.usg.ed/.

Deni, John R. 2004. NATO Versus Terrorism: Is the Alliance Ready? Paper presented at the annual international meeting for the International Studies Association, 2004, in Montreal, Canada. http://proxygsu-val1.galileo.usg.ed/.
Derleth, J. William. 2000. *The Transition in Central and Eastern European Politics.* Upper Saddle River, New Jersey: Prentice Hall.
DN. 2007a. USA-bomb dödade britter. August 24. http://www.dn.se/.
— 2007b. Finlänsk soldat dödad i Afghanistan. May 23. http://www.dn.se/.
— 2007c. Norden i tortyrens gråzon. October 9. http://www.dn.se/.
— 2007d. Norge kan inte räkna med NATO. September 24. http://www.dn.se/.
DN. 2008a. Dansk soldat dödad i Afghanistan. July 25. http://www.dn.se/.
— 2008b. Ryssland testar ny robot. September 18. http://www.dn.se/.
DN. 2009a. Nytt Krigshot i Svarta havet. September 16. http://www.dn.se/.
— 2009b. Ökat hot även mot svenska Isafstyrkan. July 21. http://www.dn.se/.
— 2009c. Afghanska kvinnor tar första svåra stegen mot ett jämställt land. November 6. http://www.dn.se/.
— 2009d. Obama söker ryskt stöd för att stoppa Irans missiler. March 4. http://www.dn.se/.
— 2009e. Putin vill ha mer efter missilbeslut. September 18. http://www.dn.se/.
— 2009f. USA skrotar robotplaner. September 17. http://www.dn.se/.
DN. 2010. Sverige skickar en ny pluton till Afghanistan. February 10. http://www.dn.se/.
DPA/AP/Reuters. 2008. Gewaltausbruch im Kosovo: UN-Polizei unter Beschuss. March 17. http://www.dpaapreuters.com/.
Dürr, Jakub. 2000. *Volby '98.* Brno: Pavel Šaradin. ec. 2008. Northern Dimension. March 3. http://www.ec.europa.eu/.
Eglitis, Daina Stukuls. 2008. The Baltic States: Remembering the Past, Building the Future. In *Central and East European Politics: From Communism to Democracy,* ed. Sharon L. Wolchik & Jane L. Curry, 233–52. New York: Rowman & Littlefield Publishers.
Estonia: Estonian Prime Minister Disapproves of the Actions of the British Council in Russia. 2008. *U.S. Federal News Service, Including U.S. State News* January 17.
Europe: Airy Disdain; Lithuania and Russia. 2005. *The Economist* 377(8446): 39.
Europe: New boots for NATO. 2007. *The Economist* 383(8535): 50.
Europe: Self-Strangulation; Latvia and Russia. 2003. *The Economist* 367(8327): 42.
Fawn, Rick. 2003. Reconstituting a National Identity: Ideologies in Czech Foreign Policy after the Split. *Journal of Communist Studies and Transition Politics* 19(3): 204–28.
Friedman, George. 2008. The Russo-Georgia War and the Balance of Power: The Russians seize an opportunity to flex their geopolitical muscle. *The American Legion* October 2008: 14–20.
Garwin, Richar L. 2008. Evaluating Iran's missile threat. *Bulletin of the Atomic Scientists* (May/June): 40–4.
Gates, Robert M. 2007. Perseverance, Spirit, Unity. *Hampton Roads International Security Quarterly* April 15, 2007: 36–9.
Gates, William, and Katsuaki Terasawa. 2003. Reconsidering Publicness in Alliance Defence Expenditures: NATO Expansion and Burden Sharing. *Defence and Peace Economics* 14(5): 369–83. http://proxygsu-val1.galileo.usg.ed/.

Gera, Vanessa. 2009. Poles, Czechs Criticize U.S. Missile Shield 'Betrayal.' *Washington Times*, September 19.
Gledhill, John and Charles King. 2008. Romania Since 1989: Living Beyond the Past. In *Central & East European Politics: From Communism to Democracy*, eds. Sharon L. Wolchik & Jane L. Curry, 317–38. New York: Rowman & Littlefield Publishers.
Global Information Network, April 15, 2004, 1.
Gnesotto, Nicole. 1997. Common European Defence and Transatlantic Relations. In *NATO's Transformation*, ed. Philip H. Gordon. New York: Rowman & Littlefield Publishers.
Godges, John. 2007. Afghanistan on the Edge. *Rand Review* (Summer).
Golan, Galia. 1971. *The Czechoslovak Reform Movement*. Cambridge: Cambridge University Press.
Goldman, Minton F. 2005. *Russia, the Eurasian Republics, and Central/Eastern Europe*, Tenth Edition. Dubuque, Iowa: McGraw-Hill/Dushkin Company.
— 2008. *Russia, the Eurasian Republics, and Central/Eastern Europe*, Eleventh Edition. Dubuque, Iowa: McGraw-Hill.
Gower, Jackie and Graham Timmins. 2007. Introduction. In *Russia and Europe in the Twenty-First Century: An Uneasy Partnership*, ed. Jackie Gower & Graham Timmins, xix–xxiv. New York: Anthem Press.
Hallams, Ellen. 2009. The Transatlantic Alliance Renewed: the United States and NATO Since 9/11. *Journal of Transatlantic Studies* 7(1): 38–60. http://proxygsu-val1.galileo.usg.ed/.
Heinrich, Hans-Georg. 1986. *Hungary: Politics, Economics and Society*. Boulder: Lynne-Rienner Publishers.
Hendrickson, Ryan C. 2006. *Diplomacy and War at NATO: The Secretary General and Military Action after the Cold War*. Columbia: University of Missouri Press.
Hesli, Vicki L. 2007. *Government and Politics in Russia and the Post-Soviet Region*. New York: Houghton Mifflin Company.
iDNES. 2006a. Čeští chemici jsou v pohotovosti, chrání summit v Rize. November 27. http://www.idnes.cz/.
— 2006b, c. Trojice balkánských zemí uzavřela partnerství s NATO. December 15. http://www.idnes.cz/.
— 2006d. Čeští vojáci kontrolují v Kosovu těžbu dřeva. June 5. http://www.idnes.cz/.
— 2006e. Neubauer: Bezpečnostní situace v Iráku se zhoršuje. June 20. http://www.idnes.cz/.
— 2006f. Výzkum: Češi by povolili americký radar, rakety nechtějí. December 15. http://www.idnes.cz/.
— 2006g. NATO začalo budovat protiraketovou obranu. November 28. http://www.idnes.cz/.
iDNES. 2007a. Americký Senát schválil rozšíření NATO. March 29. http://www.idnes.cz/.
— 2007b. Češi zamíří na východ Afghánistánu možná za rok. June 25. http://www.idnes.cz/.
— 2007c. Polští vojáci v Afghánistánu se vzbouřili kvůli autům. June 22. http://www.idnes.cz/.

iDNES. 2007d. Jihokorejci prý zajaté misionáře vyplatili miliony. August 31. http://www.idnes.cz/.
— 2007e. Ministři NATO jednají o Afghánistánu a raketové obraně. June 14. http://www.idnes.cz/.
— 2007f. Český diplomat unikl střelbě v Afghánistánu. May 1. http://www.idnes.cz/.
— 2007g. Vojáci přivezli mrtvého kolegu z Afghánistánu. May 6. http://www.idnes.cz/.
— 2007h. Armáda ocení vojáka, který zahynul v Afghánistánu. May 7. http://www.idnes.cz/.
— 2007i. Češi hlídkují v afghánských horách. April 24. http://www.idnes.cz/.
— 2007j. Češi pomáhají Afghancům ze zaplavených oblastí. May 30. http://www.idnes.cz/.
— 2007k. Ptejte se velitele polní nemocnice v Afghánistánu. April 30. http://www.idnes.cz/.
— 2007l. Vláda zváží zda pošle do Afghánistán civilní experty. August 21. http://www.idnes.cz/.
— 2007m. ČR se chce postarat o část Afghánistán. Vláda je pro. August 22. http://www.idnes.cz/.
— 2007n. Afghánce motivoval i odznak, vzpomíná český policista. October 6. http://www.idnes.cz/.
— 2007o. Polák se chtěl upálit kvůli stíhání vojáků za masakr v Afghánánu. November 20. http://www.idnes.cz/.
— 2007p. Polští vojáci v Afghánistánu se vzbouřili kvůli autům. June 22. http://www.idnes.cz/.
— 2007q. NATO nechá vojáky v Afghánistán další rok. September 20. http://www.idnes.cz/.
— 2007r. Šéf Pentagonu přiletěl do Česka jednat o radaru. September 22. http://www.idnes.cz/
— 2007s,t. Scheffer: Radarem se bude zabývat summit NATO. October 31. http://www.idnes.cz/.
— 2007u. Základny aktivuje až hrozba z Íránu, navrhl Gates. October 23. http://www.idnes.cz/.
— 2007u. Ministr Schwarzenberg chce dohodu o radaru ještě v zimě. December 7. http://www.idnes.cz/.
— 2007v. USA a Rusko dohodly schůzku o raketách a radaru. May 4. http://www.idnes.cz/.
— 2007w. Rusko chce spojit svou obranu proti raketám s NATO. June 3. http://www.idnes.cz/.
— 2007x. Česko 'ano' radaru je chyba, zopakovalo Rusko. August 21. http://www.idnes.cz/.
— 2007y. Nový americký návrh k radaru Rusy neuspokojil. October 25. http://www.idnes.cz/.
— 2007z. Ruský generál pohrozil raketami v Bělorusku. November 14. http://www.idnes.cz/.
— 2007aa. Topolánek: Pokud se Evropa nebude bránit, je s ní konec. May 31. http://www.idnes.cz/.

— 2007bb. Premiér: Radar odmítneme, pokud si ho USA nezaplatí. June 3. http://www.idnes.cz/.
— 2007cc. Pozor na populismus, píše Klaus o referendu k radaru. July 13. http://www.idnes.cz/.
— 2007dd. Schwarzenberg: Radar bude pod NATO, raketu odpálí USA. October 7. http://www.idnes.cz/.
— 2007ee. Padl hlavní důvod pro radar, jednání přesto běží dál. December 5. http://www.idnes.cz/.
— 2007ff. Průzkum: Američané chtějí radar v Čechách. July 30. http://www.idnes.cz/.
— 2007gg. Komunisté obsadí brdy, zastánci radaru chystají protiakci. September 20. http://www.idnes.cz/.
— 2007hh. Komunisté agitují v Brdech proti radaru. September 21. http://www.idnes.cz/.
— 2007ii. Nekupujte americké zboží, vyzývají humanist po vzoru Gándhiho. December 10. http://www.idnes.cz/.
— 2007jj. Scheffer: Radarem se bude zabývat summit NATO. October 31. http://www.idnes.cz/.
— 2007kk. Rusko zrazilo vývoz surovin do Estonska na polovinu. July 17. http://www.idnes.cz/.
iDNES. 2008a. VIDEO: Do Kosova odletělo šedesat českých vojáků. July 18. http://www.idnes.cz/.
— 2008b. Česko a USA podepsaly hlavní smlouvu o radaru. July 8. http://www.idnes.cz/.
— 2008c. Bush po schůzce s Topolánkem: Dohoda o radaru je blízko. February 27. http://www.idnes.cz/.
— 2008d. Rusko znovu apelovalo na přitomnost svých vojáků u českých radaru. April 8. http://www.idnes.cz/.
— 2008e. S radarem se můžeme smířit, nebo na něj zamířit, pravil ruský general. September 10. http://www.idnes.cz/.
— 2008f. Ruský velvyslanec: Česká vláda prodala bezpečnost lidí za radar. September 19. http://www.idnes.cz/.
— 2008g. Vojáci o ruském zájmu o půdu v Brdech mlčí, varují před agenty Íránu i Kosova. September 29. http://www.idnes.cz/.
— 2008h. Nejedete do USA podepsat radar? Ptá se Paroubek premiéra. January 30. http://www.idnes.cz/.
— 2008i. Topolánek: Prohlášení Parkanové o radaru je předčasné. March 10. http://idnes.cz/.
— 2008j. Exprezident Havel: Američanům umístění radaru dlužíme. March 24. http://www.idnes.cz/.
— 2008k. Opozice hrozí kvůli smlouvě o radaru Ústavním soudem. April 15. http://www.idnes.cz/.
— 2008l. V Praze protestovaly proti radaru stovky lidí. May 5. http://www.idnes.cz/.
— 2008m. Odpůrci radaru budou Riceové spílat k večeři. July 7. http://www.idnes.cz/.
— 2008n. Ruský vpad do Gruzie podporu radaru nepřinesl, ukázal průzkum. October 3. http://www.idnes.cz/.

iDNES. 2008o. Česko se dohodlo s USA na radaru, smlouvu podepiše za měsíc. April 3. http://www.idnes.cz/.
— 2008p. Smlouva o radaru podepiše v Praze Riceová, zřejmě začátkem května. April 7. http://www.idnes.cz/.
— 2008q. Schwarzenberg: Rakety u nás v případě polského odmítnutí neskončí. July 7. http://www.idnes.cz/.
— 2008r. Nesmíme opakovat selhání z minulosti, hájl Topolánek radar. July 8. http://www.idnes.cz/.
— 2008s. Česko a USA podepsaly hlavní smlouvu o radaru. July 8. http://www.idnes.cz/.
— 2008t. Klaus: Smlouvu o radaru podepíšu bez váhání. July 9. http://www.idnes.cz/.
— 2008u. Vláda schválila smlouvu SOFA, radar i půda pod ním zůstane Česku. September 10. http://www.idnes.cz/.
— 2008v. Vláda schválila dohodu o zapojení Česka do budování protiraketového štítu. October 1. http://www.idnes.cz/.
— 2008w. Litva zakázala srp a kladivo. Rusko zuří. June 19. http://www.idnes.cz/.
iDNES. 2009a. V Gruzii to jiskří, na granáty Tbilisi odpověděla Moskva záborem území. August 3. http://www.idnes.cz/.
— 2009b. Obama žáda Rusko o pomoc s Íránem, obětoval by radar v Brdech. March 2. http://www.idnes.cz/.
— 2009c. Teror sílí a NATO se blíží, varoval Medveděv a ohlásil ruské Přezbrojení. March 17. http://www.idnes.cz/.
— 2009d. Fischer: Radar nebude, sdělil mi 21 minut po půlnoci. September 17. http://www.idnes.cz/.
— 2009e. Přehledně: USA "zamázly" radar v Brdech, Češi litují a oslavují. September 17. http://www.idnes.cz/.
— 2009f. Bojme se Ruska méně než EU, prohlásil president Klaus. September 22. http://www.idnes.cz/.
— 2009g. O konci radaru debatuje se čtenáři iDNES.cz general Jiří Šedivý. September 17. http://www.idnes.cz/.
— 2009h. Zrušení radaru v Česku je zodpovědné, chválí Rusové Obamu. September 17. http://www.idnes.cz/.
— 2009i. V Česku by mohlo být velitelství nového protiraketového system. October 8. http://www.idnes.cz/.
— 2009j. Česko se na protiraketové obraně chce podílet, řekl Fischer Bidenovi. October 23. http://www.idnes.cz/.
iDNES. 2010a. Dvouleté Kosovo neuznává 127 států světa. Postrčí je Haag? February 17. http://www.idnes.cz/.
— 2010b. Vláda chce vyslat do Afghánistánu posily s radarem Arthus, ČSSD je proti. February 1, 2010. http://www.idnes.cz/.
— 2010c. Američané chtějí podepsat dohodu o jaderném odzbrojení v Česku.
— 2010d. Při sebevražedných útocích zemřelo v Pákistánu nejméně 47 lidí. April 5. http://www.idnes.cz/. March 24. http://www.idne.cz/.
Innes, Michael. 2010. A New Command Structure in Afghanistan. *Foreign Policy* March 18.
Ispek, Pinar. 2007. Challenges for Democratization in Central Asia: What Can the United States Do? *Middle East Policy* 14(1): 95–107.

IZVESTIYA. 2006a. Yushchenko and Yanukovych do not agree about NATO (translated). September 25. http://www.izvestiya.ru/.
IZVESTIYA 2007a. Lithuania closes down the only remaining Russian TV news show (translated). July 16. http://www.izvestiya.ru/.
— 2007b. Summer Lightening for Hitler Youth (translated). August 8. http://www.izvestiya.ru/.
— 2007c. Genocide that never was (translated). September 26. http://www.izvestiya.ru/.
IZVESTIYA. 2008. Who will defend the defenders of the bronze soldier? (translated). January 15. http://www.izvestiya.ru/.
IZVESTIYA. 2009a. Scheffer recognizes the impossibility of accepting Ukraine and Georgia into NATO (translated). July 21. http://www.izvestiya.ru/.
— 2009b. Confirmation of a Representative of Georgia to NATO (translated). June 26 http://www.izvestiya.ru/.
— 2009c. Nino Burzhanadze: Saakashvili intended to take Tschinvali in one night (translated). August 10. http://www.izvestiya.ru/.
— 2009d. the exercise VMS Ukraine began in Crimea (translated). September 8. http://www.izvestiya.ru/.
— 2009e. A Russian military base will guarantee the sovereignty of Abkhazia (translated). October 9. http://www.izvestiya.ru/.
— 2009f. The Pentagon is constructing two military bases in Eastern Europe (translated). October 22. http://www.izvestiya.ru/.
— 2009g. Medvedev promised to open the border with Georgia (translated). December 9. http://www.izvestiya.ru/.
— 2009h. Director of the Institute for the Solution of International Problems Aleksei Pushkov: the admission of Ukraine to NATO would not be advantageous for Kiev, Moscow, or the West (translated). June 24. http://www.izvestiya.ru/.
— 2009i. Ukraine requests help from NATO in the battle with swine flu (translated). November 2. http://www.izvestiya.ru/.
— 2009j. NATO attempts to entice Russia on Afghanistan (translated). December 16. http://www.izvestiya.ru/.
— 2009k. Head of the Lithuanian Ministry of Foreign Affairs is not content with the decision of the United States on the missile shield (translated). September 18. http://www.izvestiya.ru/.
— 2009l. Poland does not question participation in the new missile shield project of the United States (translated). October 21. http://www.izvestiya.ru/.
— 2009m. Poland asks NATO to encourage Eastern Europe with troops (translated). November 5. http://www.izvestiya.ru/.
— 2009n. Inspection of trucks blocks up highway on the Russian-Latvian Border (translated). December 18. http://www.izvestiya.ru/.
— 2009o. In January, the President of Poland took part in an energy summit in Georgia (translated). December 29. http://wwwo.izvestiya.ru/.
— 2009p. Black Sea Oil (translated). December 29. http://www.izvestiya.ru/.
IZVESTIYA. 2010a. Serbia recalls its ambassador from Montenegro (translated). January 15. http://www.izvestiya.ru/.
— 2010b. Germany wants to increase its contingent in Afghanistan (translated). January 25. http://www.izvestiya.ru/.

IZVESTIYA. 2010c. Dutch prime minister confirms plans to withdraw troops from Afghanistan (translated). February 21. http://www.izvestiya.ru/.
— 2010d. The United States seeks out a place for Turkey in NATO missile shield (translated). February 9. http://www.izvestiya.ru/.
— 2010e. Romania will distribute 24 rockets of the American missile shield on its territory (translated). March 5. http://www.izvestiya.ru/.
— 2010f. NATO acknowledges the unrealism of the new war doctrine of Russia (translated). February 8. http://www.izvestiya.ru/.
— 2010g. Russia and NATO: Confluence of Values (translated). February 3. http://www.izvestiya.ru/.
— 2010h. Afghanistan flag is raised in Sevastopol on the day of defense of the Fatherland (translated). February 23. http://www.izvestiya.ru/.
— 2010i. Yanukovych anticipates a turning point in relations with Russia (translated). March 5. http://www.izvestiya.ru/.
— 2010j. Georgia presents its strategy for relations with Abkhazia and South Ossetia to the U.N. (translated). February 22. http://www.izvestiya.ru/.
— 2010k. Medvedev confirms the law for guarding the border of South Ossetia And Abkhazia (translated). April 5. http://www.izvestiya.ru/.
Jentleson, Bruce W. 2007. *American Foreign Policy: The Dynamics of Choice in the 21st Century*, Third Edition. New York: W.W. Norton & Company.
Jervis, Robert. 2009. Unipolarity: A Structural Perspective. *World Politics* 61(1): 188–213. http://proxygsu-val1.galileo.usg.ed/.
Joch, Roman. 2007. Je-a má být-česká zahraniční politika proamerická. *Mezinárodní Politika* XXXI(2): 1–20.
Karlas, Jan. 2006. Mezinárodní organizace a přenos moci: pravidla dělby moci v bezpečnostních organizacích. *Mezinárodní vztahy* 41(2): 23–48.
Kazocins, Colonel Janis. 1999. The Baltic Battalion Five Years On: Cornerstone of Baltic Military Cooperation or Expensive White Elephant? *Baltic Defense Review* 2: 47–54.
Keohane, Daniel. 2006. Unblocking EU-NATO Co-operation. *CER Bulletin* Issue 48.
King, Charles. 2008. The Kosovo Precedent. *News Net* 48(3): 1–3.
Klaban, Vladimír. 2007. Americký radar, Evropská unie, Rusko a my. *Mezinárodní Politika* XXXI(10): 19–21.
Kscm. 2009. KSČM proti základnám USA v ČR. March 17. http://www.kscm.cz/.
Kulish, Nicholas. 2010. Dutch Government Falls Over Stance on Troops. *New York Times*, February 21.
latimes. 2007a. NATO's Afghanistan Role Defended. May 22. http://latimes.com/.
Leff, Carol Skalnik. 1997. *The Czech and Slovak Republics*. Boulder: Westview Press.
Lewis, George N. and Theodore A. Postol. 2008. Why Countermeasures Will Defeat National Missile Defense. *Bulletin of the Atomic Scientists* (May/June): 38–9.
Lijphart, Arend. 1980. *Democracy in Plural Societies: A Comparative Exploration*. New Haven: Yale University Press.
Lischer, Sarah Kenyon. 2007. Military Intervention and the Humanitarian Force Multiplier. *Global Governance* 13(1): 99–118.
Lowe, Christian. 2007. Russia gives Gazprom right to form armed units. *Reuters*, July 5. http://www.news.scotsman.com/.

Lugar, Richard. 2007. Energy Security: A NATO Article 5 Mission. *Hampton Roads International Security Quarterly* January 15, 2007: 11–16.
Lukyanov, Fyodor. 2009. Interview with Mikhail Gorbachev. *Russia in Global Affairs* 4 (October–December).
MacQuarrie, Brian. 2009. Military Situation in Afghanistan Will Get Worse, Petraeus Says. *Boston Globe*, April 22.
Mahncke, Dieter. 2004. Transatlantic Security: Joint Venture at Risk? In *Redefining Transatlantic Security Relations: The Challenge of Change*, ed. Dieter Mahncke, Wyn Rees, & Wayne C. Thompson, 15–92. New York: Manchester University Press.
McCain, John. 2007. NATO's Litmus Test in Afghanistan. *Hampton Roads International Studies Quarterly* April 15, 2007: 29–33.
McCormick, James M. 2010. *American Foreign Policy and Process*, Fifth Edition. Wadsworth: Boston, Massachusetts.
McGuigan, Mark. 2007. NATO and Russia: Progress or Process. In *Russia and Europe in the Twenty-First Century: An Uneasy Partnership*, ed. Jackie Gower & Graham Timmins, 149–68. New York: Anthem Press.
Michaels, Jim. 2009. Security plan looks to Afghan villages. *New York Times*, November 12.
Michta, Andrew W. 2006. *The Limits of Alliance: The United States, NATO, and the EU in North and Central Europe*. New York: Rowman & Littlefield Publishers.
MIL. 2007a. NATO musí do Afghanistanu vyslat viac vojakov. July 18. http://www.mil.sk/.
MIL. 2008. The Baltic Air Surveillance Network. March 3. http://www.mil.ee/.
Ministry of Defense of Bulgaria 2010a,b. Peace Support Operations. February 18. http://www.md.government.bg/.
Ministry of Defense of the Czech Republic. 2006a. Zahraniční mise: aktuální mise. July 5. http://www.army.cz/.
— 2006b. Operace NATO 'Joint Enterprise' Kosovo. August 31. http://www.army.cz/.
Ministry of Defense of the Czech Republic. 2007a. SOG. August 29. http://www.army.cz/.
— 2007b. PRT (Provinční rekonstrukční tým. August 29. http://www.army.cz/.
— 2007c. Vzácná návštěva. August 31. http://www.army.cz/.
— 2007d. Malá skupina s velkým posláním—Meteo ISAF. July 18. http://www.army.cz/.
— 2007e. Vojáci 5. Kontingentu ISAF-PRT očkovali afghánské děti. July 7. http://www.army.cz/.
— 2007f. Ukončená rotace v misi ISAF-PRT. August 13. http://www.army.cz/.
— 2007g. Celebration. August 30. http://www.army.cz/.
— 2007h. Navazování spolupráce v Afghánistánu. November 27. http://www.army.cz/.
— 2007i. Winter Race—humanitární operace NATO v Pákistánu. August 29. http://www.army.cz/.
Ministry of Defense of the Czech Republic. 2010a. History of Czech Military Operations Abroad (1990–2010). January 13. http://www.army.cz/.

Ministry of Defense of the Czech Republic. 2010b. NATO Operation "Joint Enterprise" in Kosovo. February 19. http://www.army.cz/.
— 2010c. 1st ACR Contingent—ISAF HELI UNIT, Paktika Province Afghanistan. February 19. http://www.army.cz/.
— 2010d. ISAF—Provincial Reconstruction Team in Logar. February 19. http://www.army.cz/.
Ministry of Defense of Estonia. 2010a. Estonia: A Member of NATO. February 17. http://www.mod.gov.ee.
— 2010b. The last Estonian recce platoon completed service in Kosovo. February 9. http://www.mod.gov.ee/.
Ministry of Defense of Latvia. 2010a. Latvia and NATO. February 17. http://www.mod.gov.lv/
Ministry of Defense of Lithuania. 2010a. Reporter of NATO Channel visited Lithuania-led Ghowr PRT. February 10. http://www.kam.lt.
Ministry of Defense of Romania. 2010a. Missions—NATO. February 18. http://www.mapn.ro/.
— 2010b. Romanian paratroopers: the integrant part of KFOR family. February 18. http://www.mapn.ro/.
— 2010c. Press Information. February 18. http://www.mapn.ro/.
Ministry of Defense of Slovakia. 2007a. Operace ISAF, Afganistan. September 21. http://www.mil.sk/.
Ministry of Foreign Affairs of Bulgaria. 2010a,b,c,d,e. The Participation of the Republic of Bulgaria In NATO. February 18. http//www.mfa.bg/.
Ministry of Foreign Affairs of the Czech Republic 2002a,b. Evaluation of the State of the Czech Republic's Integration into NATO. May 24. http://www.mzv.cz/.
Ministry of Foreign Affairs of the Czech Republic. 2005a. Česká republika a SZBP EU. September 8. http://www.mzv.cz/.
— 2005b. Dohody mezi Českou republikou a NATO. August 20. http://www.mzv.cz/.
— 2005c. Piloti vrtulníků odlétají do Bosny. September 21. http://www.msv.cz/.
Ministry of Foreign Affairs of the Czech Republic. 2007a. NATO in Afghanistan. http://www.mzv.cz/.
— 2007b. ISAF. September 24. http://www.mzv.cz/.
Ministry of Foreign Affairs of the Czech Republic. 2009a. Mapa předpokládného rozšíření system protiraketové obrany. March 17. http://www.mzv.cz/.
Ministry of Foreign Affairs of the Czech Republic. 2010a. Evaluation of the State of the Czech Republic's Integration into NATO. February 19. www.mzv.cz/.
Ministry of Foreign Affairs of Estonia. 2010a. Estonia's contribution to rebuilding Afghanistan. February 17. http://www.vm.ee/.
Ministry of Foreign Affairs of Germany. 2007a. Afghanistan-Koncept 2007: Kein Wiederaufbau und keine Entwicklung ohne Sicherheit. September 4. http://www.auswaertiges_amt.de/.
— 2007b. Humanitäre Hilfe in Afghanistan. September 21 http://www.auswaertiges_amt.de/.
— 2007c. Deutsches militärisches Engagement in Afghanistan. September 4. http://www.auswaertiges_amt.de/.
— 2007d. Deutsches Engagement beim Wiederaufbau der afghanischen Polizei. August 31. http://www.auswertiges_amt.de/.

Ministry of Foreign Affairs of Hungary. 2010a. History of Hungarian-NATO Relations. February 19. http://www.mfa.gov.hu/.
— 2010b. NAT0—Strategic Airlift Capability. February 19. http://www.mfa.gov.hu/.
— 2010c. History of Hungarian-NATO Relations. February 19. http://www.mfa.gov.hu/.
— 2010d. Hungary's role in Afghanistan (ISAF, PRT). February 19. http://www.mfa.gov.hu/.
— 2010e. Hungary's role in the stabilization of Iraq. February 19. http://www.mfa.gov.hu/.
Ministry of Foreign Affairs of Latvia 2010a. Latvia and NATO. February 17. http://www.mod.gov.lv/.
— 2010b,d. Participation in International Operations. February 16. http://www.am.gov.lv/.
— 2010c. Foreign Minister Maris Riekstins welcomes Government decision to support Latvia's increased engagement in Afghanistan. February 16. http://www.am.gov.lv/.
Ministry of Foreign Affairs of Lithuania. 2010a,b,c,d. Lithuania's Participation in NATO-led Operations. February 17. http://www.urm.lt/.
Ministry of Foreign Affairs of Romania. 2010a. Romania, an active ally within an active and solid alliance. http://www.mae.ro/.
Ministry of Foreign Affairs of the Russian Federation. 2008a. BEAC (Barents Euroarctic Council) (translated). http://www.mid.ru/.
Ministry of Foreign Affairs of Slovakia. 2002a. MSU Trains Slovenians and Romanians. April 25. http://www.mzv.sk/.
Ministry of Foreign Affairs of Slovakia. 2004a. SFOR Slovenian Airways. December 2. http://www.mzv.sk/.
— 2004b. Goodbye SFOR, Hello EUFOR. December 2. http://www.mzv.sk/.
— 2004c. Nations of SFOR. December 2. http://www.mzv.sk/.
Ministry of Foreign Affairs of Slovakia. 2005a. Multinational Brigade North East. October 21. http://www.mzv.sk/.
— 2005b. Multinational Brigade East. September 28. http://www.mzv.sk/.
— 2005c. Multinational Brigade Southwest. September 27. http://www.mzv.sk/.
— 2005d. Účast SR v operáciách na podporu vedením NATO. September 27. http://www.mzv.sk/.
Ministry of Foreign Affairs of Slovakia. 2010a,b,c,d. Slovakia's Engagement for Peace in the World. February 17. http://www.foreign.gov.sk/.
Ministry of Foreign Affairs of Slovenia. 2010a. Transformation of NATO. February 17. http://www.mzz.gov.si/.
Ministry of Foreign Affairs of Sweden. 2008a. Nordisk-baltisk samarbete. March 5. http://www.ud.se/.
— 2008b. Cristina Husmark Pehrsson träffar Lettlands talman. March 5. http://www.ud.se/.
— 2008c. Landstrategi: Estland, Lettland, Litauen 2002–04. March 5. http://www.ud.se/.
— 2008d. Ryssland. March 5. http://www.ud.se/.
— 2008e. Samarbete i Östersjöregionen. March 5. http://www.ud.se/.
— 2008f. Welcome to Baltic Sea States Subregional Co-operation; Union of the Baltic Cities. March 5. http://www.ud.se/.

Ministry of Foreign Affairs of Sweden. 2008g. Den Nordliga dimensionen. March 5. http://www.ud.se/.
Ministry of National Defense of Poland. 2010a. Commander IJC welcomed MNCNE Team in Kabul. February 19. http://www.mon.gov.pl/.
Misiunas, Romuald J. 1990. The Baltic Republics: Stagnation and Strivings for Sovereignty. In *The Nationalities Factor in Soviet Politics and Society*, ed. Lubomyr Hajda and Mark Bessinger, 204–27. Boulder: Westview Press.
Moore, Rebecca R. 2007. Euro-Atlantic and "Free World" Alliance? The Evolution of NATO in a Globalized World. Paper presented at the annual meeting for the International Studies Association, 2007.
Móller, Major T.D. 2000. BALTBAT—Lessons Learned and the Way Ahead. *Baltic Defense Review* 3: 38–42.
MSNBC. 2008. Kosovo declares independence. February 18. http://www.msnbc.com/.
National Program. 2000. Prague.
NATO 2005a. Fact Sheet on the NATO Training Implementation Mission. February 11. http://www.nato.int/.
NATO 2007a,b. International Security Assistance Force (ISAF). July 18. http://www.nato.int/.
— 2007c. The Afghanistan Compact. July 18. http://www.nato.int/.
— 2007d. International Security Assistance Force (ISAF). July 18. http://www.nato.int/.
— 2007e. NATO's Senior Civilian Representative in Afghanistan. July 18. http://www.nato.int/.
— 2007f. NATO's Afghanistan Priorities. July 19. http://www.nato.int/.
— 2007g. UN in Afghanistan. July 19. http://www.nato.int/.
— 2007h. UN, NATO Chart Afghanistan Approach at Rome Conference. July 18. http://www.nato.int/.
— 2007i. NATO Reaffirms Commitment to Afghanistan. July 18. http://www.nato.int/.
NATO 2008a. Statement: Meeting of the North Atlantic Council at the level of Foreign Ministers Held at NATO Headquarters, Brussels. August 19. http://www.nato.int/.
— 2008b. Statement by the North Atlantic Council on the Russian recognition of South Ossetia and Abkhazia regions of Georgia. August 27. http://www.nato.int/.
— 2008c. Statement: Meeting of the North Atlantic Council at the level of Foreign Ministers Held at NATO Headquarters, Brussels. August 19. http://www.nato.int/.
— 2008d. NATO's Relations with Georgia. August 19. http://www.nato.int/.
— 2008e. Statement: Meeting of the North Atlantic Council at the level of Foreign Ministers Held at NATO Headquarters, Brussels. August 19. http://www.nato.int/.
— 2008f. Statement by North Atlantic Council on the Russian recognition of South Ossetia and Abkhazia regions of Georgia. August 27. http://www.nato.int/.
— 2008g. Chairman's Statement. August 27. http://www.nato.int/.
— 2008h. NATO's Relations with Georgia. August 19. http://www.nato.int/.

NATO 2009a. NATO Member Countries. December 10. http://www.nato.int/.
— 2009b. Membership Action Plan. December 8. http://www.nato.int/.
— 2009c. NATO Ministers invite Montenegro to join MAP and encourage Bosnia and Herzegovina to step up reforms. December 10. http://www.nato.int/.
— 2009d. NATO Secretary General condemns terrorist attack in Turkey. April 30. http://www.nato.int/.
— 2009e. NATO Military Committee concludes two days meetings in Brussels. May 13. http://www.nato.int/.
— 2009f. NATO-Ukraine relations. April 3. http://www.nato.int/.
— 2009g. NATO Military Committee concludes two days meetings in Brussels May 13. http://www.nato.int/.
— 2009h. Membership Action Plan. December 8. http://www.nato.int/.
— 2009i. NATO Ministers invite Montenegro to joint MAP and encourage Bosnia and Herzegovina to step up reforms. December 4. http://www.nato.int/.
— 2009j. NATO Secretary General Visits Western Balkans. November 27. http://www.nato.int/.
— 2009k. NATO-Russia Council. March 5. http://www.nato.int/.
— 2009l. NATO-Ukraine relations. April 3. http://www.nato.int/.
— 2009m. NATO Secretary General condemns terrorist attack in Turkey. April 20. http://www.nato.int/.
— 2009n. NATO Military Committee concludes two days meetings in Brussels. May 7. http://www.nato.int/.
— 2009o. Statement by the NATO Secretary General on situation in Moldova. April 8. http://www.nato.int/.
— 2009p. NATO's relations with the Republic of Macedonia. April 10. http://www.nato.int/.
— 2009q. NATO Deputy Secretary General visits Armenia. April 28. http://www.nato.int/.
NATO 2010a,b,c. Peace Support Operations in Bosnia and Herzegovina. February 18. http://www.nato.int/.
— 2010d,e,f,g,h,i,j,k,l,m. International Security Assistance Force and Afghan National Army strength and laydown. February 19. http://www.nato.int/.
— 2010n. NATO's Assistance to Iraq. February 18. http://www.nato.int/.
NATO's Riga Summit Confirms Present Commitments and Looks Ahead. 2007. *Hampton Roads International Security Quarterly* January 15, 2007: 4.
New NATO Nations Should Find Niche Military Capability, Secretary General Says. 2004. *Defense Daily* 221(58)1.
Newton, Julie M. 2007. Shortcut to Great Power: France and Russia in Pursuit of Multipolarity. In *Russia and Europe in the Twenty-First Century: An Uneasy Partnership*, ed. Jackie Gower & Graham Timmins, 185–206. New York: Anthem Press.
Noetzel, Timo, and Benjamin Schreer. 2009. Does a multi-tier NATO matter? The Atlantic alliance and the process of strategic change. *International Affairs* 85(2): 211–26. http://proxygsu-val2.galileo.usg.ed/.
NORDEN. 2008. The Nordic Council of Ministers. March 3. http://www.norden.org/.
Novak, Lisa M. 2010. DoD takes over Afghan Police training after IG cites State Dept. failures. *Stars and Stripes*, February 25.

Novotný, Jaromír. 2002. DCI (Defense Capabilities Initiative) a Česká Republika. March. http://www.mzv.cz/.
Nuland, Victoria. 2006. NATO's Mission in Afghanistan: Putting Theory into Practice. October 23. http://www.nato.int/.
Obama, Barack. 2009. A Just and Lasting Peace. *USATODAY*. December 10. http://www.usatoday.com/.
O'Flynn, Kevin. 2005. Baltic Grudge Match. *Newsweek, Atlantic Edition* September 12: 45.
Ost, David. *Solidarity and the Politics of Anti-Politics*. Philadelphia: Temple University Press.
Pabriks, Artis. 2007. Five Challenges Facing NATO Today. *Hampton Roads International Security Quarterly* January 15–17, 2007: 31–2.
Palata, Luboš. 2008. A Radar and 250 Yanks. *Review of the Czech Republic* 15(5): 8–11.
Paulikas, Steven. 2005. Baltics: Brothers, Up in Arms; Perceptions to the Contrary, There is No "Baltic Bloc." *Newsweek*, Atlantic Edition February 21: 27.
Pease, Kelly-Kate. 2008. *International Organizations: Perspectives on Governance in the Twenty-First Century*, Third Edition. Upper Saddle River, New Jersey: Pearson-Prentice Hall.
Pelletière, Stephen C. 2007. *Losing Iraq: Insurgency and Politics*. Westport, Connecticut: Praeger Security International.
Pezl, Karel. 1994. Česká republika a západoevropské aspekty. *Mezinárodní Politika* 18: 25–6.
Photius, Photius. May 13. http://www.photius.com/.
Pick, Otto. 2000. NATO, evropská obrana a poučení Kosova. In *ČR po vstupu do NATO: Úvahy a problémy*. Praha: Česká Atlantická Komise ÚMV.
Pincus, Walter. 2009. What's The News? Just Ask Secretary Gates. *Washington Post*, September 22.
Politics: Russia Mapping New Strategy to Face NATO Expansion. 2004. *Global Information Network* New York (April 15): 1.
Raik, Kristi. 2007. A Europe Divided by Russia?: The New Eastern Member States and the EU's Policy towards the East. In *Russia and Europe in the Twenty-First Century: An Uneasy Partnership*, ed. Jackie Gower & Graham Timmins, 207–25. New York: Anthem Press.
Ratesh, Nestor. 1991. *Romania: The Entangled Revolution*. New York: Praeger.
Rees, Wyn. 2004. Emerging Security Challenges. Conclusion: The Challenge of Change. In *Redefining Trasnsatlantic Security Relations: The Challenge of Change*, ed. Dieter Mahncke, Wyn Rees, & Wayne C. Thompson, 163–217. New York: Manchester University Press.
Rees, Wyn and Dieter Mahncke. 2004. Introduction. In *Refedining Transatlantic Security Relations: The Challenge of Change*, ed. Dieter Mahncke, Wyn Rees, & Wayne C. Thompson, 1–14. New York: Manchester University Press.
Remington, Robin Alison. 1984. Yugoslavia. In *Communism in Eastern Europe*, Second Edition, ed. Teresa Rakowska-Harmstone, 238–82. Bloomington: Indiana University Press.
RIA NOVOSTI. 2009. Report of the Russian Experts for the Valdai Discussion Club Conference. London: Council on Foreign and Defense Policy, December 8–10.

Rinkevics, Edgar. 2007. Global NATO: Overdue or Overstretch? *Hampton Roads International Security Journal* January 15, 2007: 29–30.
Rogin, Josh. 2009. *The Cable (thecable.foreignpolicy.com)*, September 21.
Roskin, Michael G. 2002. *The Birth of East Europe*, Fourth Edition. Upper Saddle River, New Jersey: Prentice Hall.
Rubin, Barnett R. 2009. Afghanistan and Pakistan. In *Great Decisions*, 17–28. New York: Foreign Policy Association.
Rupp, Richard E. 2006. NATO after 9/11: An Alliance in Decline. Paper presented at the annual meeting for the International Studies Association, 2006. http://proxygsu-val1.galileo.usg.ed/.
Rychlík, Jan and Matyáš Zrno. 2008. Má Česká republika uznat Kosovo? *Mezinárodní Politika* XXXII(04): 20.
Saikal, Amin. 2006. Afghanistan's Transition: ISAF's Stabilisation Role. *Third World Quarterly* 27(3): 525–34.
Scheffer, Jaap de Hoop. 2009. Acceptance Speech. April 24. http://www.nato.int/.
Schwartzenberg, Karel. 2007. NATO Must Continue to Change. *Hampton Roads International Security Quarterly* April 15, 2007: 43–5.
Shankar, Thom. 2007. Iran May Know of Weapons for Taliban, Gates Contends. *New York Times*, June 14.
Simon, Steven. 2008. The Price of the Surge: How U.S. Strategy is Hastening Iraq's Demise. *Foreign Affairs* 87(3): 57–76.
Sky, Emma. 2007. Increasing ISAF's Impact on Stability in Afghanistan. *Defense and Security Analysis*. March 2007.
SME. 2005a. Multinational Specialized Unit. October 20. http://www.sme.sk/.
SME. 2006a,d. NATO rozšíri svoju členskú základňu. November 29. http://www.sme.sk/.
— 2006b. Ivanov: Krajiny NATO nelegálne dodávali Gruzínsku zbrane. September 29. http://www.sme.sk/.
— 2006c. Ukrajina rozhodne o vstupe do NATO referendum. December 29. http://www.sme.sk/.
SME. 2007a. Britská armada ide v Iraku aj Afganistane na maximum. August 18. http://www.sme.sk/.
— 2007b. Česko má záujem o našich zdravotníkov v Afganistane. August 17. http://www.sme.sk/.
— 2007c. Do Afganistanu a Kosova odchádza 90 profesionálnych vojakov. December 3. http://www.sme.sk/.
— 2007d. Rusko zatvorí radarové stanice na Ukrajine. July 12. http://www.sme.sk/.
— 2007e. NATO varuje Rusko, aby neodstúpilo od zmluvy od odzbrojení. November 30. http://www.sme.sk/.
— 2007f. Ruský parlament schválil zmluvu o hraniciach s Lotyšskom. September 19. http://www.sme.sk.
— 2007g. Ruský bombardéry opäť nad Severným morom. July 20. http://www.sme.sk/.
— 2007h. Estónsky minister: Rusko je čoraz nebezpečnejšie. October 9. http://www.sme.sk/.
SME. 2008a. Na Balkáne sa striedajú slovenské jednotky. July 11. http://www.sme.sk/.

SME. 2008b. Srbská cirkev: Očakávame na Balkáne ďalšiu vojnu. October 17. http://www.sme.sk/.
— 2008c. Český vojak zahynul v Afganistane po útoku na konvoj. March 17. http://www.sme.sk/.
— 2008d. Rusko a Bielorusko chcú zjednotiť protivzdušnú obranu. October 8. http://www.sme.sk/.
— 2008e. Európská únie nepodporila raketový štít USA. June 10. http://www.sme.sk/.
SME. 2009a. Rusko sa vyhráža zrušením stretnutia s veliteľmi NATO. April 20. http://www.sme.sk/.
— 2009b. Ukrajina požiadala USA o financie na jadrovéodzbrojenie. April 6. http://www.sme.sk/.
— 2009c. Ukrajina vraj zaplatí, Rusi varujú, že vypnú plyn. June 5. http://www.sme.sk/.
— 2009d. Nová kosovská armada začala pôsobiť pod dohľadom NATO. January 21. http://www.sme.sk/.
— 2009e. Slovenskí vojaci dorazili do Afganistanu. March 17. http://www.sme.sk/.
— 2009f. Kazachstan povolil transit zásob NATO do Afganistanu. February 9. http://www.sme.sk/.
— 2009g. Pakistanskí vojaci sa zmocnili kľúčového mesta Talibanu. November 2. http://www.sme.sk/.
— 2009h. Do Afganistanu vyšleme dvojnásobný počet vojakov. December 15. http://www.sme.sk/.
— 2009i. Rusko: Nový americký štít vzbudzuje viac otázok ako odpovedí. October 9. http://www.sme.sk/.
— 2009j. Putin: Rusko musí vyvíjať útočné zbrane. December 29. http://www.sme.sk/.
— 2009k. Ukrajina požiadala USA o financie na jadrovéodzbrojenie. April 6. http://www.sme.sk/.
— 2009l. Rusko sa vyhráža zrušením stretnutia s veliteľmi NATO. April 20. http://www.sme.sk/.
— 2009m. Ukrajina vraj zaplatí, Rusi varujú, že vypnú plyn. June 5. http://www.sme.sk/.
SME. 2010a. Janukovyč zrušil komisiu pre prípravu Ukrajiny do NATO. April 5. http://www.sme.sk/.
— 2010b. Šéf NATO: Zaplatiť Talibanu je investícia do mieru. February 4. http://www.sme.sk/.
— 2010c. Komunisti vyhlásili petíciu za stiahnutie vojakov z Afganistanu. February 8. http://www.sme.sk/.
— 2010d. Medvedev obvinil zahraničie z vyzbrojovania Gruzínska. March 5. http://www.sme.sk/.
— 2010e. Militanti zaútočili na americké zastupiteľstvo v Pakistane. April 5. http://www.sme.sk/.
Snow, Donald M. 2004. *National Security for a New Era: Globalization and Geopolitics.* New York: Pearson Longman.
State Department Issues Statement on Latvia-Russia Border. 2007. *U.S. Federal News Service, Including U.S. State News.* December 18.

Štěpanovský, Jiří. 2008. Mezinárodní aspekty nezávislosti Kosova. *Mezinárodní Politika* XXXII(03): 18–22.
Stillman, Richard II. 2004. *The American Bureaucracy: The Core of Modern Government*, Third Edition. Belmont, California: Thomson/Wadsworth.
Stokes, Gale. 1993. *The Walls Came Tumbling Down: The Collapse of Communism In Eastern Europe*. New York: Oxford University Press.
Suchý, Petr. 2007. Protiraketová obrana a ruská paranoia. *Mezinárodní Politika* XXXI(7): 4–6.
sueddeutsche. 2007a. Militäroffensive fordert erstes Opfer. March 6. http://www.sueddeutsche.de/.
— 2007b. Luftschläge und Zivilistenhass. August 9. http://www.sueddeutsche.de/.
— 2007c,d. Die NATO plant Strategiewechsel. July 30. http://www.sueddeutsche.de/.
sueddeutsche. 2009a. US-Zeitung: Taliban planen gemeinsame Offensive. March 27. http://www.sueddeutsche.de/.
— 2009b. Afghanistaqn-Konferenz: Iran will sich am Wiederaufbau beteiligen. March 9. http://www.sueddeutsche.de/.
— 2009c. Drei deutsche Soldaten getötet. June 23. http://www.sueddeutsche.de/.
— 2009d. Wahlkommission erklärt Karsai zum Sieger. November 2. http://www.sueddeutsche.de/.
— 2009e. Brown erhöht Druck auf Karsai. November 6. http://sueddeutsche.de/.
— 2009f. Rasmussen will Neustart mit Russland. September 18. http://www.sueddeutsche.de/.
sueddeutsche. 2010a. Keine zusätzlichen Kampftruppen. January 22. http://www.sueddeutsche.de/.
— 2010b. Was heist hier Krieg? April 5. http://www.sueddeutsche.de/.
— 2010c. Clinton says no—and stirs up the Russians. February 5. http://www.sueddeutsche.de/.
Suja, Miroslav. 2008. Irán a základny—test unipolarity. *Mezinárodní Politika* XXXII (03): 32–5.
Svěrák, Antonín. 1999. Vnejší a vnitřnaspekty začlenování resort obrany ČR do NATO. *Mezinárodní Vztahy* 2: 13–31.
Szayna, Thomas S. 1999. The Czech Republic: A Small Contributor or a 'Free Rider'? In *America's New Allies: Poland, Hungary, and the Czech Republic in NATO*, ed. Andrew A. Michta, 112–48. Seattle: University of Washington Press.
Terzuolo, Eric. 2006. *NATO and Weapons of Mass Destruction: Regional Alliance, Global Threats*. New York: Routledge.
Thompson, Wayne C. 2004. Transatlantic responses to global challenges. In *Redefining transatlantic security relations: The challenge of change*, ed. Dieter Mahncke, Wyn Rees, & Wayne C. Thompson, 93–159. New York: Manchester University.
USATODAY. 2007a. As U.S. steps up presence in Iraq, its coalition partners scale back. January 12. http://www.usatoday.com/.
— 2007b. Afghan civilian deaths stir NATO unease. May 25. http://www.usatoday.com/.
— 2007c. Afghans shut down private security firms. October 11. http://www.usatoday.com/.

USATODAY. 2007d. Afghanistan executes 15 prisoners, first in 3 years. October 12. http://www.usatoday.com/.
— 2007e. Gates wins pledge for more troops in Afghanistan. October 22. http://www.usatoday.com/.
— 2007f. Bush: Missile defense need is 'urgent.' October 23. http://www.usatoday.com/.
— 2007g. U.S. might delay missile defense plan. October 23. http://www.usatoday.com/.
— 2007h. NATO mulling safety against cyberattacks. June 14. http://www.usatoday.com/.
— 2007i. U.K., Norway monitor Russian bombers. July 20. http://www.usatoday.com/.
USATODAY. 2008a. U.N. reopens court in Kosovo's tense north. October 3. http://www.usatoday.com/.
— 2008b. Gates asks allies to send troops to Afghanistan. October 8. http://www.usatoday.com/.
— 2008c. Gates: Troop withdrawal may pause after summer. February 11. http://www.usatoday.com/.
— 2008d. Canada extends Afghan mission, with conditions. March. http://www.usatoday.com/.
— 2008e. U.S. Marines deploy in south Afghanistan. March 18. http://www.usatoday.com/.
— 2008f. Afghanistan 'most important issue' for NATO. March 30. http://www.usatoday.com/.
— 2008g. Russia says 'nyet' to U.S. missile defense. March 18. http://www.usatoday.com/.
— 2008h. Medvedev vows response to U.S. missile defense plans. July 15. http://www.usatoday.com/.
USATODAY. 2009a. Medvedev criticizes NATO exercise in Georgia. May 15. http://www.nato.int/.
— 2009b. Kosovo marks first anniversary of independence. February 17. http://www.usatoday.com/.
— 2009c. NATO rejects Amnesty call for war crimes probe. April 24. http://www.usatoday.com/.
— 2009d. NATO to scale down Kosovo force. June 11. http://www.usatoday.com/.
— 2009e. Obama's war: Deploying 17,000 raises stakes in Afghanistan. February 17. http://www.usatoday.com/.
— 2009f. Commander: Troops 'stalemated' in Afghanistan. February 18. http://www.usatoday.com/.
— 2009g. Clinton hints at possible talks with Iran on Afghanistan. March 5. http://www.usatoday.com/.
— 2009h. Poll: More view Afghan war as 'mistake'. March 16. http://www.ustoday.com/.
— 2009i. France to boost aid to Afghanistan. March 31. http://www.usatoday.com/.
— 2009j. U.S. general seeks help in Afghan war. April 3. http://www.usatoday.com/.

— 2009k. NATO allies endorse Obama's Afghan plan. April 4. http://www.usatoday.com/.
— 2009l. Gates evokes WWII unity, resolve in Afghan fight. June 10. http://www.usatoday.com/.
— 2009m. Obama to measure progress of Afghan war. September 16. http://www.usatoday.com/.
— 2009n. Presidential ballot recount begins in Afghanistan. October 4. http://www.usatoday.com/.
— 2009o. Slovakia to add 250 NATO troops to Afghan mission. November 17. http://www.usatoday.com/.
— 2009p. U.K. confirms 500 more troops heading to Afghanistan. November 30. http://www.usatoday.com/.
— 2009q. NATO allies confirm troops pledge. December 17. http://www.usatoday.com/.
— 2009r. Gates sees heavy U.S. role in Afghanistan for 2–4 years. December 6. http://www.usatoday.com/.
— 2009s. Pentagon: Obama adjusting European missile shield. September 17. http://www.usatoday.com/.
— 2009t, u. Obama scraps Bush missile-defense plan. September 17. http://www.usatoday.com/.
— 2009v. Russia scraps plan for missiles near Poland. September 20. http://www.usatoday.com/.
— 2009w. Untitled. September 30. http://www.usatoday.com/.
USATODAY. 2010a. AP: U.S. aid goes to small nations in Afghan war. April 1. http://www.usatoday.com/.
— 2010b. Most U.S. forces in Afghanistan to be under NATO. March 17. http://www.usatoday.com/.
— 2010c. Germany to increase Afghan contingent by up to 850. January 26. http://www.usatoday.com/.
— 2010d. Russia criticizes U.S., NATO over Afghan drug trafficking fight. March 12. http://www.usatoday.com/.
— 2010e. International talks eye exit strategy from Afghanistan. January 28. http://www.usatoday.com/.
— 2010f. German friendly fire kills 6 Afghan soldiers. April 5, 2010. http://www.usatoday.com/.
— 2010g. Afghan 'war' to continue, Germany defense minister says. April 5. http://www.usatoday.com/.
— 2010h. Czechs torn over U.S. nuclear treaty with Russia. April 6. http://www.usatoday.com/.
Velinger, Jan. 2006. Czechs hand training over to Iraqis at policy academy. Czech Radio 7, Radio Prague. November 8, 2006. http://www.radio.cz/.
Volgyes, Ivan. 1986. *Politics in Eastern Europe*. Chicago: The Dorsey Press.
Vondra, Alexandr. 2006. Česká zahraniční politika: tři princepy, trojí směrování, a tři témata. *Mezinárodní Politika* XXX(11): 16–19.
Vondrous, J. 2002. Regionální dimenze českého atlantismu. March. http://www.mzv.cz/.

Wall Street Journal. 2008a. Attack Spotlights Taliban Strength. July 15. http://www.defensenews.com/.
— 2008b. U.S. Blames Pakistan as Afghanistan Incursions Rise. July 11. http://www.wallstreetjournal.com/.
Walt, Stephen M. 2009. Alliances in a Unipolar World. *World Politics* 61(1): 86–120. http://proxygsu-val1.galileo.usg.ed/.
Wasby, Stephen L. 1970. *Political Science: The Discipline and its Dimensions: An Introduction*. New York: Charles Scribner's Sons.
Washingtonpost. 2008a. Gates: to Remain in Kosovo through Late 2009. October 7. http://www.washingtonpost.com/.
— 2008b. Gates: Expanding US Command in Afghanistan is Possibility. May 2. http://www.washingtonpost.com/.
Webber, Mark. 2007. Russia and the European Security Governance Debate. In *Russia and Europe in the Twenty-First Century: An Uneasy Partnership*, ed. Jackie Gower & Graham Timmins, 267–88. New York: Anthem Press.
White, Stephen and Margot Light. 2007. The Russian Elite Perspective on European Relations. In *Russia and Europe in the Twenty-First Century: An Uneasy Partnership*, ed. Jackie Gower & Graham Timmins, 41–56. New York: Anthem Press.
Wolchik, Sharon L. and Jane L. Curry. 2008. Democracy, the Market, and the Return to Europe: From Communism to the European Union and NATO. In *Central & East European Politics: From Communism to Democracy*, ed. Sharon L. Wolchik & Jane L. Curry, 3–32. New York: Rowman & Littlefield Publishers.
Zachar, Marián. 2008. Prečo má Kosovo nárok na samostatný stat? *Mezinárodní Politika* XXXII(04): 37–9.
Zelikow, Philip. 1997. The Masque of Institutions. In *NATO's Transformation*, ed. Philip H. Gordon. New York: Rowman & Littlefield Publishers.
Žižka, Jan. 2009. The Czech Republic: Ten Years in NATO. *Review of the Czech Republic* 16(1): 12–15.

Index

Afghan National Army 83, 85, 95
ALTHEA 26, 64, 76
Arctic Council 151, 160, 163
axis of evil 1, 116

Baltic Air Surveillance Network
 (BALTNET) 160–1
Baltic Battalion (BALTBAT) 160–1
Barents Euro-Artic Council
 (BEAC) 160, 163
Black Sea Economic Cooperation Pact
 (BSEC) 47, 177
Black Sea NGO Network 177
Black Sea Studies Center 177
Bosnian War 20, 29, 62, 69, 80
 and Kosovo 47, 71, 129
 western nations 5, 130
Brdo 127, 134, 136, 138, 140–1
Bremer, Paul 47, 113–14
Brezhnev, Leonid 53, 59, 120

Clinton administration 61, 63, 69
 partnership for peace (PfP) 10, 21,
  130, 169
Common Foreign and Security Policy
 (CFSP) 22–3, 26, 133
containment 2, 4, 6, 125
Council of the Baltic Sea States 151,
 162, 178
Croatian minority 65, 182
Czechoslovakia 3, 39, 133, 136, 169

Dayton Accord 26, 63–5, 120
democratic peace 129

European Security and Defense Policy
 (ESDP) 69
European Union Force (EUFOR) 26, 42,
 65–6, 73
 and NATO 64, 67, 182

failed state 17, 101
Federally Administered Tribal Areas 47,
 104, 147, 183
free market principles 21, 69

Gorbachev, Mikhail 11, 59, 148

Havel, Václav 10, 21–3, 139
Helmand Province 90, 95, 107
Holbrooke, Richard 105, 109

Implementation Force (IFOR) 26,
 64–5
interceptors 127, 139, 143, 146, 153

Kabul Airport 92, 94
Kandahar 90, 95, 99, 107, 121
Karzai, Hamid 82, 100, 106–7,
 109, 126
Klaus, Václav 21, 23–4, 138, 143, 145
Kosovo Constitution 73–5
Kosovo Defense Force (KDF) 79
Kosovo Force (KFOR) 69, 71, 73,
 79, 179
Kosovo Security Force (KSF) 79
Kurds 114, 167

McCrystal, Stanley 108
McKiernan, David 105
Medvedev, Dmitry 50, 53, 144, 149, 175
 concepts 52, 148
 U.S. 145, 181
membership selection process to
 NATO 32–3
Milosevic, Slobodan 19, 29, 61, 63, 70
 aggression 20, 28
 Bosnia 5, 61, 68
 and Saddam 5–6
Muslims 36, 59
 Bosnia 38, 61, 63, 65, 182

National Training Mission—Iraq (NTM-I) 27, 42, 122–3, 182
NATO-Georgia Commission 50, 175
NATO Response Force 41, 56, 96, 158, 176
NATO-Russia Council 50, 136, 149, 175
NGOs 86, 91, 93
Nordic Council of Ministers 151, 160–1
Northern Dimension 151, 160, 164

oil politics 100–1
Operation Allied Force 68–71, 74, 79, 182
Operation Deliberate Force 63
Organization for Security and Cooperation Europe (OSCE) 10, 22, 64, 74, 150
  Russia 148, 149

Petraeus, David 106–7, 121, 195
Provincial Reconstruction Team (PRT) 27, 83–5, 94–6

radar station 130, 136, 153
Rambouillet Conference 68
Rasmussen, Anders Fogh 58, 108, 146, 149
rogue leaders 4, 6, 19, 130
Russian minority 171
  Latvia 14, 35, 155–6
  Lithuania 165, 92

Saakvashili, Mikheil 50, 53, 175
Scheffer, Jaap de Hoop 82, 110, 122
  speeches 45, 130, 142, 176, 179

Serbian minority 49, 68, 71, 73
Shiites 38, 113–14
shock therapy 21, 101, 129
soft power 148
Srebrenica 61–2, 65
Stabilization Force (SFOR) 26, 42, 64–6
Status of Forces Agreement (SOFA) 142–3
summits of NATO 33–4, 41, 141, 176
Sunnis 114
surge strategy 90, 106, 108, 113, 121
  Afghanistan 107
  Iraq 106–7, 115, 147

totalitarian 20–1
Truman Doctrine 2

unilateral policy 117–18
United Nations Assistance Mission in Afghanistan (UNAMA) 87
United Nations Protection Force (UNPROFOR) 41, 62, 66

Visegrad 22–3

Warsaw Pact 4, 15–16, 29
Weapons of Mass Destruction (WMD) 132
Western European Union (WEU) 22, 25
World Court 35, 57, 63, 80

Yanukovych, Viktor 54–6, 58, 172, 181